American Marriage
A Changing Scene?

American Marriage

A Changing Scene?

Second Edition

Frank D. Cox
Santa Barbara City College

wcb

WM. C. BROWN COMPANY PUBLISHERS
Dubuque, Iowa

Contents

Section 4

The Family and Its Alternatives

Preface

This book attempts to supply perspective to the reader by presenting a diversity of opinion and thought about marriage and morals. This is accomplished by examining current patterns of American marriage, scientific advances in our knowledge of biology influencing the male-female relationship, and alternate marital patterns as found in other cultures. The book's major purpose is to provoke meaningful debate over the questions raised rather than to supply the reader with answers to the questions. Creative thoughtful discussion is important to the success of every marriage, regardless of the exact form of the family institution. Such discussion helps one to function realistically in the marriage relationship. A second purpose is to stimulate the reader to hypothesize about what one might expect of the family in the future.

The first section, "Tomorrow's Morality," attempts to excite and stimulate thought by presenting both a wide variety of ideas concerning marriage and morals in America, and some of the biological breakthroughs that have widened our knowledge of reproduction and the creation of life. The controversies aroused are placed into a time and data perspective so that the reader will understand that marriage is a historically evolving institution that is still very much alive and viable in America.

Section 2, "The Romantic Ideal: Love and Marriage in America," seeks to clarify just what the romantic ideals are for the bulk of Americans, regardless of how realistic or erroneous such ideals may be. One important thesis of the book is that to the degree that the individual accepts the unrealistic stereotyped images of his culture and its institutions, i.e., marriage, his chances for success in the institution diminish. If an individual expects one thing of marriage but meets something else in reality, the incongruence between reality and expectation will likely cause a disruption in the real situation. The better one understands what the stereotyped images are, the better the chances of keeping one's expectation realistic.

Section 3, "The Romantic Ideal: Ethnic, Cultural and Class Differences," attempts to help the reader appraise his romantic ideals by introducing him to alternate ethnic and cultural systems, as well as to class differences within America. This section attempts to help the reader step out of his own forest so as to better see the trees. Examining other systems of family helps one to better understand one's own system since it allows a broadened perspective.

The final section, "The Family and Its Alternatives," leads the reader to examine some of the new and changing forms that the American family is or may be taking. For example, E. E. LeMasters points out that, in thinking about parents, it is easy to assume a model of what might be termed "the biological parent team" of mother and father. What is not realized by many is the fact that a considerable proportion of contemporary American parents do not operate from this model. These parents include "parents without partners" (mostly divorced or separated women); widows and widowers with children; unmarried mothers; adoptive parents; stepparents; and foster parents. Some of these groups are surprisingly large. During the 1960s approximately one out of every nine American children was a stepchild.

In essence, the book examines the new pressures being placed on the marriage institution by both societal change and scientific breakthrough. Speculations as to the changes that may result within the social mores and hence the family institution are then made. Additional comparative materials about alternate marriage patterns are included to give the reader a broader perspective.

Thirteen of the twenty-five articles in the second edition are new as is much of the material written by your author. Sixteen of the articles were written in the 1970s. Three of the articles were written expressly for this book. As with the first edition of the book, the author supports a broad conception of the meaning of family and is generally supportive of the institution. Although it is fun and easy to debunk existing social institutions, it is far more difficult to build better institutions. It is hoped that the broad, critical yet supportive tone of this book will help the reader to build better social institutions rather than helping him to only tear down the existing ones.

Unlike many books of readings, *American Marriage: A Changing Scene?* flows logically from beginning to end. Although the readings may be perused individually, they become more meaningful when read in context. The readings are tied together by the author's running commentary. Comments serve to amplify and relate the various readings and, hopefully, give the book a sense of unity and purpose. In many cases the readings have been condensed, but the essence of each writer's meaning remains.

So that the reader can distinguish the author's commentaries from the readings, two different typefaces have been used.

Acknowledgments

The author wishes to express his deep gratitude to the many fine writers represented by this volume and to all those who helped in the synthesis and preparation of this book. Special thanks must go to Brigitte Cox whose intellectual stimulation and dissatisfaction with first conclusions have led to many of my best insights and writings. Special thanks must also go to Pamela Slagle through whom I learned the meaning of care and sensitivity.

Frank D. Cox

Introduction

I would like to get married because of my own personality traits and because I believe the benefits outweigh the drawbacks. Being married would give me a feeling of security and a permanence of the relationship between my spouse and myself. I've been in love before and I am sure that when I become attracted again I will completely and absolutely adapt my plans and aims to include my love. The advantages of a well-matched, compatible, and financially secure marriage are readily apparent, but I know that my emotions will be the final judge.

Male—19 years old

I plan to get married someday because I feel that on my own, I'm incomplete. I want someone to love and someone to love me. I want to be committed to someone and give myself totally to that person. I have basic sexual desires that I need to have satisfied, yet I want this to be within the marriage experience. And someday, if possible, I want to give the man I love a child who belongs only to us. As a woman I don't think that I could be happy for a lifetime without having the man I love beside me. I need someone and my life won't be complete until I can be committed and united with that person. Marriage for me means a deep personal relationship for life with the person I love. Marriage is what we will make of it and I know that it requires effort, skill, compatibility, and love.

Female—19 years old

When I get married I will have to be positively in love with the man. By this, I mean, I will have to have a very deep feeling for him. I'm going to get married so that I can have some of the love, tenderness, and kindness I never had. I need a person I can trust and rely on.

Female—17 years old

I want to have a son. I'm looking for a girl who wants one too. When I find her and if she has certain qualities that I require, we'll have a child. To avoid pressure, hurt feelings of families, and legal trouble, we will eventually get married. But marriage itself isn't that important to me.

Male—20 years old

I don't particularly want to get married and if perchance I do, it won't be for at least another ten years. The only real reason I can see to marry is reproduction. However, there happens to be a serious population explosion taking place and I feel it my duty to try not to have children unless I adopt. Therefore, I find marriage unnecessary at the present time. The older generation has been too hypocritical about marriage for me to see it in a good light. They tell us that a piece of paper makes it O.K. with the society for us to have sex. I believe in premarital sex whether it leads to marriage or not. It seems to me that a lot of people don't trust themselves to stay in love with one person. Therefore, they insure themselves with the commitment of marriage. No one likes to be humiliated by being told they aren't desirable any more so they make sure the spouse can't leave without a fight. The younger generation is above that.

Female—18 years old

Such comments are among hundreds that have been gathered from marriage classes in response to the question, "What place does marriage play in your life at the present time?" The diversity of opinion represented by these comments indicates something of the diversity of thought concerning marriage and morals within the American culture. It seems as if marriage, sex, and morality are among the major topics of debate in twentieth-century America if one judges the publicity given to these topics. Books about sexuality remain on the best-seller lists month after month. Pornography becomes a nationwide debate with the issuance of the National Commission of Obscenity and Pornography report in 1970. The Commission found little evidence that pornography was harmful, and it recommended the repeal of laws prohibiting its dissemination to adults who want it. Much of the American citizenry, including the President, rejected the report, denouncing its "morally bankrupt conclusions."

One reads of the biological sciences unlocking increasing numbers of life's secrets. Such possibilities as selecting a child's general physical characteristics before conception and then, via genetic surgery, producing the desired characteristics, are within the realm of future achievement.

"The times they are a-changin'," wails Bob Dylan. Communal living and consensual marriage are not only discussed but are attempted in communes scattered across America. Staid and traditional colleges and universities are integrating their dormitories into coeducational living quarters. Homosexuals form Gay Liberation leagues and proclaim their rights to live together. The once rigid adoption agencies now allow single persons to adopt a child. The United States government forms a special agency to disseminate birth-control information. Parents view the film, "Woodstock," and, if they survive three hours of 100-decibel sound, wonder at the young lady standing nude in the pond shaving her armpits while thousands of people stroll past.

Despite all of the ferment and change, marriage remains popular with more than nine out of ten Americans marrying sometime in their lives. Remarriage rates for those divorced and widowed are very high. Notwithstanding the fact that many married couples have serious difficulty and that about 1 in 3½ marriages ends in divorce, marriage remains a dominant and popular goal for most Americans. In the 1960s the number of U.S. families grew at a greater rate than the population. According to the 1970 census, over 80 percent of Americans live in families that include two parents. A recent survey utilizing 384 in-depth interviews with a cross section of men and women in 43 cities across America and 239 interviews with leading experts in the field of marriage and the family concludes that marriage is enjoying a revival in the mid-1970s.[1]

This is not to say that marriage today is the same institution that it has been in the past. It is much more of a "companionship marriage," based on intimacy, equity, and flexible interaction than on institutionalized roles. As some experts put it when discussing the change to companionship marriage:

> A generation of men and women turned eagerly to the concept of companionship marriage; but multitudes of them failed dismally because, instead of being trained in interpersonal competence, they were fed with romantic notions that being "in love" would assure them unending bliss.
> What we have been calling "the failure of marriage" has rather been the failure of large numbers of individual marriages as they tried to undertake a transition for which the partners concerned simply lacked the basic equipment.[2]

It is true that the family institution has changed dramatically in the past century. It has moved from an extended rural family that performed many basic functions, including reproduction, protection and care of children, economic production of goods and services, socialization of children, recreation, religion, affection-giving and education, to the nuclear urban family which has lost most of these functions. Yet change does not necessarily mean deterioration. Indeed, a family that does not have educational and economic production functions *per se* may be better able to devote itself to its remaining functions, such as giving affection.*

Debate and controversy have always accompanied the topics of marriage and morals. Usually such debate is informal, represented by "bull sessions," dinner-table debates, popularized articles, talk shows, and panel discussions in the media as well as in hundreds of schools, churches,

---

*The term "family" designates a social group offering at least three characteristics, according to Claude Lévi-Strauss: (1) it finds its origin in marriage; (2) it consists of husband, wife, and children though it can be conceived that other relatives may also find a place close to this nuclear group; and (3) the family members are united together by (*a*) legal bonds, (*b*) economic, religious, and other kinds of rights and obligations, (*c*) a precise network of sexual rights and prohibitions, and a varying amount of psychological feelings, such as love, affection, respect, etc.

YMCA's, etc. Often such debates are piecemeal, and consider only one aspect such as birth control. Broader consideration of the social milieu, however, must be given if such specific topics are to be meaningful. Often, lack of perspective characterizes popular debate. For example, discussion of premarital sexual behavior centers on the apparent increase in premarital sexual relations. Such discussion often ignores the fact that there has always been premarital sexual activity and that there has always been debate about it in our society. Maintaining a broad perspective contributes to enlightenment by reducing the tendency to exaggerate the newness and/or extent of the problem under discussion.

Section 1

Tomorrow's Morality

1 Science, Sex, and Tomorrow's Morality

Albert Rosenfeld

Albert Rosenfeld is science editor of *Saturday Review* and visiting profes-
sor of medical humanities at The University of Texas Medical Branch in
Galveston. The following article is adapted from his book, *The Second
Genesis: The Coming Control of Life,* published by Prentice-Hall, Inc.

Wrenching changes in the nature of the ties that bind one human being to
another. Radically different meanings for old words and acts—sex and love,
for instance. Perhaps even the end of institutions such as marriage and the
family. Startling advances in the science of reproductive biology may bring
about a sweeping transformation in the style of man's life on earth. We have
lived so long with our traditions, it is hard to realize how much of our morality
—at least that part of it concerned with sex, marriage and the family—rests
solidly on the basic and unarguable facts of reproductive biology. Long before
the study of obstetrics and gynecology began, people understood that a man
and a woman must unite sexually in order to produce a child; that the embryo
develops on its own during the long, dark, quiet months before it is ejected into
the shock of life outside; and that the helpless human infant requires an
unusually prolonged period of parental protection and training before it can
cope, on even a minimal basis, with its environment. An infant horned toad
bursts forth from the maternal sac all ready to fend for itself. A newborn giraffe
or zebra can run beside its mother within a very few hours. But the human
baby is helpless.

All this being so, it was inevitable that certain sets of conventions would
evolve. Thus grew our institutions of marriage and the family, buttressed by
religion, law, politics, philosophy, education, commerce and the arts—an
interdependent social edifice endowed with an aura of self-evident immutabil-
ity.

For the rearing of the young there had to be some continuity of place and
the assignment of responsibility. The mother could not give her baby the care
and attention it needed to survive and, at the same time, be the one to fight
and protect, to feed and clothe and shelter. So the father had to be discouraged
from straying. Society channeled sexual urges toward one goal—procreation
—devising complicated systems of prescriptions and proscriptions.

Everyone in the family, from infants to uncles to grandmothers, had his
assigned role and was aware of his rights, duties and privileges. Courtship was
ritualized, wedding vows were solemnized, family support was enforced. Par-

"Science, Sex and Tomorrow's Morality" by Albert Rosenfeld, *Life* magazine, June 13,
1969, © 1969 Time Inc. Reprinted by permission of Albert Rosenfeld.

ents were to be obeyed, elders respected, children protected. Spouses were to be the exclusive sexual property of one another. Theologians labored to inculcate in man and woman alike a deep sense of sin regarding the pleasures of the flesh. But if religious taboos were insufficiently inhibiting, more practical fears were at hand: the fear of impregnating or of becoming pregnant, the fear of contracting a venereal disease, the fear of losing a spouse's devotion, the fear of earning the disapproval of one's friends and the condemnation of society.

Exceptions to convention were never uncommon, human powers of self-discipline being what they are, but such departures have, on the whole, fared rather badly. Romantic love and other cultural variants have influenced people's attitudes from time to time and from place to place, yet at no time and in no place—not, at any rate, until modern times—has there existed for very long a widespread belief that a stable society of responsible citizens could be maintained without marriage and the family.

True, these institutions clamped undeniable restrictions on individual freedom (or at least on individual license), but they also served the individual's essential needs. For a man, they served his need for sex, his need for a mate who would provide progeny to carry on his name, his need for status, his need to be needed, his need for a physical and psychical base of operations. For a woman, they served her need for security during her periods of maximum vulnerability—pregnancy and child-rearing—her need for a man and a mate to provide her with children, her need for status, her perhaps even greater need than a man's to be needed.

The system was never perfect, but it worked better than any other that men had been able to devise—and most of us have been raised in the belief that things would always go on more or less the same way. It was possible to believe this—almost impossible to believe otherwise—because there was no reason to doubt that the facts of life on which the whole moral structure rested would also remain essentially unchanged forever.

But in the sciences forever has a way of turning out to be not so everlasting after all. We are now entering an era when, as a result of new scientific discoveries, some mind-boggling things are likely to happen. Children may routinely be born of geographically separated or even long-dead parents, virgin births may become relatively common, women may give birth to other women's children, romance and genetics may finally be separated, and a few favored men may be called upon to father thousands of babies.

What has been far less widely discussed, however, are the implications of this approaching revolution, particularly the fact that traditional morality will experience a far more severe and far more profound shaking up than most people have yet imagined. If the biological foundations of present-day morality are removed, can it not logically be argued that this morality, every last time-honored shred of it, has become nothing but a useless anachronism?

Consider, as an indication of the current rapid pace of change, the matter of birth control. The potentialities for control are better understood than ever before. In addition to techniques for the *prevention* of conception, techniques are now available for the *encouragement* of conception. Where other therapies have failed, the doctor can intervene directly in two ways to promote conception. He can implant in the wife the husband's own sperm or that of an anonymous donor—a commonplace procedure these days; or he can implant an egg taken from the tubes or uterus of another woman—a technique so far applied only in animal experiments. The further refinement of freezing techniques will, moreover, permit the establishment of sperm banks and egg banks. Long-term storage would mean that proximity in space and time of donor, recipient and middleman (doctor) would no longer be required.

More and more man is beginning to unlock the secrets of life. Artificial insemination is not new, but the preserving of male sperm for up to three years by freezing is. Dr. S. J. Behrman, director of the University of Michigan's Center for Research in Reproductive Biology, has been able to achieve pregnancy in his subjects with sperms that have been frozen for up to two and one-half years. He feels that indefinite preservation will be possible one day. This brings forth the hypothesis that we might be able to preserve the sperm of an Einstein or a Beethoven for reproduction in future times. Commercial semen banks have suggested that men about to undergo vasectomy might store their semen as fertility insurance.

Beyond artificially assisted fertilization, there could be (and has been, experimentally) fertilization *in vitro*—i.e., in laboratory glassware. An egg thus prefertilized could be implanted in any woman. Furthermore, it might well be possible eventually to grow babies entirely *in vitro*, with the protecting and nourishing presence of a human mother nowhere in evidence.

There are also other variations to be played upon this theme, variations which nature has already played spontaneously, at least with the lower orders of animals, and which biologists can now duplicate in the laboratory. There is, for one, the phenomenon of parthenogenesis or virgin birth, in which, without the presence of a male sperm, the egg spontaneously doubles its supply of chromosomes, thus in effect fertilizing itself. When parthenogenesis takes place, all the child's genetic traits are maternal and there is only one true parent. And a bit of microsurgery could easily make the father the one true genetic parent. In that case the resulting child would have no genetic mother at all.

Among other controls bestowed by medical science will be the power to determine in advance the sex of one's offspring. There are two kinds of sperm —one (androsperm) that produces males, the other (gynosperm) females. Several scientists have claimed success in separating the two—and, after artificially inseminating animals with the separated sperm, getting a significantly higher proportion of the desired sex.

Finally, there is the distinct possibility of raising people without using sperm or egg at all. Could people be grown, for example, in tissue culture? In a full-grown, mature organism, every normal cell has within itself all the genetic data transmitted by the original fertilized egg cell. There appears, therefore, to be no theoretical reason why a means might not be devised to make all of a cell's genetic data accessible. And when that happens, should it not eventually become possible to grow the individual all over again from any cell taken from anywhere in the body? A number of scientists believe so.

Dr. Frederick Steward of Cornell University, working with plants such as carrots and tobacco, has in effect bypassed the sexual process of pollination. He routinely takes single cells from adult plant tissues and treats them with complex growth-stimulating substances, thereby causing them to grow into mature plants. In this manner he can make any cell from almost anywhere on the body of a mature carrot behave as if it were the "original fertilized egg."

J. B. Gurdon of Oxford University has experimented with various kinds of nuclear cell transplantations. One example is the development of adult frogs from the nuclei of single somatic cells. Gurdon took single donor cells from frog embryos at various stages of development through the tadpole stage. By using special techniques he transplanted the nuclei and obtained mature frogs 9 to 12 months later. Seventy-six percent of the frogs so produced (when the donor nuclei came from an early developmental stage) were normal in size and reproductive capacity.[1] Such experiments have been successful with other animals as well, including rabbits. In each case the newly produced animal is of the same sex and genetic makeup as the animal from which the donor cell is taken. Gurdon's experiment was also proof of what has long been suspected: that all of the genetic information necessary to produce an organism is coded into the nucleus of every cell in that organism.[2]

Thus, it is not altogether absurd to imagine the day when a single cell taken from the skin of a genius might be grown into a second individual who is identical in every respect. In the following Rosenfeld speculates about the changes that might occur in sexual mores if procreation and sexual intercourse become separated. There are many social pressures that influence society's mores and although such speculations as Rosenfeld's are sensationalistic and question-provoking, they should not be confused with scientific speculations about what our future may be.

Even more startling would be the production of human beings whose characteristics can be specified in advance. Breakthroughs in genetic knowledge make such speculations anything but preposterous, and when this kind of biochemical sophistication has been attained, man's powers will have become truly godlike. Just as he has been able, through chemistry, to create a variety of synthetic materials that never existed in nature, so may he, through genetic surgery, bring into being new species of creatures never before seen or imagined in the universe—beings better adapted, if he wishes, to survive on the surface of Jupiter, or on the bottom of the Atlantic Ocean.

If, then, the so-called facts of life are going to be subject to change in these startling ways, we can expect a chain reaction of related changes in social attitudes and institutions. This means, of course, that if we are to manage the new controls that scientists will soon be handing us, the nature of human relationships must be thoroughly re-examined—and, some think, radically reconstructed.

All this may sound unduly alarmist to those who assume that people would automatically resist as bizarre the idea of subjecting themselves to bio-engineering. But would they really? Take *in vitro* embryology. While it is not likely to be available to us soon, the technical obstacles to its attainment are surely surmountable. And when they *are* surmounted, someone somewhere is going to produce *in vitro* offspring. Once the first full and safe success has been achieved, it will not be long before some couples in special circumstances start raising babies in this fashion. Imagine what the reaction must have been to the first outlandish suggestions that human beings might one day be conceived through artificial insemination. Yet, today husbands and wives by the thousands collaborate in this manner with doctors and anonymous sperm donors to produce progeny.

So would it be with *in vitro* babies. Research in this direction will undoubtedly be accelerated by the new interest in prenatal medicine—doctoring the fetus while still in its mother's womb. Many medical scientists believe they could do much more than they now can, perhaps preventing hundreds of thousands of birth defects, if the embryo and fetus could be developed *in vitro,* as visible and accessible to diagnosis and therapy as any other patient is. Hitherto reluctant parents might opt for *in vitro* babies to increase their chances of having a normal, healthy child. Some mothers, too, might simply find it more convenient to skip the whole process of pregnancy and childbearing. There would, of course, remain staunch, old-fashioned types who consider this more a deprivation than a convenience—but have very many women ever turned down labor-saving devices? Besides, sex as recreation, as opposed to sex as procreation, is not exactly a new idea.

A quick look around confirms that a startling transformation is already taking place in our attitudes toward sex—long in advance of most of the techniques we have been talking about. In fact, where sex is concerned it is hard to say any more what is "normal" and what is not. All sorts of behavior which only a few years ago were considered wrong, or at least questionable, now seem reasonable. Playwrights and novelists do not hesitate to describe any kind of sexuality they can imagine in whatever terms seem suitable to them. Books once available only by mail in plain brown wrappers now flourish on paperback racks in card shops and at your local pharmacy. Sex in the movies leaves little to the imagination. And if sex is talked about much more openly these days, there is no reason to doubt that it is practiced much more uninhibitedly, too. On the college campus, where a goodnight kiss at the dormitory door was once considered a bit wicked, premarital sex—while not indulged in universally—is now taken for granted. (It is difficult to remember that as recently as 1960 the University of Illinois fired a biology professor for suggesting that premarital sex might be ethically justifiable.) Around a few campuses free-sex clubs featuring nude parties have sprung up. In the scientific laboratory sexual activity is studied clinically, recorded and measured by instruments and photographed in color by motion-picture cameras, and many people already accept this as logical: men and women of various ages, alone or with partners, with or without the aid of artificial devices, are willing to perform sexually and even earn a modest fee for their contribution to scientific knowledge.

If all this has taken place in the context of the familiar facts of life, essentially unaltered by science, what even greater change will occur when the new facts of life take over? Chances are we haven't seen anything yet.

Even before the current sexual revolution, there were problems aplenty in interpersonal relationships. Today, however, the problems are more evident than ever. The divorce rate is high and would be even higher if many couples did not work hard to "make a go of it." Unfortunately, the "go" they make of it frequently amounts to nothing more than a borderline accommodation to a minimally tolerable arrangement. Under the best of circumstances the chronic failure of communication that besets so many marriages creates a nagging sense of discontent and insecurity. Add an ingredient—the prevailing liberalized attitudes toward sex—and you compound all the existing confusions and insecurities. Dependable standards of fidelity are getting harder to come by. How are married couples to fix them, even for themselves, with convincing validity, let alone arrive at standards that apply to other people? And in their own state of uncertainty, what standards do they fix for their growing children—and how do they make their criteria credible? It is difficult enough even for confident parents, in a stable era, to impart what is traditionally assumed to be their superior, experience-based wisdom. In a chaotic time like ours, how do you persuade teen-agers to "behave"—or even that they ought to?

The moral sanctions of religion once served as a sufficient guide for most people. But those sanctions, and the grounds on which they are based, have been increasingly called into question, even by theologians, so that more and more laymen have come to feel that sexually they are on their own.

But if the wrath of God is no longer to be feared, what then? We may soon reach a time when venereal disease is no longer any threat, and when contraception is so cheap and easy as to remove any risk of an unwanted pregnancy. Once physiological immunity is thus assured, we can suppose that, with changing attitudes, there may also be social immunity; that is, if one is found out, no one will care. In fact, there would be no point in secrecy at all.

Any man or woman living in this changed moral environment will clearly have greatly increased opportunities for sexual adventures—though enhancing the opportunities may diminish the adventure. For any husband or wife so inclined, the temptation to philander may be overpowering. The man or woman who is not personally tempted, but who is subject to jealous apprehensions, is bound to become more uneasy with the awareness that the second party may not be resisting temptations with equal success. A jealous person traditionally has at least had the sympathy of friends. But he might find that most of his friends think it absurd to expect anyone to be faithful. The effect of all these pressures would vary with the individual, of course, but in the case of a marriage already precarious these added concerns could easily finish it.

With old fears replaced by new freedoms, do the foundations of fidelity then fall? Does fidelity become an outmoded concept? And if sex outside the marriage bed is O.K., what happens to marriage itself? Do we marry for love, companionship, security? And are these lasting? Should we be prepared to change partners whenever there is a feeling on the part of either one that it's time for a change? Are the legal bonds of marriage nonsense? Is the ideal to be a purely personal arrangement without law or ceremony, a companionate arrangement such as those that are becoming increasingly common among college students?

Dr. Margaret Mead, an anthropologist who has long studied the folkways of marriage, underscores the relevance of such questions by pointing up the enormous obstacles to staying married for life, especially in the U.S. where marriage undergoes extraordinary strains because of the romantic expectations it must uphold. "The ideal is so high," says Dr. Mead, "and the difficulties so many . . . that a very rigorous re-examination of the relationship between ideals and practice is called for."

But what about the rearing of children? Is it not vital to maintain marriage and the current family structure for that reason alone? Not necessarily. Many observers have raised serious questions about how well children fare under current circumstances anyway. They may fare considerably less well as biology begins to displace tradition. That tradition has been to regard a child as a product of the marriage bed—and therefore, in some way, sacred. "Moved by the force of love," Père Teilhard de Chardin, the priest-scientist, once wrote, "fragments of the world seek out one another so that a world may be." The fragments of the world he was talking about were the sperm and the egg—the sperm fresh-sprung from the father's loins, the egg snug in its warm, secret place; the propelling force being conjugal love, the new world being the child itself.

But the force of love may henceforth have little to do with the process. The crucial fragments of the world may simply be taken out of cold storage on demand. Even if the scientist or technician who brings the fragments together in the laboratory managed to maintain an attitude of reverence toward the life he was thus creating, love in the old sense would no longer be a part of the procreative process.

Assuming that the father's own sperm and the mother's own egg were used, the mere fact of conception outside themselves—conception in which they did not personally participate—might make a vast difference in their later attitudes toward their children. If the sperm or egg—or both—belonged originally to someone else, it would add to the impersonality of the transaction. How much of any mother's feeling toward a child is bound up in the physical fact of having carried it inside the womb for those long months, providing nourishment with her own body, fulfilling herself physiologically and spiritually as a woman? With this gone, would her maternal feelings be the same?

There are, of course, some people for whom this question is quite irrelevant: those who are capable of giving genuine love and affection to a child who has been adopted, who is not their genetic product at all. Might the answer—or a partial answer—then be to restrict childrearing privileges to couples who really want them? "People brought up without parental love," A. S. Makarenko, the Soviet counterpart of Dr. Spock, reminds us, "are often deformed people."

When family units were larger—in older, less urbanized days, when there were grandparents in the house, or even aunts and uncles—a child had alternate sets of adults to turn to, and therefore a wider chance of getting the kind of love and attention he needed, at the time he needed it. Even when there was not a large family living under one roof, people used to stay put longer in their communities, so that lots of long-time friends, who were almost like relatives, were in the immediate neighborhood during the years when a child was growing up. Among the many peoples she has studied, Dr. Mead believes the Samoans are by far the best adjusted sexually and maritally, for the very reason that "the relationship between child and parent is early diffused over many adults. . . . He is given food, consoled, carried about, by all the women of the large households, and later carried about the village by child nurses who cluster together with their charges on their hips."

In the U.S. today, however, the typical family is a "nuclear" one, with only the married couple and their immediate children living in a separate house or apartment. They probably have not lived there very long and may contemplate moving again soon. Chances are that no relatives live with them—or even close by—and that they are not really "involved" with their friends and neighbors. The result is that the children are dependent for emotional sustenance solely on their single set of parents, and their human experience is thus considerably restricted.

Such nuclear marriages are termed "longer marriages" by some because they are, in a sense, analogous to what the psychologist describes as the "loner" individual. This individual operates quite well as long as his narrow frame of reference fits the reality situation. If, however, the reality should change, it is difficult for him to judge the change because of his isolation. The same holds true for the "loner" marriage. The statistics show that married couples who enjoy many contacts with the society around them—club memberships, church activities, family ties, etc., tend to have more stable marriages. This would imply that the stability of the "loner" marriage is less. When an argument occurs in the "loner" marriage, the spouses tend to react to it in light of their own limited frame of reference. If their frame of reference is not appropriate to the new reality, then they have no place to turn to correct their reaction because of the private quality of their marriage.

Rosenfeld continues:

Except in our nostalgic fantasies, the large, tribal, multiparental household or community is a thing of the past. But one day might friends or relatives arbitrarily decide to live together in groups again, sharing expenses, households and parental duties (just as neighbors now trade around babysitting chores on occasion)? In Sweden as well as in the U.S. and Canada today a few groups are currently experimenting with such arrangements, and many communes in this country have been trying it. But could this form of tribalism ever really work in our highly mobile, technological society? Far-fetched though the idea may be, it is perhaps not to be dismissed out of hand. [See Reading 24.]

If we were to enter an era when permanent marriages became a rarity and children were raised only by volunteer parents, what would happen to the child when the parents separated? Whose children would they be? Would they be reassigned to some other group or couple for a while? Or, for stability's sake, would they have to be raised by the state—perhaps in small, familylike units? And in the new era what would be the role of sex? If it were as casual as any other harmless pleasure (assuming the harmlessness of it), what would be wrong with anyone having sex with anyone else for no other reason than their mutual desire? Some people have been saying, in effect, "Good! It's about time sex was devalued and put in its place. Now maybe people will marry for more sensible reasons." But this kind of freedom could bring about a drastic decline in the quality of sexual experience—as well as a drastic reversal in the roles of both the male and the female.

Such a reversal would give neither sex much to rejoice at. Traditionally the male has been much more free about sex than the female. He was expected to delight in sex, to be the aggressor, the panting pursuer, the sower of wild oats. In the sex act it was the woman who bestowed the favors, the man who won them. The woman treasured her chastity, used it as a lure to marriage. One of the reasons a man married was to assure himself secure possession of a pleasure that was otherwise hard to get. The woman submitted to his passion as her wifely duty.

Women have increasingly emancipated themselves from this mystique. They hear and read a great deal about the female orgasm, what a monumental experience it can and should be, their inalienable right to intense and frequent sexual pleasure—yea, even into their 70s and 80s. We now know that the sexual needs of women are at least as great as those of men, and that the female climax is more intense and longer-lasting.

The male sexual capacity, despite the Casanovas and Don Juans of history, seems to be essentially more limited than the female's and his need more easily satisfied. It will be satisfied even more easily if the female goes on the prowl. He will not have to pursue at all. Soon, in fact, he may find himself fleeing as opportunities surpass his ability to deal with them.

The woman, who formerly competed for males as marriage partners, may find herself competing for them as sexual partners. She will have become the aggressive pursuer of coy, hesitant males (even if the coyness and hesitancy are due merely to satiation—or to boredom with a commodity so totally available). Even today, as a woman grows older, she finds there are fewer and fewer men to go round. (For one thing, they tend to die earlier than women do.) With so many enhanced opportunities for dissipation, the men may begin to wear out even sooner. To preserve them longer, women—especially if they can begin to have their babies without having to carry them, thus freeing them from their ancient bondage—may wind up working while the more delicate male stays home and takes care of himself. And as the supply of available males dwindled in a world where sexual satisfaction was every woman's right, what would women do? Would there be a return of polyandry? Would they turn to each other?

However it all went, the concept of adultery would disappear, words like "premarital" and "extramarital" would become meaningless, and no one would think of attaching a label like "promiscuity" to sex activities. After all, why not be as free to experiment with a variety of sexual partners as with a variety of foods and restaurants? Love, marriage and the family have been around a long time and have served us very well. But it is clear that they may not survive the new era unless we really want them to.

Whatever our attitude, a more liberalized sexuality does seem to be here to stay, and it finally seems to be established, even among many churchmen, that sex is, or ought to be, a good and joyous thing. In this atmosphere most authorities tend to agree with the judgment of Dr. Joseph Fletcher, an Episcopal theologian: "It is doubtful that love's cause is helped by any of the sex laws that try to dictate sexual practices for consenting adults." It looks very much as if we will have to abandon our old habit of insisting that sex must serve the same purpose for everyone, or even for the same person at different times of his life. As long as sex is practiced in private between fully consenting adults who do no physical harm to one another, is it really a matter for the police or for criminal statutes?

A good many authorities have suggested that it might help, too, if we stopped thinking of sex as consisting only of intercourse, if we thought, instead, of sex as something a person *is* rather than something he *does,* as something incidental to his or her total sexuality—that is, to all the experiences and all the thoughts, from childhood to old age, that have contributed to his or her maleness or femaleness. Sexual feeling does not, after all, invariably or even usually involve only sexual intercourse; rather, it involves a whole range of attitudes and actions, from a mother's tenderness to a father's pride in the development of a child.

A man of our time, feeling overburdened by his confusions and responsibilities, might see distinct advantages in the more carefree kind of world that the new biology could make feasible. He might even envy his imaginary counterpart in one of the possible societies of the not-too-far-off future—a man grown *in vitro,* say, and raised by a state nursery. Such a man, it is true, might never know who his genetic parents were, nor would he have any brothers or sisters he could call his own. On the other hand, if he considered all men his brothers, what need would he have for a few specifically designated siblings who happen to be born in the same household? Think how carefree he might be: no parents to feel guilty about neglecting, no parental responsibilities of his own, no marriage partner to whom he owes fidelity—free to play, work, create, pursue his pleasures. In our current circumstances the absence of a loved one saddens us, and death brings terrible grief. Think how easily the tears could be wiped away if there were no single "loved one" to miss that much—or if that loved one were readily replaceable by any of several others.

And yet if you (the hypothetical *in vitro* man) did not miss anyone very much, neither would anyone miss *you* very much. Your absence would cause little sadness; your death little grief. You too would be readily replaceable.

A man needs to be needed. Who, in the new era, would need you? Would your mortality not weigh upon you even more heavily, though your life span were doubled or tripled?

"Which of us has known his brother?" wrote Thomas Wolfe. "Which of us has looked into his father's heart? Which of us has not remained forever prison-pent? Which of us is not forever a stranger and alone?"

The aloneness many of us feel on this earth is assuaged, more or less effectively, by the deep and abiding relationships we have with other human beings—with our parents, our children, our brothers and sisters, our wives, husbands, sweethearts, lovers, closest friends. These relationships are not always as close as we would like them to be, and communication is often distressingly difficult. Yet there is always the hope that each man and woman who seeks this special warmth will eventually find it.

But in the *in vitro* world, the tissue-culture world, even this hope might be difficult to sustain. Could society devise adequate substitutes? Could the trans-humans of post-civilization survive without love as we have known it in the institutions of marriage and the family? If each of us is "forever a stranger and alone" here and now, then how much more strange, how much more alone, would one feel in a world where we belong to no one, and no one belongs to us?

The following reading expands Rosenfeld's discussion to include a more specific analysis of possible effects that the biological as well as social changes might have on the family of the future. In the course of this the author calls into question certain basic assumptions that our society tends to make about the family. It should be noted that when the author uses the term "family," she usually means a nuclear family of father, mother, and their children. Some of her basic criticisms of the "family" are really criticisms of one kind of family structure—that idealized by American society. A broader definition of the term "family" tends to obviate some of her arguments. See page 8 for another definition of "family."

2 Does the Family Have a Future?

Suzanne Keller

. . .

Parenthood and above all maternity are the pivots in the anatomy of marriage and the family. If these change so must the familial organization that contained them.

There is good reason to suppose that such changes are now upon us. The malaise of our time reflects not simply a temporary disenchantment with an ancient institution but a profound convulsion of the social order. The family is indeed suffering a seachange.

It is curious to note how much more quickly the popular press, including

"Does the Family Have a Future?" by Suzanne Keller, *Journal of Comparative Family Studies*, Spring 1971. Reprinted by permission.

the so-called women's magazines, have caught on to changing marital, sexual, and parental styles. While many of the experts are still serving up conventional and tradition-bound idols—the hard-working, responsible, breadwinner husband-father, the self-effacing, ministering, wife-mother, the grateful, respectful children—these magazines tempt the contemporary reader with less standard and more challenging fare. Whether in New York or in Athens, the newsstands flaunt their provocative titles—"Is This the Last Marrying Generation?", "Alimony for Ex-Husbands," "Why We Don't Want to Have Children," "Are Husbands Superfluous?"—in nonchalant profusion. These and other assaults on our sexual and moral codes in the shape of the new theater, the new woman, the new youth, and TV soap operas akin to a psychiatrist's case files, persuade us that something seems to be afoot in the whole sphere of marriage and family relations which many had thought immune to change. In point of fact the question is not *whether* the family is changing but how and how much; how important are these changes, how permanent, how salutary? The answers depend largely on the way we ask our questions and define our terms.

The family means many things to many people but in its essence it refers to those socially patterned ideals and practices concerned with biological and cultural survival of the species. When we speak of the family we are using a kind of shorthand, a label for a social invention not very different, in essence, from other social inventions, let us say the Corporation or the University, and no more permanent than these. This label designates a particular set of social practices concerned with procreation and child rearing; with the heterosexual partnerships that make this possible and the parent-child relations that make it enduring. As is true of all collective habits, once established, such practices are exceedingly resistant to change, in part because they evoke strong sentiments and in part because no acceptable alternatives are offered. Since most individuals are unable to step outside of their cultures, they are unable to note the arbitrary and variable nature of their conventions. Accordingly, they ascribe to their folkways and creeds an antiquity, an inevitability, and a universality these do not possess.

The idea that the family is universal is highly misleading despite its popularity. All surviving societies have indeed found ways to stabilize the processes of reproduction and child care else they would not have survived to tell their tale. But since they differ greatly in how they arrange these matters (and since they are willing to engage in Hot and Cold Wars to defend such differences) the generalization does not help us explain the phenomenon but more nearly explains it away.

In truth there are as many forms of the family as there are forms of society, some so different from ours that we consider them unnatural and incomprehensible. There are, for example, societies in which couples do not share a household and do not have sole responsibility for their offspring; others in which our domestic unit of husband and wife is divided into two separate units, a conjugal one of biological parents and a brother-sister unit for economic sustenance. There are societies in which children virtually rear each other and societies in which the wise father does not know his own child. All of these are clearly very different from our twentieth century, industrial-urban conception of the family as a legally united couple, sharing bed and board, jointly responsible for bearing and rearing their children, and formally isolated from their next of kin in all but a sentimental sense. This product of a long and complicated evolutionary development from prehistoric times is no simple replica of the ancient productive and reproductive institutions from which it derives its name and some of its characteristic features. The contemporary family really has little in common with its historic Hebrew, Greek, and Roman ancestors.

The family of these great civilizations of the West was a household community of hundreds, and sometimes thousands, of members ("familia" is the Latin term for household). Only some of the members were related by blood and by far the larger part were servants and slaves, artisans, friends, and distant relations. In its patriarchal form (again culturally variable), this large community was formally held together by the role of eldest male who more nearly resembled the general of an army than a modern husband-father. In its prime, this household community constituted a miniature society, a decentralized version of a social organization that had grown too large and unwieldy for effective management. In this it resembles the giant bureaucracies of our own day, and their proposed decentralization into locally based, locally staffed subsystems, designed to offset the evils of remote control while nevertheless maintaining their connection with it. Far from having been universal, this ancient family type, with its gods and shrines, schools and handicrafts, was not even widely prevalent within its own social borders. Confined to the landed and propertied upper classes, it remained an unattainable ideal for the bulk of common men who made up the society.

The fallacy of universality has done students of human behavior a great disservice. By leading us to seek and hence to find a single pattern, it has blinded us to historical precedents for multiple legitimate family arrangements. As a result we have been rather impoverished in our speculations and proposals about alternative future arrangements in the family sphere.

A second common fallacy asserts that the family is *the* basic institution of society, hereby revealing a misunderstanding of how a society works. For as a social institution, the family is by definition a specialized element which provides society with certain needed services and depends on it for others. This means that you cannot tamper with a society without expecting the family to be affected in some way and vice versa. In the contemporary jargon, we are in the presence of a feedback system. Whatever social changes we anticipate, therefore, the family cannot be kept immune from them.

A final fallacy concerns the presumed naturalness of the family in proof of which a motley and ill-assorted grab bag of anecdotal evidence from the animal kingdom is adduced. But careful perusal of ethological accounts suggests that animals vary as greatly as we do, their mating and parental groupings including such novelties as the love death, males who bear children, total and guilt-free "promiscuity," and other "abnormal" features. The range of variation is so wide, in fact, that virtually any human arrangement can be justified by recourse to the habits of some animal species.

In sum, if we wish to understand what is happening to the family—to our family—in our own day, we must examine and observe it in the here and now. In so doing it would be well to keep in mind that the family is an abstraction at best, serving as guide and image of what a particular society considers desirable and appropriate in family relations, not what takes place in actual fact. In reality there are always a number of empirical family types at variance with this, though they usually pay lip service to the overarching cultural ideal.

Challenges to the Contemporary Industrial Family

In the United States, as in other industrial societies, the ideal family consists of a legally constituted husband-wife team, their young, dependent children, living in a household of their own, provided for by the husband's earnings as main breadwinner, and emotionally united by the wife's exclusive concentration on the home. Probably no more than one-third of all families at a particular moment in time, and chiefly in the middle and would-be middle classes, actually live up to this image. The remaining majority all lack one or more of the essential attributes—in lacking a natural parent, or in not being economically self-sufficient, or in having made other necessary modifications.

One contrasting form is the extended family in which the couple share household arrangements and expenses with parents, siblings, or other close relatives. The children are then reared by several generations and have a choice of models on which to pattern their behavior. This type, frequent in working class and immigrant milieus, may be as cohesive and effective as the ideal type but it lacks the cultural legitimacy and desirability of the latter.

A third family type, prevalent among the poor of all ethnic and racial backgrounds, is the mother-child family. [See Reading 23.] Contrary to our prejudices this need not be a deviant or distorted family form, for it may be the only viable and appropriate one in its particular setting. Its defects may stem more from adverse social judgments than from intrinsic failings. Deficient in cultural resources and status, it may nevertheless provide a humane and spirited setting for its members, particularly if some sense of stability and continuity has been achieved. Less fortunate are the numerous non-families, ex-families, and non-intact families such as the divorced, the widowed, the unmarriageables, and many other fragmented social forms, who have no recognized social place. None of these, however, threaten the existing order since they are seen and see themselves as involuntarily different, imperfect, or unfortunate. As such they do not challenge the ideals of family and marital relations but simply suggest how difficult it is to live up to them. When we talk of family change or decline, however, it is precisely the ideal standards which we have in mind. A challenge to them cannot be met by simple reaffirmations of old truths, disapproval, shock, or ridicule of the challengers, or feigned indifference. Such challenges must be met head on.

Today the family and its social and psychological underpinnings are being fundamentally challenged from at least three sources: (1) from accumulated failures and contradictions in marriage; (2) from pervasive occupational and educational trends including the changing relations between the sexes, the spread of birth control, and the changing nature of work; and (3) from novel developments in biology. Let me briefly examine each.

It is generally agreed that even in its ideal form, the industrial-urban family makes great, some would say excessive, demands on its members. For one thing it rests on the dyadic principle or pair relationship which, as Georg Simmel observed long ago, is inherently tragic and unstable. Whether in chess, tennis, or marriage, two are required to start and continue the game but only one can destroy it. In this instance, moreover, the two are expected to retain their separate identities as male and female and yet be one in flesh and spirit. No wonder that the image of the couple, a major source of fusion and of schism in our society, is highly contradictory according to whether we think of the sexes as locked in love or in combat. Nor do children, the symbols of their union, necessarily unify them. Their own growing pains and cultural demands force them into mutually exclusive sociosexual identities, thereby increasing the intimate polarity. In fact, children arouse parental ambivalence in a number of ways, not the least of which is that they demand all but give back all too little. And yet their upbringing and sustenance, the moral and emotional climate, as well as the accumulation of economic and educational resources needed for survival, all rest on this small, fragile, essential but very limited unit. Held together by sentimental rather than by corporate bonds, the happiness of the partners is a primary goal although no one is very sure what happiness means nor how it may be achieved and sustained.

To these potentials for stress and strain must be added the loss of many erstwhile functions to school, state, and society, and with it something of the glamour and challenge of family commitments. Few today expect the family to be employment agency, welfare state, old age insurance, or school for life. Yet once upon a time, not too long ago at that, it was all that and more. At the same time, however, with fewer resources, some new burdens have been added stemming from rising standards of child health, education, and welfare. This makes parents even more crucially responsible for the potential fate of their children over whom they have increasingly less exclusive control.

Like most social institutions in the throes of change, moreover, the modern family is also beset by numerous internal contradictions engendered by the conflict between traditional patterns of authority and a new egalitarianism between husbands and wives and parents and children. The equality of the spouses, for example, collides with the continuing greater economic responsibilities, hence authority, of the husband. The voluntary harness of love chafes under the constraint of numerous obligations and duties imposed by marriage, and dominance patterns by sex or age clash with new demands for mutuality, reciprocity, equity, and individualism. These, together with some unavoidable disillusionments and disappointments in marriage, set the stage for the influence of broader and less subjective social trends.

One such trend, demographic in nature but bound to have profound social implications, concerns the lengthened life expectancy and the shortened reproductive span for women. Earlier ages at marriage, fewer children per couple, and closer spacing of children means: the girl who marries at 20 will have all her children by age 26, have all her children in school by her early thirties, have the first child leave home for job, schooling, or marriage in her late thirties, and have all her children out of the home by her early forties. This leaves some thirty to forty years to do with as personal pleasure or social need dictate. The contrast with her grandmother is striking: later marriage, and more children spaced farther apart, meant all the children in school no earlier than her middle or late thirties and the last to leave home (if he or she ever did) not before her early fifties. At which time grandmother was probably a widow and close to the end of her own lifespan. The empty nest thus not only occurs earlier today but it lasts longer, affecting not this or that unfortunate individual woman but many if not most women. Hence what may in the past have been an individual misfortune has turned into a social emergency of major proportions. More unexpected free time, more time without a socially recognized or appreciated function, more premature retirements surely puts the conventional modern wife, geared to the domestic welfare of husband, home, and children, at a singular disadvantage relative to the never-married career woman. Destined to outlive her husband, stripped of major domestic responsibilities in her prime years, what is she to do with this windfall of extra hours and years? Surely we must expect and prepare for a major cultural shift in the education and upbringing of female children. If women cannot afford to make motherhood and domestic concerns the sole foci of their identities, they must be encouraged, early in life, to prepare themselves for some occupation or profession not as an adjunct or as a last resort in case of economic need but as an equally legitimate pursuit. The childrearing of girls must increasingly be geared to developing a feminine identity that stresses autonomy, non-dependency, and self-assertion in work and in life.

Some adjunct trends are indirectly stimulating just such a reorientation. When women are compelled, as they often are, to earn their own living or to supplement inadequate family resources necessitated by the high emphasis on personal consumption and the high cost of services increasingly deemed essential as national standards rise, conventional work-dependency patterns are shattered. For, since the male breadwinner is already fully occupied, often with two jobs, or if he cannot or will not work, his wife is forced to step in. Thus there is generated internal family pressure—arising from a concern for family welfare but ultimately not confined to it—for wives to be gainfully employed outside of the home. And fully three-fourths in the post-childbearing ages already are, albeit under far from ideal conditions. Torn between home and job, between the precepts of early childhood with its promise of permanent security at the side of a strong male and the pressures of a later reality, unaided by a society unaware or indifferent to her problems, the double-duty wife must manage as best she can.

That this need not be so is demonstrated by a number of modern societies whose public policies are far better meshed with changing social realities. Surely one of our more neglected institutions—the single-family household which, despite all the appliances, remains essentially backward and primitive in its conditions of work—will need some revamping and modernizing. More household appliances, more and more attractive alternatives to the individually run household, more nursery schools, and a total overhaul of work-schedules not now geared to a woman's life and interests cannot be long in coming. While these will help women in all of their multiple tasks they may also of course further challenge the presumed joys of exclusive domesticity.

All in all, it would appear that the social importance of the family relative to other significant social arenas will decline. Even today when the family still exerts a strong emotional and sentimental hold its social weight is not what it once was. All of us ideally are still born in intact families but not all of us need to establish families to survive. Marriage and children continue to be extolled as supreme social and personal goals but they are no longer—especially for men—indispensable for a meaningful existence. As individual self-sufficiency, fed by economic affluence or economic self-restraint, increases, so does one's exemption from unwanted economic as well as kinship responsibilities. Today the important frontiers seem to lie elsewhere, in science, politics, and outer space. This must affect the attractions of family life for both men and women. For men, because they will see less and less reason to assume full economic and social responsibilities for four to five human beings in addition to themselves as it becomes more difficult and less necessary to do so. This, together with the continued decline of patriarchal authority and male dominance—even in the illusory forms in which they have managed to hang on—will remove some of the psychic rewards which prompted many men to marry, while the disappearance of lineage as mainstays of the social and class order will deprive paternity of its social justification. For women, the household may soon prove too small for the scope of their ambitions and power drives. Until recently these were directed first of all to their children, secondarily to their mates. But with the decline of parental control over children a major erstwhile source of challenge and creativity is removed from the family sphere. This must weaken the mother-wife complex, historically sustained by the necessity and exaltation of motherhood and the taboo on illegitimacy.

Above all, the move towards worldwide population and birth control must affect the salience of parenthood for men and women, as a shift of cultural emphasis and individual priorities deflates maternity as woman's chief social purpose and paternity as the prod to male exertions in the world of work. Very soon, I suspect, the cultural presses of the world will slant their messages against the bearing and rearing of children. Maternity, far from being a duty, not even a right, will then become a rare privilege to be granted to a select and qualified few. Perhaps the day is not far off when reproduction will be confined to a fraction of the population, and what was once inescapable necessity may become voluntary, planned, choice. Just as agricultural societies in which everyone had to produce food were once superseded by industrial societies in which a scant 6 per cent now produce food for all, so one day the few may produce children for the many. This along with changing attitudes towards sex, abortion, adoption, illegitimacy, the spread of the pill, better knowledge of human behavior, and a growing scepticism that the family is the only proper crucible for childrearing, creates a powerful recipe for change.

Although both Keller and Rosenfeld stress the impact that improved birth-control methods have had on sexual mores, it must be remembered that enlightened birth-control technology is relatively limited throughout the world. Even within the industrialized nations such as the United States, unwanted pregnancies still occur frequently. In addition, in most countries population growth continues at a dangerously high rate. The theoretical impact of improved methods of birth control is not the same as the practical impact. In most of the underdeveloped countries infant mortality rates are still so high that a family must have numerous children in order to insure that some will reach adulthood. Such families are really not interested in birth control. In many countries the methods are either too complicated or too costly to be practical.

For most countries birth-control technology is more vitally related to the problems of overpopulation than to changing sexual mores. Aside from the possibility of man's population outgrowing the Earth's capacity to support life, sheer numbers of people vastly complicate man's efforts to improve his lot. Large population also necessitates greatly increased bureaucratization in order to control behaviors that would be no problem if there were only a few people involved. Indeed, increased numbers of people usually mean diminished individual freedom if for no other reason than efficiency.

In addition, it is again numbers of people that cause man's ecological problems. Many experts now believe that the world is at an ecological crisis point. Paul and Anne Ehrlich in their recent book, *Population, Resources, Environment: Issues in Human Ecology,* state:

> The explosive growth of the human population is the most significant terrestrial event of the past million millennia. Three and one-half billion people now inhabit the Earth, and every year this number increases by 70 million. Armed with weapons as diverse as thermonuclear bombs and DDT, this mass of humanity now threatens to destroy most of the life on the planet. Mankind itself may stand on the brink of extinction; in its death throes it could take with it most of the other passengers of Spaceship Earth. No geological event in a billion years —not the emergence of mighty mountain ranges, nor the submergence of entire subcontinents, nor the occurrence of periodic glacial ages—has posed a threat to terrestrial life comparable to that of human overpopulation.

Population growth intimately influences marriage and family development. If a young couple is concerned about overpopulation, their decision about having children, when, and how many, will be affected. Birth control and family planning become important marital factors.

Just how threatening is the overpopulation problem? Estimates range from the black pessimism that Earth will reach a point of being unable to contain its human population within the next 100–200 years, to the sanguine optimism that great new food sources (such as ocean agriculture) will minimize overpopulation problems in the foreseeable future.

Indeed, great strides have been made in the more efficient production of food. At the second meeting of the World Food Congress, there was much less emphasis on the scarcity of food than concern for the problem of abundance. The World Food Congress finds that with new miracle grains and advanced technologies the world's agricultural potential is great enough to feed 157 billion people (present world population is 3.5 billion). One example of these advances is to be found in the rice crop. After some years of experimentation, researchers have produced improved rice strains that have greatly increased production. Only five years ago, the Philippines imported over one million tons of rice annually. Today they are self-sufficient and will soon begin to export rice. West Pakistan has increased wheat production by 17 percent and rice production by 162 percent. In Mexico, wheat yields have grown from 150 pounds per acre in 1950 to 2300 pounds today.[1,2]

The reader will have to decide for himself just how threatening overpopulation will be in the near future. Figures 1 and 2 show some of the statistics of population growth. Naturally, if such birth trends continue indefinitely, there will come a catastrophic time when the earth can no longer support its population.

Doubling Times

Date	Estimated world population	Time for population to double
8000 BC	5 million	
		1,500 years
1650 AD	500 million	
		200 years
1850 AD	1,000 million (1 billion)	
		80 years
1930 AD	2,000 million (2 billion)	
		45 years
1975 AD	4,000 million (4 billion)	
	Computed doubling time around 1970	35–37 years

Fig. 1   Doubling Times for World Population

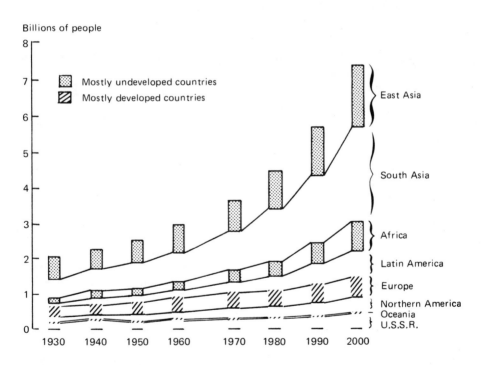

Projected growth of world population, based on the United Nations "constant fertility" projection. [After Population Bulletin, vol. 21, no. 4.]

Fig. 2

In the United States, the current birthrate has fallen to its historical low, being just below zero population growth. It takes about 2.1 children per family to maintain the population. Because of the past years of higher birthrate, it will be about 35 years before the population in the United States ceases to grow, assuming the low birthrate remains and immigration is discounted.

Keller continues,

The trends that I have sketched would affect marriage, male-female, and parent-child relations even if no other developments were on the horizon. But there are. As yet barely discernible and still far from being applicable to human beings, recent breakthroughs in biology—with their promise of a greatly extended life span, novel modes of reproduction, and dramatic possibilities for genetic intervention—cannot be ignored in a discussion devoted to the future of the family.

Revolution in Biology

If the early part of this century belonged to physics and the middle period to exploratory ventures into outer space, the next few decades belong to biology. The prolongation of life to double or triple its current span seems virtually assured, the extension of female fertility into the sixties is more than a distinct possibility, and novel ways of reproducing the human species have moved from science fiction to the laboratory. The question then arises, What will happen when biological reproduction will not only be inadvisable for the sake of collective well-being but superseded by new forms and eventually by non-human forms of reproduction?

A number of already existing possibilities may give us a foretaste of what is to come. For example, the separation of conception from gestation means that motherhood can become specialized, permitting some women to conceive and rear many children and others to bear them without having to provide for them. Frozen sperm banks (of known donors) are envisioned from which prospective mothers could choose the fathers of their children on the basis of particularly admired or desired qualities, thereby advancing an age-old dream of selecting a distinguished paternity for their children based on demonstrated rather than potential male achievement. And it would grant men a sort of immortality to sire offspring long after their biological deaths as well as challenge the implicit equation now made between fathers and husbands. Finally, the as yet remote possibility to reproduce the human species without sexual intercourse, by permanently separating sex from procreation, would permit unmarried women (and men) to have children without being married, reduces a prime motive for marriage and may well dethrone—inconceivable as this may seem—the heterosexual couple. All of these pose questions of legal and social policy to plague the most subtle Solon. Who is the father of a child—the progenitor or the provider where these have become legitimately distinct roles? Who is the mother—the woman who conceives the child or the one who carries it to term? Who will decide on sex ratios once sex determination becomes routine? Along with such challenges and redefinitions of human responsibility, some see the fate of heterosexuality itself to be in the balance. In part of course this rests on one's assumptions about the nature of sexuality and sexual identity.

. . .

Some are speculating about a future in which only one of the current sexes will survive, the other having become superfluous or obsolescent. Depending on the taste, temperament—and sex—of the particular writer, women and men have alternately been so honored (or cursed). It is not always easy to tell which aspect of sex—the anatomical, psychological, or cultural—the writer has in mind but as the following comment suggests, much more than anatomy is at stake.

> Does the man and woman thing have a future? The question may not be hypothetical much longer. Within 10 years . . . we may be able to choose the sex of our offspring; and later to reproduce without mating male and female cells. This means it will someday be possible to have a world with only one sex, woman, and thereby avoid the squabbles, confusions, and headaches that have dogged this whole business of sex down the centuries. A manless world suggests several scientific scenarios. The most pessimistic would have society changing not at all, but continuing on its manly ways of eager acquisition, hot competition, and mindless aggression. In which case, half the women would become "men" and go right on getting ulcers, shouting "charge" and pinning medals on each other.[3]

Long before the demise of heterosexuality as a mainstay of the social order, however, we will have to come to terms with changing sexual attitudes and mores ushered in by what has been called the sexual revolution. This liberalization, this rejection of old taboos, half-truths, and hypocrisies, also means a crisis of identity as men and women, programmed for more traditional roles, search for the boundaries of their sexual selves in an attempt to establish a territoriality of the soul.

Confusion is hardly, of course, a novel aspect of the human condition. Not knowing where we have come from, why we are here, nor where we are headed, it could hardly be otherwise. There have always been dissatisfied men and women rejecting the roles their cultures have assigned them or the responsibilities attached to these. But these are the stuff of poetry and drama, grist for the analyst's couch or the priest's confessional, in other words private torments and agonies kept concealed from an unsympathetic world. It is only when such torments become transmuted into public grievance and so become publicly heard and acknowledged that we can be said to be undergoing profound changes akin to what we are experiencing today.

Returning now to our main question—Does the family have a future?—it should be apparent that I expect some basic and irreversible changes in the decades ahead and the emergence of some novel forms of human togetherness. Not that the current scene does not already offer some provocative variations on ancient themes, but most of these gain little public attention, still less approval, and so they are unable to alter professed beliefs and standards. Moreover, every culture has its own forms of self-justification and self-righteousness and in our eagerness to affirm the intrinsic superiority of our ways, we neglect to note the magnitude of variations and deviations from the ideals we espouse. What are we to make, for example, of such dubious allegiance to the monogamous ideal as serial marriages or secret adulteries? Or, less morally questionable, what of the quasi-organized part-time family arrangements necessitated by extreme occupational and geographic mobility? Consider for a moment the millions of families of salesmen, pilots, seacaptains, soldiers, sailors, and junior executives where the man of the house is not often *in* the house. These absentee husbands-fathers who magically re-enter the family circle just long enough to be appreciated, leaving their wives in charge of the homes they pay for and of the children they sired, are surely no more than part-time mates. If we know little about the adjustments they have had to make or their children's responses, this is because they clearly do not fit in with our somewhat outmoded stereotyped notions of what family relations ought to be. Or consider another home-grown example, the institution of governesses and boarding schools to rear upper-class children. Where is the upper-class mother and how does she spend her time between vacations and homecoming weekends? Then there are of course many countries around the world—Israel, Sweden, the Socialist countries, some of the African societies—where all or nearly all women, most of them mothers, work outside of the home as a matter of course. And because these societies are free from guilt and ambivalence about the working mother, they have managed to incorporate these realities more gracefully into their scheme of things, developing a number of useful innovations along the way. Thus even in our own day, adaptions and modifications exist and have not destroyed all notions of family loyalty, responsibility, and commitment.

In fact, people may be more ready for change than official pronouncements and expert opinions assume. The spread of contraceptive information and the acceptance of full birth control have been remarkable. The relaxation of many erstwhile taboos has proceeded at breakneck speed, and the use of public forums to discuss such vital but previously forbidden topics as abortion, homosexuality, or illegitimacy is dramatic and startling in a society rooted in Puritanism. A number of studies, moreover, show that the better educated are more open to re-examination and change in all spheres, including the family. Since these groups are on the increase, we may expect greater receptivity to such changes in the future. Even such startling proposed innovations as egg transplants, test-tube babies, and cloning are not rejected out of hand if they would help achieve the family goals most Americans prize. . . . (See Reading 1.)

. . . If we dare to speculate further about the future of the family we will be on safe ground with the following anticipations: (1) a trend towards greater, legitimate variety in sexual and marital experience; (2) a decrease in the negative emotions—exclusiveness, possessiveness, fear and jealousy—associated with these; (3) greater room for personal choice in the kind, extent, and duration of intimate relationships, which may greatly improve their quality as people will both give and demand more of them; (4) entirely new forms of communal living arrangements in which several couples will share the tasks of childrearing and economic support as well as the pleasures of relaxation; (5) multi-stage marriages geared to the changing life cycle and the presence or absence of dependent children. Of these proposals, some, such as Margaret Mead's, would have the young and the immature of any age test themselves and their capacities to relate to others in an individual form of marriage which would last only so long as it fulfilled both partners. In contrast to this, older, more experienced and more mature couples who were ready to take on the burdens of parenthood would make a deeper and longer lasting commitment. Other proposals would reverse this sequence and have couples assume parental commitments when young and, having discharged their debt to society, be then free to explore more personal, individualistic partnerships.

For the immediate future, it appears that most Americans opt for and anticipate their participation in durable, intimate, heterosexual partnerships as anchors and pivots of their adult lives. They expect these to be freer and more flexible than was true in the past, however, and less bound to duty and involuntary personal restrictions. They cannot imagine and do not wish a life without them.

Speculating for the long-range future, we cannot ignore the potential implications of the emerging cultural taboo on unrestricted reproduction and the shift in public concern away from the family as the central preoccupation of one's life. Hard as it may seem, perhaps some day we will cease to relate to families just as we no longer relate ourselves to clans, and instead be bound up with some new, as yet unnamed, principle of human association. If and when this happens, we may also see a world of Unisex, Multi-sex, or Nonsex. None of this can happen, however, if we refuse to shed some of our most cherished preconceptions, such as that monogamy is superior to other forms of marriage or that women naturally make the best mothers. Much as we may be convinced of these now, time may reveal them as yet another illusion, another example of made-to-order truths.

Ultimately all social change involves moral doubt and moral reassessment. If we refuse to consider change while there still is time, time will pass us by.

Only by examining and taking stock of what is can we hope to affect what will be. This is our chance to invent and thus to humanize the future.

Effective birth control separates sexual intercourse from procreation and it is this separation rather than the overpopulation problem that evokes the continuing debate about a sexual revolution and changing mores.

The thoughtful students of human nature will, however, need to assess the impact of successful birth control on the social mores and in particular on the marital relationship. Many years ago Walter Lippmann made such an assessment and with his usual clarity he discussed love in the great society where birth-control methods have freed both man and woman from the responsibility of children unless desired. A few excerpts from his essay may help the reader to understand better the kind of ethical problems man faces when sexual intercourse is separated from procreation. It also points up the fact that such problems are not new.

3 Love in the Great Society

Walter Lippmann

For many years Mr. Lippmann has been a brilliant political analyst and commentator in which capacity he has often influenced public policy in America. The following reading comes from an older work in which he has written incisively about the foundations of belief and conduct. He addresses the question of "love" as a humanist and moralist.

. . .

We know that the old conventions have lost most of their authority because we cannot know about, and therefore can no longer regulate, the sexual behavior of others. It may be that there is, as some optimists believe, a fine but candid restraint practiced among modern men and women. It may be that incredible licentiousness exists all about us, as the gloomier prophets insist. It may be that there is just about as much unconventional conduct and no more than there has always been. Nobody, I think, really knows. Nobody knows whether the conversation about sex reflects more promiscuity or less hypocrisy. But what everybody must know is that sexual conduct, whatever it may be, is regulated personally and not publicly in modern society. If there is restraint it is, in the last analysis, voluntary; if there is promiscuity, it can be quite secret.

.   .   .

With contraception established as a more or less legitimate idea in modern society, a vast discussion has ensued as to how the practice of it can be rationalized. In this discussion the pace is set by those who accept the apparent logic of contraception and are prepared boldly to revise the sexual conventions accordingly. They take as their major premise the obvious fact that by contraception it is possible to dissociate procreation from gratification, and therefore to pursue independently what Mr. Havelock Ellis calls the primary and secondary objects of the sexual impulse. They propose, therefore, to sanction two distinct sets of conventions: one designed to protect the interests of the offspring by promoting intelligent, secure, and cheerful parenthood; the other designed to permit the freest and fullest expression of the erotic personality. They propose, in other words, to distinguish between parenthood as a vocation involving public responsibility, and love as an art, pursued privately for the sake of happiness.

.   .   .

They ask public opinion to sanction what contraception has made feasible. They point out that "a large number of the men and women of today form sexual relationships outside marriage—whether or not they ultimately lead to marriage—which they conceal or seek to conceal from the world." These relationships, says Mr. Ellis, differ from the extramarital manifestations of the sexual life of the past in that they do not derive from prostitution or seduction. Both of these ancient practices, he adds, are diminishing, for prostitution is becoming less attractive and, with the education of women, seduction is becoming less possible. The novelty of these new relations, the prevalence of which is conceded though it cannot be measured, lies in the fact that they are entered into voluntarily, have no obvious social consequences, and are altogether beyond the power of law or opinion to control. The argument, therefore, is that they should be approved, the chief point made being that by removing all stigma from such unions, they will become candid, wholesome, and delightful. The objection of the reformers to the existing conventions is that the sense of sin poisons the spontaneous goodness of such relationships.

The actual proposals go by a great variety of fancy names such as free love, trial marriage, companionate marriage. When these proposals are examined it is evident they all take birth control as their major premise, and then deduce from it some part or all of the logical consequences. Companionate marriage, for example, is from the point of view of the law, whatever it may be subjectively, nothing but a somewhat roundabout way of saying that childless couples may be divorced by mutual consent. It is a proposal, if not to control, then at least to register publicly, all sexual unions, the theory being that this public registration will abolish shame and furtiveness and give them a certain permanence. Companionate marriage is frankly an attempt at a compromise between marriages that are difficult to dissolve and clandestine relationships which have no sanction whatever.

. . .

It is one thing, however, to recognize the full logic of birth control and quite another thing to say that convention ought to be determined by that logic. One might as well argue that because automobiles can be driven at a hundred miles an hour the laws should sanction driving at the rate of a hundred miles an hour. Birth control is a device like the automobile, and its inherent possibilities do not fix the best uses to be made of it.

What an understanding of the logic of birth control does is to set before us the limits of coercive control of sexual relations. The law can, for example, make divorce very difficult where there are children.

. . .

On the other hand the law cannot effectively prohibit infidelity, and as a matter of fact does not do so today.

. . .

But sexual conventions are not statutes, and it is important to define quite clearly just what they are. In the older world they were rules of conduct enforceable by the family and the community through habit, coercion, and authority. In this sense of the word, convention tends to lose force and effect in modern civilization. Yet a convention is essentially a theory of conduct and all human conduct implies some theory of conduct. Therefore, although it may be that no convention is any longer coercive, conventions remain, are adopted, revised, and debated. They embody the considered results of experience: perhaps the experience of a lonely pioneer or perhaps the collective experience of the dominant members of a community. In any event they are as necessary to a society which recognizes no authority as to one which does. For the inexperienced must be offered some kind of hypothesis when they are confronted with the necessity of making choices: they cannot be so utterly open-minded that they stand inert until something collides with them. In the modern world, therefore, the function of conventions is to declare the meaning of experience. A good convention is one which will most probably show the inexperienced the way to happy experience.

Just because the rule of sexual conduct by authority is dissolving, the need of conventions which will guide conduct is increasing. That, in fact, is the reason for the immense and urgent discussion of sex throughout the modern world. It is an attempt to attain an understanding of the bewilderingly new experiences to which few men or women know how to adjust themselves. The true business of the moralist in the midst of all this is not to denounce this and to advocate that, but to see as clearly as he can into the meaning of it, so that out of the chaos of pain and happiness and worry he may help to deliver a usable insight.

It is, I think, to the separation of parenthood as a vocation from love as an end in itself that the moralist must address himself. For this is the heart of the problem: to determine whether this separation, which birth control has made feasible and which law can no longer prevent, is in harmony with the conditions of human happiness.

. . .

The sexual conventions which they (proponents of freer sexual involvements) have proposed are really designed to cure notorious evils. They do not define the good life in sex; they point out ways of escape from the bad life. Thus companionate marriage is proposed by Judge Lindsey not as a type of union which is inherently desirable, but as an avenue of escape from corrupt marriages on the one hand and furtive promiscuity on the other. The movement for free divorce comes down to this: it is necessary because so many marriages are a failure. The whole theory that love is separate from parenthood and home-building is supported by the evidence in those cases where married couples are not lovers. It is the pathology of sexual relations which inspires the reformers of sexual conventions.

There is no need to quarrel with them because they insist upon remedies for manifest evils. Deep confusion results when they forget that these remedies are only remedies, and go on to institute them as ideals. It is better, without any doubt, that incompatible couples should be divorced and that each should then be free to find a mate who is compatible. But the frequency with which men and women have to resort to divorce because they are incompatible will be greatly influenced by the notions they have before and during marriage of what compatibility is and what it involves. The remedies for failure are important. But what is central is the conception of sexual relations by which they expect to live successfully.

They cannot—I am, of course, speaking broadly—expect to live successfully by the conception that the primary and secondary functions of sex are in separate compartments of the soul. I have indicated why this conception is self-defeating and why, since human nature is organic and experience cumulative, our activities must, so to speak, engage and imply each other. Mates who are not lovers will not really cooperate, in bearing children; they will be distracted, insufficient, and worst of all they will be merely dutiful. Lovers who have nothing to do but love each other are not really to be envied; love and nothing else very soon is nothing else. The emotion of love, in spite of the romantics, is not self-sustaining; it endures only when the lovers love many things together, and not merely each other. It is this understanding that love cannot successfully be isolated from the business of living which is the enduring wisdom of the institution of marriage. Let the law be what it may be as to what constitutes a marriage contract and how and when it may be dissolved. Let public opinion be as tolerant as it can be toward any and every kind of irregular and experimental relationship. When all the criticisms have been made, when all supernatural sanctions have been discarded, all subjective inhibitions erased, all compulsions abolished, the convention of marriage still remains to be considered as an interpretation of human experience. It is by the test of how genuinely it interprets human experience that the convention of marriage will ultimately be judged.

The wisdom of marriage rests upon an extremely unsentimental view of lovers and their passions. Its assumptions, when they are frankly exposed, are horrifying to those who have been brought up in the popular romantic tradition of the Nineteenth Century. These assumptions are that, given an initial attraction, a common social background, common responsibilities, and the conviction that the relationship is permanent, compatibility in marriage can normally be achieved. It is precisely this that the prevailing sentimentality about love denies. It assumes that marriages are made in heaven, that compatibility is instinctive, a mere coincidence, that happy unions are, in the last analysis, lucky accidents in which two people who happen to suit each other happen to have met. The convention of marriage rests on an interpretation of human nature which does not confuse the subjective feeling of the lovers that their passion is unique, with the brutal but objective fact that, had they never met, each of them would in all probability have found a lover who was just as unique. . . .

This is the reason why the popular concept of romantic love as the meeting of two affinities produces so much unhappiness. The mysterious glow of passion is accepted as a sign that the great coincidence has occurred; there is a wedding and soon, as the glow of passion cools, it is discovered that no instinctive and preordained affinity is present. At this point the wisdom of popular romantic marriage is exhausted. For it proceeds on the assumption that love is a mysterious visitation. There is nothing left, then, but to grin and bear a miserably dull and nagging fate, or to break off and try again. The deep fallacy of the conception is in the failure to realize that compatibility is a process and not an accident, that it depends upon the maturing of instinctive desire by adaptation to the whole nature of the other person and to the common concerns of the pair of lovers.

The romantic theory of affinities rests upon an immature theory of desire. It springs from an infantile belief that the success of love is in the satisfactions which the other person provides. What this really means is that in child-like fashion the lover expects his mistress to supply him with happiness. But in the adult world that expectation is false. Because nine-tenths of the cause, as Mr. Santayana says, are in the lover for one-tenth that may be in the object, it is what the lover does about that nine-tenths which is decisive for his happiness. It is the claim, therefore, of those who uphold the ideal of marriage as a full partnership, and reject the ideal which would separate love as an art from parenthood as a vocation, that in the home made by a couple who propose to see it through, there are provided the essential conditions under which the passions of men and women are most likely to become mature, and therefore harmonious and disinterested.*

They need not deny, indeed it would be foolish as well as cruel for them to underestimate, the enormous difficulty of achieving successful marriages under modern conditions. For with the dissolution of authority and compulsion, a successful marriage depends wholly upon the capacity of the man and the woman to make it successful. They have to accomplish wholly by under-standing and sympathy and disinterestedness of purpose what was once in a very large measure achieved by habit, necessity, and the absence of any practicable alternative. It takes two persons to make a successful marriage in the modern world, and that fact more than doubles its difficulty. For these reasons alone the modern state ought to do what it would none the less be compelled to do: it ought to provide decent ways of retreat in case of failure.

But if it is the truth that the convention of marriage correctly interprets human experience, whereas the separatist conventions are self-defeating, then the convention of marriage will prove to be the conclusion which emerges out of all this immense experimenting. It will survive not as a rule of law imposed by force, for that has now, I think, become impossible. It will not survive as a moral commandment with which the elderly can threaten the young. They will not listen. It will survive as the dominant insight into the reality of love and happiness, or it will not survive at all. That does not mean that all persons will live under the convention of marriage. As a matter of fact in civilized ages all persons never have. It means that the convention of marriage, when it is clarified by insight into reality, is likely to be the hypothesis upon which men and women will ordinarily proceed. There will be no compulsion behind it except the compulsion in each man and woman to reach a true adjustment of his life.

It is in this necessity of clarifying their love for those who are closest to them that the normal problems of the new age come to a personal issue. It is in the realm of sexual relations that mankind is being schooled amidst pain and worry for the novel conditions which modernity imposes. It is there, rather than in politics, business, or even in religion, that the issues are urgent, vivid, and inescapable. It is there that they touch most poignantly and most radically

---

*Disinterested—not influenced by selfish motives or personal interest.

the organic roots of human personality. And it is there, in the ordering of their personal attachments, that for most men the process of salvation must necessarily begin.

For disinterestedness in all things, as Dean Inge says, is a mountain track which the many are likely in the future as in the past to find cold, bleak, and bare: that is why "the road of ascent is by personal affection for man." By the happy ordering of their personal affections they may establish the type and the quality and the direction of their desires for all things. It is in the hidden issues between lovers, more than anywhere else, that modern men and women are compelled, by personal anguish rather than by laws and preachments or even by the persuasions of abstract philosophy, to transcend naive desire and to reach out towards a mature and disinterested partnership with their world.

Realizing that Walter Lippmann wrote this piece in 1929 makes it clear that our current debate over sex, marriage, and the family is hardly new. "The family as a sacred union of husband and wife, of parents and children, will continue to disintegrate. Divorces and separations will increase until any profound difference between socially sanctioned marriages and illicit sex-relationships disappears." Pitirim Sorokin, a Harvard sociologist, wrote this in 1937. (See Reading 4.)

Although it is clear that there has been great change in the family during the past fifty years, the family has hardly disappeared. Most people live most of their lives in a married state. Most children grow up within a family. Both Rosenfeld and Keller shared the common assumption that marriage and morals were undergoing dramatic revolutionary changes. When one considers the lengthy history of criticism leveled at the Western family, one begins to suspect that the changes in morals and family structure are not as revolutionary as Rosenfeld and Keller suggest. Only time will tell how revolutionary the changes will really be. Hopefully, perspective may be gained by reading earlier criticisms of marriage and family and by judging their validity in light of what has actually occurred during the intervening years. Atlee L. Stroup, a sociologist at the College of Wooster, discusses some of the earlier criticisms of the family in the following reading.

4 Are Marriage and the Family About to Disappear?

Atlee L. Stroup

. . .

Marriage and family life are "not what they used to be." One can legitimately ask: "Do we have before us a system which is in its dotage (old age)? Is the family an example of cultural lag, an outmoded institution which is dead but not yet buried?" A number of writers have given attention to such questions. For convenience they can be labeled as liberal and conservative critics, it being granted that each group is concerned with movement toward a more satisfying life as it sees it.

Two Harvard sociologists have been outstanding critics of the modern family from a position which is to the right of center. Sorokin takes the stand that western society has been in transition from a sacred, stable type of culture (ideational) to a contract-sensate style of life.[1] This latter type of society emphasizes values that are essentially false and weak. Materialism, happiness, security, comfort, and indulgence are substituted for the more basic values developed in Greece of the eighth to fifth centuries B.C. or the medieval period of Europe. Basic causal factors involved in this transition to a sensate culture have been Protestantism, paganism, capitalism, and utilitarianism.

The possibilities for a family life worthy of the name in a sensate* culture are not good. Writing in 1937, Sorokin declared:

> The family as a sacred union of husband and wife, of parents and children, will continue to disintegrate. Divorces and separations will increase until any profound difference between socially sanctioned marriages and illicit sex-relationships disappears. Children will be separated earlier and earlier from parents. The main socio-cultural function of the family will further decrease until the family becomes a mere incidental cohabitation of male and female while the home will become a mere overnight parking place mainly for sex-relationship.[2]

Zimmerman, a colleague of Sorokin for a number of years, holds that the family has been in transition from the large extended *trustee* type through the *domestic* to the *atomistic*. He believes that the old trustee type had to give way in the West under the revolutionary pressures at work in the religious and economic realms of society. However, the domestic type family is most favor-

Atlee L. Stroup, *Marriage and Family: A Developmental Approach,* © 1966, pp. 52–54. Reprinted by permission of Prentice-Hall, Inc., Englewood Cliffs, New Jersey.
*Sensate—having the power of physical sensation, registering on the senses.

able for society. It is a solid, stable, patriarchal unit performing many functions. It produces many children. The roles within the family are clear-cut. Duty and fidelity as against love and freedom are stressed.

The atomistic family is weak and cannot last as a system according to Zimmerman. It is nihilistic and carries within it the seeds of its own destruction. Divorce, adultery, homosexuality, and other such aberrations, are correlates of the atomistic family, and symptoms of the decay which has set into the domestic system. The real cause of the trouble is that the general populace is giving up its faith in the values of familism. Zimmerman is a family determinist, holding that family change is the "final decisive force" in historical change. As he notes in reference to Greece and Rome, if the family becomes atomistic the whole country is eventually doomed to decay.[3]

. . .

On the liberal side, strong criticisms of monogamous marriage and family life as we know it came in the twenties. Writers such as Key, Russell, Calverton, Lindsey, and others stirred up a storm of controversy by their writings which called into question many beliefs about monogamous marriage.[4] A number of themes were common to the writers cited above, especially the first three. Marriage is an outmoded institution. Signs of decay are everywhere in abundance. Conventional marriage and family patterns represent bourgeois carry-overs which have no meaning in our present world. A new moral system is needed which will separate love in marriage and the childbearing function.

As university teacher of mathematics and as a lay philosopher, Russell observed the behavior of youth around him.[5] Many seemed to be possessed by sex to the point that their studies were affected. He proposed that trial marriages should be allowed, to be followed by more regular marriages at later periods. Russell was more conservative than some writers regarding children born of such trial marriages. He insisted that they be cared for adequately. Actually what he proposed in essence was trial marriage with liberal divorce for the childless who did not wish to continue the marriage.

Russell's most radical proposal involved extramarital sex relations. Where marriage is successfully established, "The expectation ought to be that it will be lifelong, but that it will not exclude other sex relations."[6] Temporary alliances should be accepted by both parties. The problem is to develop a high level of control lest "orgies of jealousy" ensue.

Lindsey, for many years a nationally known divorce court judge in Denver, proposed the concept of "companionate marriage."[7] Noting the kinds of problems that came before him and, especially, the sexual pressures on the unmarried, Judge Lindsey favored youthful marriage and the use of contraceptives so that parenthood could be delayed. If the partners were satisfied with each other, well and good. The couple would move along normally and children would come. But the system "would also afford a line of retreat in case the marriage failed." With no children to consider, the divorce would be by mutual consent with no provision for alimony.

A modern critic, Moore, takes a more moderate point of view, but he writes in the intellectual tradition of Russell, as he acknowledges. Moore feels that the family is not making up for its lost functions of the past by an emphasis on social-psychological functions. The duty of affection to relatives and family members is to him a barbaric relic. Parents are increasingly unable to exert authority over their children. Motherhood really is frequently a degrading experience and it is useless to try to raise the social value of the role of housewife and mother. Moore feels that parents will have to assert authority much more vigorously if the family structure is to regain any semblance of solidarity. He doubts that this more conservative approach will offer any real solution. The task of child care and supervision could be handled by specialized institutions with the help of machinery such as the Skinner box. We need not worry about the absence of fondling, the giving of affection, and the early socialization. "A nurse can perform these tasks . . . just as well as parents, often better."[8] Certain adaptations to shore up the middle-class family are also considered by Moore but he believes that like the old soldier, the family may not die but will just fade away.

Such criticism sounds surprisingly similar to the criticisms voiced by the authors of the preceding readings, despite the fact that they were sounded 25 to 50 years ago. For example, Bertrand Russell's tradition-breaking criticism of the Western system of marriage and morals appeared in book form in 1929. Much of his criticism sounds modern and up to date. Indeed, in describing the importance of alcohol prohibition to the changes he found in morals, he sounds surprisingly like the modern critics who decry the evils of marijuana prohibition. His point of view about marriage is well summarized by the following passage:

> For my part, while I am quite convinced that companionate marriage would be a step in the right direction, and would do a great deal of good, I do not think that it goes far enough. I think that all sex relations which do not involve children should be regarded as a purely private affair, and that if a man and a woman choose to live together witout having children, that should be no one's business but their own. I should not hold it desirable that either a man or a woman should enter upon the serious business of a marriage intended to lead to children without having had previous sexual experience. There is a great mass of evidence to show that the first experience of sex should be with a person who has previous knowledge. The sexual act in human beings is not instinctive. And apart from this argument, it seems absurd to ask people to enter upon a relation intended to be lifelong without any previous knowledge of their sexual compatibility. It

is just as absurd as it would be if a man intending to buy a house were not allowed to view it until he had completed the purchase. The proper course, if the biological function of marriage were adequately recognized, would be to say that no marriage should be legally binding until the wife's first pregnancy. At present a marriage is null if sexual intercourse is impossible, but children, rather than sexual intercourse, are the true purpose of marriage, which should therefore be not regarded as consummated until such time as there is a prospect of children. This view depends, at least in part, upon that separation between procreation and mere sex which has been brought about by contraceptives. Contraceptives have altered the whole aspect of sex and marriage, and have made distinctions necessary which could formerly have been ignored. People may come together for sex alone, as occurs in prostitution, or for companionship involving a sexual element, as in Judge Lindsey's companionate marriage, or, finally, for the purpose of rearing a family. These are all different, and no morality can be adequate to modern circumstances which confounds them in one indiscriminate total.[9]

In Reading 3, Walter Lippmann broadened the conception of marital love to include more than sexual love alone. The general nature of the relationship between spouses is very important to conjugal happiness. It is essential to understand that there are several kinds of love, of which sexual love is only one. "Eros," the drive to procreate or create—the urge toward higher forms of being and relationship—adds the creative dimension to conjugal love. "Philia," or friendship, is a necessary ingredient to successful conjugal love; so is "agape," or love devoted to the welfare of the other. Authentic, satisfying love is a blend, in varying proportions, of these four kinds of love.[10] Lippmann made an important contribution to the understanding of the marital relationship by going beyond the mere fact that scientific birth control will influence that relationship to the deeper philosophical analysis of what contributes to an enduring relationship between a man and a woman.

In many ways, Lippmann's discussion of the change in values wrought by the separation of sex and procreation due to contraceptives shows more insight than much contemporary writing on the subject. He recognizes "that whether or not birth control is eugenic, hygenic, or economic, it is the most revolutionary practice in the history of sexual morals." Significantly, however, he arrived at this conclusion more than 40 years ago. Perhaps this revolution in sexual mores is no revolution at all, but rather a trend that has slowly been evolving over the past century.

Other experts, such as Ira Reiss, share this view.

The popular notion that America is undergoing a sexual "revolution" is a myth. The belief that our more permissive sexual code is a sign of general breakdown or morality is also a myth. . . .

What has been happening recently is that our young people have been assuming more responsibility for their own sexual standards and behavior. The influence of their parents has been progressively declining. The greater independence given to the young has long been evident in other fields—employment, spending, and prestige, to name three.[11]

Not only is there some question as to how new all of the revolutionary changes in marriage and morals are, but there are numerous thoughtful students of modern marriage who believe that American marriage is healthier than ever before. Rather than citing the high divorce rate as evidence of family decay, they point out that a high divorce rate must accompany a family system that emphasizes a high quality of human relationship. It may be true, they argue, that an Oriental arranged marriage will endure longer statistically than an American marriage based on romantic love and attraction, but what is the quality of the relationship? As Paul Landis states, "failure often reflects high hopes." Americans demand more of marriage, hence the higher rate of failure. Indeed, Landis begins his marriage textbook (and has done so through several editions), with a chapter entitled "Marriage Has Improved." He ends his latest edition with a chapter entitled "Better Marriages." He points to the goals of a more complete development of the individual person and a closer, more understanding and harmonious relationship between husbands and wives and between parents and children, as unique to the American marital system. This American invention—the "love marriage"—is proving to be one of the most marketable products of our culture. Even the Japanese throne cast aside more than 2,600 years of tradition to permit the 1959 marriage of the prince to the girl he loved, a commoner. Marriage now hinges upon the ability of the husband and wife to meet each other's psychological, emotional, and companionship needs, rather than on the more practical aspects of industry and domestic skills. Landis offers numerous data to substantiate the success of the American marriage.

5 Marriage Has Improved

Paul H. Landis

Dr. Landis is a well-known sociologist who has written extensively in the field of marriage and the family. He is a professor at Washington State University.

A philosophy teacher gifted with both optimism and realism told his class, "If you wish to worship the past, don't study history too closely." This bit of advice is particularly timely in the area of marriage and the family. Although it is primarily by psychological standards that improvement is measured, progress is also evidenced in the duration of marriage and increased privacy and greater material comforts surrounding the married pair and their off-spring.

The Lasting Quality of Marriage

Pessimism of young people about marriage is in considerable part engendered by our much-advertised divorce rate. It makes many feel that marriage is a highly risky venture. Divorce is a measure of failure, yet the fact remains that the average marriage lasts longer today than ever before. Divorce has replaced premature death as a factor in terminating marriages, but fewer are terminated early than at any time in history.

In 1890, when the United States Census Bureau first took a census of marriage and divorce, 33 marriages per thousand were terminated annually; now the figure is down to 29 per thousand (see Figure 3). At that time 30 of the 33 broken homes were due to death of husband or wife, only 3 to divorce. Of the 29 broken annually now about 19 will be by divorce, only 10 by death.

Now at age 20, young people can look forward to approximately 55 years of life. White persons in their marriage in 1900 could expect about 30 years of married life before a mate died, now a couple can expect about 45 years.[1] The chances of a golden wedding anniversary, taking only the death rate into account, are twice as great as in 1900. The chances will be even greater for those now in college.

Our present divorce rate, about 2.3 per 1,000 marriages per year compared with 4.3 in 1946,[2] has remained fairly constant for several years since reaching an all-time high in the post World War II period. Parke and Glick[3] think it will probably decline with the increase in affluence of the lower socioeconomic

NUMBER OF MARRIAGES BROKEN PER 1,000 ANNUALLY. Source: Table B, "Divorce Statistics Analysis, United States, 1963," National Center for Health Statistics, Series 21, No. 13, Washington, D.C., October, 1967.

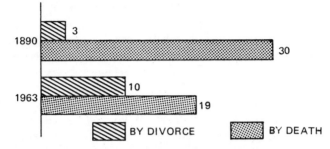

The average marriage lasts longer than it did in 1890 because of the decreasing death rate. In 1890, 33 marriages per thousand were terminated annually; in 1963, 29. Life expectancy permitted 30 years of married life in 1900 compared to 45 years today.

Fig. 3

layers of our society. The rapid decline in poverty, a stated national objective, should also bring greater marriage stability. Another factor in the probable decline in divorce is the falling rate of teenage marriages.* These marriages and poverty have been the two most important social factors in the nation's high divorce rate.

Marriage lasts so long today that the Roys[4] proposed that we allow couples to have marriages of fifteen years each with perhaps a five-year single break between marriages.

Landis made these predictions about increased marriage stability in 1970. Since that time, however, divorce rates have begun to rise again. The Census Bureau reported that there were 63 divorced persons in 1974 for every 1,000 married persons living with their spouses. In 1970, Landis reported the number was only 47, and in 1935 the number was 35. Presently, the divorce rate per thousand marriages per year is again close to the post-World War II high.

Part of our divorce rate today must be attributed to the greater length of life. We speak of menopause divorces—which take place in midlife—when psychological stress is not unusual for women and when husbands and wives

*There are fewer girls marrying under 18 years of age today than there were 15 to 20 years ago. At the peak 15 years ago, 23 percent of the girls were marrying before they were eighteen. Today that percentage has dropped to only fifteen.[3]

both may feel a letdown as they find life together without purpose after children leave the home. Few pairs lived to go through the middle-aged slump together at the beginning of the century. One was already in the graveyard, usually the wife who had died in childbirth or been worn out by too frequent pregnancy for which she had no effective control, and the husband had already taken a young bride. Even then, of course, there was the occasional sturdy woman who lived to marry a succession of husbands, having survived the first or subsequent husbands.

Divorce in middle age, after children are reared, is certainly a brighter prospect than death, but couples now have the alternative of twenty to thirty years more of married life together. In spite of learned theorizing to the effect that little social damage is done if couples choose to divorce and freshen up their future with a new mate, more readjust to a home without children and live together to share the joys of seeing grandchildren grow to maturity and marry, carrying the family line into the third generation. The majority of couples complete these long modern marriages still enjoying a great deal of happiness in each other's companionship.

The Equalitarian Trend

The status of women and children in most cultures has been that of inferiors, sometimes even property. One of the great achievements of this century has been the elevation in the position of women and children in the American family. The stern patriarch has been eliminated and with his passing, the rule of fear based on punishment has disappeared from the average family. Women and men share as equals to an increasing extent.

"The Pill" age, using this concept broadly to embrace all forms of contraception, has arrived and may well mark the final and most significant step in the emancipation of women.

Freedom from the penalty of unwanted pregnancy produces genuine equality in the sense that sexual activity brings no greater biological consequences to the female than to the male. It is almost impossible to envision the full psychological, social, moral, and economic consequences of the removal of this threat to women's freedom of action, and to the mutuality made possible in the physical union of marriage.

American women have been freed from the belief that reproduction is their primary function. They can be individuals in a sense they never could have been before. The population explosion has given them the moral right to make use of the new birth control technology. Limiting children in numbers and scheduling their appearance during a brief portion of the life span—the twenties—leaves them some fifty years of life after childbearing is over. Not least of the developments has been the weakening of the authority of the Catholic Church in this area, liberating millions from the guilt of disobedience and giving many communicants the courage to use effective means of family spacing and limitation.

Security for Children

Although youth think of marriage in terms of their own happiness and fulfillment, its ultimate purpose is the well-being of children. Marriage now gives children greater assurance of security, in terms of marriage lasting, than ever before. Today few children are orphaned. The man who marries at age 23 has 88 chances in 100 of seeing his last child marry. The girl who marries at 21 has a 94 in 100 chance of living to see the marriage of her youngest child.[5] Death rarely leaves children orphaned during their younger years. Divorce may, but as we have seen, the overall risk of broken homes is far lower than ever before.

The average family has less than half the funerals it had in 1890. Most couples never experience death in their families, even of the parents, until their own children are married. In most cases both parents live until their children are grown. Even if there is a divorce, the one denied custody still usually has some influence in helping support and train the child. Unlike death, divorce does not terminate parental influence. (There are a few cases when it would be better eliminated, if the child is kept under tension by parental visiting, but this is the exception.)

The threat to children from premature death has been drastically reduced. The deaths which do occur are usually the result of accident. The marriage is spared the fearful economic and emotional cost of having to sire many children in order to rear a few to maturity.

Divorce often gives children first consideration. Some conscientious couples divorce for the sake of their children. They can see that their own conflicts are robbing their children of peace. Tragic as divorce can be for the child, in many cases it is the better alternative, and children do find happiness many times in the remarriage which follows. Step-parent relationships are not as unpleasant as fiction has presented them to be.

Marriage Opportunity

During this century, those who wish to marry had an increased opportunity to do so. As a result of the great economic developments making early self-support possible, the chance comes earlier in life.

The typical groom of 1890 was just over 26 years of age at the time of his first marriage, the typical bride 22. Today the typical groom is just over 23 and the bride just past 20.5. In 1890, the average age difference between bride and groom was over 4 years, now it is about 2.5 years.

Compare the prospects life offers young people in the United States, where economic circumstances and customs permit early marriage, with Ireland, where economic hardship and religious taboos against birth control cause more than a third of the women and almost two-thirds of the men to delay marriage past thirty years of age. Many there must postpone marriage until they have passed the childbearing age.[6]

In 1960 the U.S. census showed that only 7.2 percent of males had never married by age 45–49, 6.5 percent of females. In 1965, 64 percent of all women 55–64 were married and living with a husband (first or subsequent). According to predictions this figure will be 72 percent by 1980. Of women now 65 to 74 years of age, only 64 percent were married at age 25, now 93 percent of women age 25 are married; for men the figures are 42 percent and 72 percent respectively.[7]

Although it is still too early to tell if a new trend is developing in opposition to Landis' predictions about the number of married persons, it is true that many young persons are stating their preference for the single life. It is also true that approximately one-fourth of American college students are having living-together experiences before marriage, and it may be that some opt for this style of life on a permanent basis. Whether this is really something different than marriage, however, is another question. They may not be legally married, but prolonged living together is in almost every other way similar to marriage.

In the United States, about 94 percent of all women are or have been married by the end of the childbearing age.[8] This is the highest record in American history. Except for the sick and badly crippled, the deformed, the emotionally warped, and the mentally defective, almost everyone has an opportunity to marry. Even the handicapped often marry, thanks to social security, to routine machine-powered jobs, and to labor-saving devices in the home.

The Marriage-Family Environment

It is not popular today to measure improvement by material standards, and yet the environmental circumstances of marriage and family living are important to success. Degree of privacy, quantity and quality of environmental space, and adequacy of material goods are influential in the lives of couples and their children.

Improvements have been so many and so far-reaching in impact on marriage and the family that one would have to review the most vital aspects of the technology and welfare policy of our civilization to encompass them. Since this is not possible or desirable, only a few improvements can be mentioned.

Broad social and economic programs of state, federal, and voluntary organizations have come to the aid of couples, particularly in child care and development. Some critics resent the invasion of bureaucracy into family life, as well as the concept of the "welfare state" programs but the rapidity of social change has made such programs necessary and advantageous to the family. A great burden is lifted from parents and the growth of children is facilitated.

School lunch programs, school medical examinations, and accident insurance have been great boons to the health of children, particularly those of the lower socioeconomic classes. Innovations in teaching mathematics, spelling, reading, and the sciences, and the use of computer techniques have brought such progress in learning as to make parental help with homework difficult, in many instances impossible. But the intellectual growth of the child is greatly enhanced.

In many aspects of life, the couple of today can expect to have the assistance and guidance of experts for their child's health and education from Head Start, through nursery school, and on through college and university. Inexpensive paperbacks of the best professional quality on child rearing, the television "Children's Doctor," women's magazines, medical columns, and features on parent-child relations all come to the mother's aid. Parents may have to struggle to keep up with the latest innovations in the area of child training but can delegate much more of the care of their child to school, clinic, and specialists in other agencies, even at the expense of spending a great deal of time transporting and waiting for children. But the child profits and the parent gains in seeing the child develop at a rate and in ways they could not have realized for him.

The general quality of everyday life has improved greatly since 1950. About 74 million people are enrolled in schools and this accounts for one-third of the population. Even from our poorest homes, 21 percent enter college. The median income in constant 1972 dollars and considering inflation has risen from $4,500 to over $11,000 in the past twenty-five years. The percentage of families below the poverty line has dropped from 22 percent in 1950 to 11 percent.[9] The food stamp program alone costs $4 billion annually and is currently helping to feed 13.5 million people.[10]

The later years of marriage, too, show improvement in living conditions. Pensions, Social Security, Medicare and other such benefits, along with increasing earned abundance on the part of more of the elderly have permitted them to maintain separate households. Since 1960 nearly one-third of new households have been one-person households,[11] and the proportion of one-person households increases with age. With Social Security and Medicare the elderly are able to live outside the families of their children and to maintain their independence. Their wish of "not having to live with our children" is realized. Increasing mobility and affluence have at the same time made visiting possible.

Not the least of these benefits has been the removal of the burden of caring for their parents from the younger generation during their childrearing period and also feelings of guilt for their neglect.

The dream of "a place of our own" is realized by young and old alike here more than in any other Western nation.[12] The separate dwelling has done much to alleviate the in-law problem and the grandparent problem. It gives the couple and their children the privacy they want to pursue individual growth. Dependence on the large family has been replaced by various forms of social insurance and social security. Burdens of ancestry and of relatives, still present in most cultures of the world, have been lifted from the modern American family.

Many even have a separate house and yard, although apartment dwelling must increase because of the high cost of land and increased crowding due to population growth. Even so, home ownership climbed from 33 million in 1960 to 37 million in 1967.

During the 20 years from 1947 to 1967, the percent of married couples living with relatives declined from 7 percent to 1.6 percent.[13] Since an important factor in the romantic marriage and the nuclear family is "a place of our own," where couples can maintain privacy, the housing trend is significant to our kind of marriage and family.

Our Problem Consciousness

As a people, we make much of our problems, and in so doing sometimes exaggerate them. Having cast aside tradition, we pursue elusive goals and entertain lofty hopes and dreams, often too romantic, and beyond reach. This is especially true of marriage. Long ago we ceased to believe that fate ruled our destiny, and began to seek remedies for our problems.

Almost every woman's magazine and some magazines written for the more general public carry articles that outline and suggest help for some critical marriage problem. Divorce statistics are much quoted and the pro and con of the sex revolution is considered.

An outsider to our culture, particularly one from the more institutionalized, custom-controlled, Asiatic cultures, where marriage adjustment is not an accepted concept and where it is never discussed, might well think our marriage institution is but the ruins of some earlier state of equilibrium. Safe and relatively unchallanged by change, the joint family system of these cultures is based on the secure foundations of centuries of custom. Little wonder that they see in our nuclear marriage family system, where so much is left to the individual choice and so little to ancestral heritage, little pattern at all.

Recognizing that problems exist is the first step toward improvement. Traditional family systems will never improve until they become problem-conscious. They are fate oriented, believing that what has been must always be. The fact that our society exhibits concern for the welfare of husbands and wives, parents and children, represents a vast leap forward. The numerous minor miseries of the pair and their children have become social concerns.

Failure Often Reflects High Hopes

If the view that couples aspire to more in marriage than they did in earlier generations is accepted then it is easy to believe (1) that the successful realize more satisfaction in marriage than did their ancestors and (2) that many suffer defeat because they expect marriage to bring more in the way of happiness than is possible.

By the same logic, it is understandable too, that failure is more likely to lead to decisive action than in earlier generations. There is little doubt that many divorces today result from overly idealistic expectations for marriage. Many expect the impossible. As English novelist Somerset Maugham has said, the American wife expects to find in her husband "a perfection English women only hope to find in their butlers." And what perfection in romantic attraction, home management, and social competence American men expect of their wives! It is doubtful that marriage has ever been asked to pass such a high test.

If a culture makes happiness the goal of marriage, it must grant the right of divorce to those who fail in its attainment. Only by this means can they be freed to seek fulfillment in another marriage, or to return to the single state. The right of divorce is important in the new system of marriage values. It recognizes two facts: first, human judgment is fallible in mate choice, and second, those who fall in love may also fall out of love.

Divorce is doubly serious when it represents the failure of high aspirations, but is not more tragic than living together in bitter conflict and frustration. In an earlier day, when a more stoic marriage philosophy prevailed, personal clashes may well have brought less torture than now when marriage values are different.

It is enough here to say that divorce is a recognized adjustment device in the modern marriage-family system—the ultimate, desperate, but sometimes necessary one. Divorce is, in fact, a part of all marriage-family institutions, historic and contemporary. In ours, its causes are related to our new marriage values.

Our much-used reason for divorce, "mental cruelty," (irreconcilable differences) is indicative that marriage is no longer judged in terms of traditional value, but by the quality of the interpersonal relationship involved. Marriage is a dynamic interrelationship of two individuals with personal destinies.

It is a remarkable testimony to our monogamous idea that marriage is still looked upon as a lifetime partnership.

Margaret Mead, as always an outspoken critic of contemporary life, often expounds on the American family. One of her better-known ideas alluded to earlier is the "two-step marriage." Several years ago she suggested that there be two types of marriages. The first would be a loose, easily dissolved marriage without the prerogative of having children. If the couple, after sufficient testing of the relationship, desired children, they would then enter into a marriage that would be much more difficult to dissolve. In a sense, the first-step marriage would act as a test of the relationship and, if successful, would prepare the couple for the responsibility of parenthood.

In the following article she focuses on the so-called generation gap, the nuclear family, and the changing roles of women.

6 Future Family   Margaret Mead

This article is based on an edited transcript of an address given by Margaret Mead to Barnard students and their parents, February 12, 1970.

There was an article by an eminent psychologist in the *New York Times* recently, saying there wasn't any generation gap, because lots of parents got on with lots of children.

But the generation gap has not got anything to do with parents and children. The generation gap is between all the people born and brought up after World War II and the people who were born before it. It's not at all about children and getting on with parents.

If you happen to be a parent who was born and brought up before World War II, and you happen to have children at the moment, you're on one side of the generation gap and they're on the other. But this is an accident. In about 15 years there'll be parents and children on this side of the generation gap. And all the people on the other side will be at least grandparents.

What we're talking about as the generation gap only happened once. It isn't about parents not getting along with children, or children rebelling or changing styles of morality. It's simply that at the time of World War II the whole world became one, so that there is a complete difference between all young people and all older people.

In New Guinea, you have children who are studying medicine whose parents were cannibals. That's quite a gap. But whether it's more or less of a gap than the gap between a sophisticated cabinet member and his son, that's a question. Or between a professor of physics and his youngest student in college.

We've mixed this gap with conflict between parents and children and professors and college students at present because the oldest members of the new generation—the inhabitants of this new post-World War II world—are just 25 now. Five years ago, the oldest members were only 20, and they were all in college, and none of them were members of the establishment. So that it looked as if this was a battle between students and parents, and students and teachers, and everybody in college. But it wasn't.

Now the oldest are 25, and a lot of them are getting to be members of the faculty. They can't be treated as traitors any more.

At the moment, two things are happening that we have to take into account. One is the fact that we're having a revolt, a new kind of revolt, which is only partly connected with the generation gap. It's particularly characteristic of the Western industrialized society. In the past, most revolutions and revolts and rebellions have been by people who were being done evil to by other people. They were being enslaved, exploited, sent down in mines, treated terribly. It was perfectly clear they were rebelling against bad treatment.

Now, we're having a revolt of all the people that are being done good to. For the first time in history children—all children, after all, are being done good to by their parents—pupils, students, mental patients, welfare mothers, and even people who are being rehabilitated in Federal prisons, are suggesting they take a share in what's going on.

This is the first time we have had this kind of rebellion, and students are included in it. In the past, the professors knew best, the doctors knew best, the social workers knew best, psychiatrists knew best. There were great numbers of professional people who knew best and did good. Then the beneficiaries were supposed to be appreciative. And they've now become extremely unappreciative. And they're all insisting on getting into the act.

. . .

Whenever there is a period of upheaval in the world, somebody's going to do something to the family. If the family's being very rigorous and puritanical, you loosen it up. And if it's being very loose, you tighten it up. But you have to change it to really feel you're accomplishing something. If we go back into history we find over and over again, in moments of revolutionary change, that people start talking about the family, and what they're doing to it, and what's wrong with it. They even predict it's going to disappear altogether. It is in fact the only institution we have that doesn't have a hope of disappearing.

No matter how many communes anybody invents, the family always creeps back. You can get rid of it if you live in an enclave and keep everybody else out, and bring the children up to be unfit to live anywhere else. They can go on ignoring the family for several generations. But such communities are not part of the main world.

As one of my sophomore students wrote the other day, when I had asked them to say where they were going to be 15 years from now: "Fifteen years from now it may not be necessary to get married; but nevertheless I expect to live with the father of my children."

And that is, strictly speaking, where we are. Girls are going to live with the fathers of their children—if they can catch them. And on the whole, they're just as interested in catching them as they've been throughout history. But there will be a great deal of discussion, and a great deal of gloom, and a great deal of talk about the family falling to pieces. In fact, we've got more families per capita than we've ever had. We're more married than we've ever been, and we're more married than most peoples. We've a terribly overmarried society, because we can't think of any other way for anybody to live, except in matrimony, as couples.

It's very, very difficult to lead a life unless you're married. So everybody gets married—and unmarried—and married, but they're all married to somebody most of the time. And so that we have, in a sense, overdepended on marriage in this country. We've vastly overdone it.

At the graveside—you know, when a woman has just lost a husband that she's been happy with 20 years, the first thing people say is, "I do hope she marries again." They don't give her two minutes to grieve before they start marrying her off again. We also have had a form of marriage that is probably one of the most precarious and fragile forms of marriage that people have ever tried. That form—the Nuclear Family—was not named after the Bomb. It was just named after the physical analogy, but calling it the Nuclear Family is very good, because it is just about as dangerous as the bomb.

The Nuclear Family is a family consisting of one adult man and one adult woman, married to each other, and minor children. The presence of any other person in the household is an insult. The only people that can come in are cleaning women and sitters. In-laws become sitters—which means that when they come in, you go out, and you never have to see them. Furthermore, today, mothers are very uncomfortable with adolescent daughters in the house. So they push them out as rapidly as possible. If they're rich, they send them to Barnard, and if they're poor, they get them married, and they work at it, very hard, because there isn't room in the kind of kitchens we've had since 1945 for two women.

We have put on the Nuclear Family an appalling burden, because young couples were expected to move as far from both sets of relatives as they could, and they had to move, a great deal of the time.

Millions and millions of Americans move every year, moving miles from relatives or anybody that they know. We know now that the chances of a postpartum depression for a woman are directly proportional to the distance she is from any female relative or friend. When we put her in a new suburb all by herself, her chances of getting a postpartum depression go way up. There are millions of young families living in such suburbs, knowing nobody, with no friends, no support of any kind.

Furthermore, each spouse is supposed to be all things to the other. They're supposed to be good in bed, and good out of it. Women are supposed to be good cooks, good mothers, good wives, good skiers, good conversationalists, good accountants. Neither person is supposed to find any sustenance from anybody else.

Young people from Europe who wanted to come to the United States had to bring their spouses with them, and leave their parents behind or they'd never have gotten here. In India or Africa, when you have a great mass of very traditional relatives, the thing to do is to take your girl and leave, and go a long way off if you want to live the way you want to live.

So it's a good style of family for change, but it's a hazardous kind of family, nonetheless. And if it is hazardous enough in the city, it's a hundred percent more hazardous in the suburbs. There's a special kind of isolation that occurs in the suburbs. So the attack on the Nuclear Family is, I think, thoroughly justified.

There is a need to have more people around: more people to hold the baby, more people to pitch in in emergencies, more people to help when the child is sick, when the mother is sick, more children for other children to play with so you don't have to spend a thousand dollars sending them to nursery school, more kinds of adults around for the children to pick models from in case father or mother can't do the things they want to do. The communes aim to supply these. Real communes, of course, are more extreme—this country was founded by many forms of communes, and it's been so with them ever since—but the bulk of people don't live in communes. One of the things the communes are emphasizing is a lot of people sharing child-care, sharing bringing up the children again, so the children have more security, and don't have to think every day, "What if something happens to Mommy; what if something happens to Daddy? Will there be anyone at all?" I think we're going to have a trend toward different kinds of living.

It will take quite a little while, because it means building new houses, on the whole—new kinds of apartments, closer together, places where you don't have to drive 15 miles to use somebody else's washing machine when yours breaks, and where people can get together more closely. We won't have this right away —but we're going to have it.

It means places where all the people can live somewhere near young people, and places where young married couples with children will be cherished and cared for and flanked on all sides by people who don't have children at the moment. Maybe they're had them before; maybe they haven't had them yet, maybe they don't want any. But it'll be a place where they, also, can find children, and won't be banished from children as they are at present. If today you don't have children of your own, you hardly ever see any. We banish our old people far away from any children at all, and the only thing we ask them to do is to live on in misery and smile, so their children won't feel guilty.

With the population explosion, the pressure on women to marry is going to be reduced, and the pressure to be mothers is going to be enormously reduced. For the first time in history we're not going to tell a woman that "Your principal glory is to be a wife and a mother."

By dint of telling women that their major job was to be wives and mothers, we told most men their major job was to be breadwinners and very much limited the number of men who could do the things they wanted to do most.

We always talk about career women, and the wonderful careers they would have had, if they hadn't had those five children. But nobody looks at fathers and thinks what a life he'd have had if he hadn't had those five children.

He might have been able to paint instead of being a stock broker. Or a musician, instead of running a jewelry store he inherited. When you shut women up in a home and require wifehood and motherhood, you shut men up and require husbandhood and fatherhood at the same time. As we reduce the requirements for motherhood, we reduce the requirements for fatherhood. And we'll release a lot of people to be individuals and to make contributions as individuals, rather than as parents.

This isn't going to happen immediately, but we get a lot of funny forerunners. The members of the Women's Liberation Movement, in its extreme form, walk around saying how well they get on without men. We're quite prepared to have a lot of women get on without men now. It won't do a bit of harm. There're too many women, and if some of them would get on without men it would relieve the pressure.

Twenty years from now, we'll have many fewer families, but children will still be brought up in families because we don't know how to bring them up any other way. The family will be just as safe as it ever was, but everybody won't have to live in it all the time. We'll recognize that the family is the perfect place for children. It is just ideal for children, and doubtfully ideal for anybody else for the whole of their lives—except in very exceptional cases. Of course we'll also recognize that when we used to have the idea of lifelong marriage, the expectation of life was 37. When one spouse died and the other was left with a batch of little children they had to marry somebody else.

Today, the expectation of life is over 30 years after the last child leaves home. In terms of rapid change, it means the rate of change for both husbands and wives is very different than in the past. We may move to an ideal of marriage, which is an ideal of people staying married until the children are grown. At present, they have an ideal of staying together forever, but in fact they get divorced very often. If instead they have as an ideal staying together until the children are grown and not having children until they were ready to do that, not picking out somebody you'd like to spend the weekend with, parenthood will probably become much more solemn, and much more of a commitment. If it doesn't, of course, we're going to have some government putting contraceptives in the drinking water.

Some people are somewhat worried by the present notion of the young that they are not going to get married, but they're going to live "in sin." It's a very funny kind of sin—because you do it with the approval of the dean of women, your minister, and both sets of parents. We used to call it common law marriage—when people are generally known to tradesmen as living together. You could sue people to get part of their property when they died, and all that sort of thing. Well, what young people in general today call an "arrangement" is an absolutely public union.

When I proposed that there be a simple marriage ceremony, which would go with the stated intention of having no children,—they said "No." They're going to experiment with "arrangements"—public, virtuous, publicly proclaimed—and then, later, they're going to get married.

We've been cheating women when, in the last ten years, we wanted women to work. We were very short of cheap labor so we told them they needed to be fulfilled. The last source of educated cheap labor was women. So finally everybody discovered that it is very unfulfilling to stay at home, and a woman, of course, when she has her children, maybe she would stay at home a few years and then she'd leave to be fulfilled. And the foundations gave money, centers were established to lure her out and get her re-educated.

But of course they weren't going to pay her like men, because after all she was more interested in her home, she wouldn't want to leave her children, and you know art lessons sometimes take up more time than little babies—and so she'd want a job from which she could get home early like being a clerk in a team-teaching outfit, instead of a teacher. Something like that—so she could go home when her children did. And of course she wouldn't want to be very ambitious, because all the strain would be bad; she'd want to keep something for home.

In the last ten years, women have been pretty well beguiled and bedazzled into becoming self-fulfilling, educated cheap labor. And I think it's not surprising if some of them are saying that they think they are exploited, and they don't want to be exploited any more.

At the end of World War II, when they wanted all the women that held jobs to go home so the men could get them back, women who'd done well in Washington were told they were overmature, overexperienced:—"Please go home."

I think we'll be bringing girls up with more sense of themselves as people, and that they're going to be people all the way through. If they choose parenthood, they'll choose it much more as they've chosen vocations, and much less as if it were just something the neighbors are doing.

Section 2

The Romantic Ideal
Love and Marriage in America

It is extremely difficult to sort out our attitudes about such basic fundamentals as marriage, and yet it is important to try to do so if we are to promote growth and fulfillment within our lives. Considering attitudes to be enduring, generalized, learned predispositions that act as foundations for many of our behaviors, it becomes crucial to analyze our attitudes if we are to understand ourselves. Hopefully, self-understanding will lead us to make better decisions about our relations with the opposite sex, whether the relation be one of casual dating or marriage.

Many of the difficulties experienced in our interpersonal relationships stem from conflicting attitudes we hold rather than from specific overt behaviors. Indeed, if attitudes are comprehensive foundations for one's behaviors, then it follows that a very efficient way to change many behaviors is to change one's attitudes. If one believes strongly in the traditional male dominant role in marriage and acts upon this belief, many overt behaviors will be affected. As a male, one would eschew housework, assume responsibility for major family decisions, insist upon the right to a "double standard" in sexual behavior, assume leadership in public, and in one hundred other small ways, would assert (traditional) male prerogatives. A change in attitude away from the traditional masculine role toward a more egalitarian position would drastically change many of these overt behaviors.

It must be remembered, of course, that attitudes generally consist of three components: the affective, cognitive, and behavioral. The affective aspect is one's emotional response resulting from an attitude such as "I like blondes." The cognitive consists of a person's beliefs and/or factual knowledge supporting a particular attitude, such as "blondes have more fun." Lastly, the behavioral component involves the person's overt behavior resulting from his attitude, "I date blondes."

Unfortunately for our understanding, these three attitudinal components are not necessarily consistent. For example, a recent survey of sexual behavior at Stanford University revealed that approximately 85 percent of both males and females who had not engaged in sexual relations reported that they planned to use contraceptive devices. Yet, of those who had actually engaged in sexual relations, 70 percent of the females and 66 percent of the males reported no birth-control measures were taken during their first act of intercourse. Even more surprising was the fact that 50 percent or more of both sexes who were engaging in sexual intercourse reported no regular use of birth-control devices during these relations.[1] We can hypothesize many reasons for the apparent split between belief (cognitive attitude) and actual behavior. One good hypothesis that might account for such apparently inconsistent behavior is attitudinal conflict. Since the culture has placed taboos around premarital intercourse, strong conflict is aroused if the taboo is broken. For the girl who has premarital relations, the conflicts and guilts that arise are far easier to handle if the encounter can be rationalized as a momentary, romantic, spontaneous act that could not be resisted—all the better if "love" can be enlisted to support it.

Thus a girl might well believe in birth control, yet for her to take the pill or by some other method protect herself against pregnancy before going out on a date would shatter her rationalizations about her behavior. How can sexual relations be a spontaneous act into which one falls because of extenuating circumstances (love?), when birth-control measures have already been taken before the date arrives? In this case conflicting cognitive level attitudes cause what appears to be inconsistent behavior.

If attitudes are an important influence on premarital behavior, they are equal if not a more important influence in determining marital behavior. Each person has some expectations and ideas as to what marriage should be. To have definite ideas about what one wants from a marriage relation is perfectly acceptable.

Yet belief in "romantic love" leads one to expect a great deal of marriage, perhaps too much. As Lippmann points out in Reading 3, basing marriage on the popular conception of romantic love produces a great deal of unhappiness. The concept of "romantic love" places before the individual a set of idealized images by which he will judge the object of his love as well as the quality of the relationship. Unfortunately, the expectations generated by idealized images usually bear little relationship to the real world. Often we project our images onto another person, exaggerating those characteristics of the person that match our internalized images and masking those characteristics that do not. Thus, the other person is transformed into an unreal person that fits our idiosyncratic idealized concept of the romantic marital partner. In essence, some individuals are in love with their own romantic images rather than with a real human being. They have "fallen in love with love." Such an individual will suffer disappointment when the real human begins to emerge in his chosen partner. Rather than meeting the emerging human with joy and enthusiasm, the partner who holds romanticized images may reject the real human in favor of his own images. He again commences to search for the proper object of his love, rejecting the real life partner as unworthy and/or changed. Although some may argue that romantic love is as innate to man as sexual arousal, cross-cultural research refutes this possibility. Love is a learned emotion. Where does it come from and what are its characteristics? Lawrence Casier[2] finds that love develops in part because of man's need of acceptance and confirmation. Such needs are heightened in a competitive, individualized society such as is found in America. Because life requires continual decision-making, we tend to feel accepted and confirmed when we meet someone whose choices coincide with our own. We tend to attach ourselves to such a person because self-validation is offered and such self-validation constitutes one important basis for love. Research has demonstrated that a person is more likely to love someone who loves him. Casier points out that the American dating game may serve to provoke love feelings in the partners more as an artifact of the game than as some innate attraction. A person, for any number of reasons including simple politeness, may pretend to like his date more than is actually true. The date, seeking self-validation, responds favorably. In turn, this favorable response of affection (love) produces self-validation in the first person, and so he now begins to feel fondness that was at first feigned.

Of course, falling in love is more complex because there are many needs to fulfill. The more needs that are satisfied by another, the more likely we are to love the person. Obviously sex is one of these needs. Thus love is elicited by self-validation from someone with sex appeal.

Society emphasizes the necessity for love to precede sex. Although many disregard this restriction, others remain frightened or disturbed by the idea of a purely sexual relationship. The only way for many sexually aroused individuals to avoid frustration or anxiety is to fall in love—as quickly as possible. More declarations of love have probably been uttered in parked cars than in any other location. Some of these are surely nothing more than seduction ploys, but it is likely that self-seduction is involved in most cases.[3]

Because our society is marriage oriented we learn early that love is a prerequisite to marriage. Thus for most Americans love, sex, and marriage go together. This is what they have learned and they believe it implicitly.

In more general terms the sources of love for Casier are (1) the need for security, (2) sexual satisfaction, and (3) social conformity. If these are the causes of love, what does Casier see as the consequences of love?

First in this culture, "being in love makes it easier to have guilt-free sex, to marry, and to view oneself as a normal healthy citizen." Love will also create the error of overevaluation (romanticized ideal images) of the love object. Love will foster dependency on the love object insofar as the love object is relied upon for much need gratification.

If maturity is, in part, establishing independence, then love, as viewed by Casier, acts as a deterrent to maturity. Although the individual who is unable to love is viewed as pathological in the American culture, Casier's conception of love can lead to an alternate interpretation. The individual who is not loving may be in excellent mental health. If, as Casier suggests, the need for love is based largely on insecurity, conformity, and sexual frustration, then the person who is secure, independent, and leading a satisfactory sex life may not need to love. Such a person will:

be a person who does not find his own company boring—a person whose inner resources are such that other persons, although they supply pleasure and stimulation, are not absolutely necessary. We have long been enjoined to love others as we love ourselves, but perhaps *we seek love relationships with others only because we do not love ourselves sufficiently.*[4]

Erich Fromm, in *The Art of Loving,* also hypothesizes that one must love himself before he can give love to others.

Love of others and love of ourselves are not alternatives. On the contrary, an attitude of love toward themselves will be found in all those who are capable of loving others. *Love, in principle, is indivisible as far as the connection between "objects" and one's own self is concerned.* Genuine love is an expression of productiveness and implies care, respect, responsibility, and knowledge.[5]

The following readings discuss general American concepts of love and marriage. Since each reader has his own unique set of attitudes about marriage and the family, this section can do no more than provoke thought, hopefully critical and analytical. It is true that the American culture holds certain generalized values and that all of us to an extent share some of these values. Section 2 examines what the American culture has traditionally and ideally said about love and marriage. This can then be compared with what other cultures say about marriage, as well as with some contrasting views held by minority groups within the American culture, presented in Section 3. Consideration of alternate attitudes and values helps to place one's personal values into perspective.

In Reading 7, the authors describe the ideals surrounding the middle-class American marriage.

7 The American Ideal of Marriage

Jeffrey K. Hadden and
Marie L. Borgatta

The United States has drawn its population from many nations and a rich range of cultural traditions. For this reason, it is not easy to delineate a composite set of values that describe an "ideal" marriage and family. The task of defining an ideal family is further complicated by the fact that our own values about marriage and the family have been changing rather dramatically during the past century. What might have represented an ideal set of values that described the American family at the turn of the century would hardly be adequate to describe the contemporary ideal family. Yet, given these rather serious limitations, a great deal of energy has been devoted to describing the dominant ideals of the American family. Many of the characteristics of the ideal family sound like platitudes. In fact, they are. Other characteristics call forth a nostalgia to reassert an ideal family of yesteryear which in reality may no more describe our ancestor's families than our own. Yet they represent an integral part of the imagery we carry around in our heads about the family and which we continue to transmit to new generations. Some of these ideal values appear to be outmoded and thus bear little relationship to the families we all know through personal experience. Other values appear to retain a dominant place in our culture and do seem to describe ideal features of the family. The purpose of this article is to outline a description of the "ideal" family. We leave to the reader the task of sifting nostalgia and myth from reality. We also pose a serious question for the reader: what are the consequences and implications of living with a set of ideal images about the family that do not correspond to reality?

Ideally, marriage in American society involves a male who is somewhat older than the female. When marrying it is assumed that the adults involved, though young, still have achieved some degree of maturity. They have finished their schooling, or he has a responsibile job, has learned a good trade, or has demonstrated competence as an adult. The popular view is that if a person does not marry young, he still should marry sometime, for marriage is "a good thing." On the other hand, marriage should not take place between persons who are too young, for they are not yet worldly-wise and do not know what the challenge of tomorrow is. The very young, the adolescent, are not expected to understand love in terms of responsibilities and mutual satisfactions, and thus their affective ties are often called by names like "puppy love."

Persons who marry in American society should do so through their own choice, and the major value that is involved is mutual affection. Each person is expected to understand both self-needs and those of the other. In a way every marriage is personalized, and every marriage is unique. The persons in love and about to be married are expected to feel as though this were a new experience, and no one has ever felt it before. The persons in the couple were made for each other, and indeed this can be seen by the fact that they were even neighbors, went to school together, or met under casual circumstances and "found" each other. Sometimes they do not realize that they should be married until after a long acquaintance. Still it is assumed marriage is for two persons who are made for each other, and often this realization may come after a short period. It is not good to marry, however, after too short an acquaintance, because the persons may not have had an opportunity to really become acquainted and know each other. But on the other hand, marriages that are born in such an aura of romance must be destined to be successful.

While opposite personalities may find each other stimulating and attractive, it is more likely that persons who can understand each other and have similar backgrounds are likely to have happy marriages. On basic factors, including race, ethnic background, religion, and education, the couples should have some meeting ground and, if they don't, at least they must provide for handling their problems in these areas. Whether or not the persons in the couple are similar or different is really not important, if they are "ideal" persons for the marriage. Each is expected to be mature and have the ability to adapt and transcend any particular situation. Each will be responsible and aware of his own motives and the needs of the other. Each will be rational and sensible, and, if not rational, will have those intuitions that make for the right decision. Each will have respect for the other and thus will not force values on the other, nor require the other to give up individuality. As the society requires the man nominally to be the head of the household, this is the primary ordering. But within this, the personalities and relationships are compatible and complementary, and decisions and participation are joint ones.

In this marriage situation each person will benefit in many ways. Each will have the companionship of the person with whom he is intimate. In this companionship there is no need for defensiveness, and communication can be open and unguarded. Each has, in a word, security in the other and the interpersonal support from the other that earmarks a good partnership. The two are together to share a life, to give to each other rather than to take from each other. And yet in this situation where each extends himself to the other there is the opportunity for personal development and all persons get better through marriage. In being able to extend oneself to the other, in reaching out, in just this way, there is growth for the person in the marriage. Maturity continues to develop. In the marriage there are many pleasures. Companionship is important, but in addition it is in the marriage that the sexual drives are gratified in a situation of kindness and understanding and freedom from guilt which can lead to ecstatic physical pleasure. Sexual gratification consists of physical pleasure, relief, serenity and closeness. Sex has a purpose within the marriage, and it is not surrounded by taboos or negative sanctions. Each person should be relatively inexperienced in sex, and it is particularly expected that the female will be a virgin. In this world of turbulence and change, many are not, but the prior experiences were of exploration, of chance, of accident, or of error, and in effect this is the first true sexual involvement.

Having children is something that is normally expected in the marriage, and two or three are good numbers. The partners in the marriage shall decide how many children they shall have, and also when. It is good to have children early, but a couple should also be given an opportunity to enjoy themselves first so that children may be delayed somewhat. There may be some reasons why a couple will not have children, but in general having children is a way of fulfillment to a richer life, and each couple should contribute to the new generation.

As the couple proceeds through life they will achieve more responsibilities in their jobs and in other social contacts. They will have friends, and they will have friendly relationships with their parents. They will be dependent upon each other, however, for their primary gratifications. Their aspirations will grow in a realistic way and every couple is expected to be upwardly mobile in socioeconomic status. While they started their life together in a tastefully decorated apartment with all the modern conveniences, they look forward to and provide themselves with more adequate and extensive housing in a stable suburban community as the family grows. Not only does the family improve its position in the community, but it accumulates less visible forms of security, such as savings and insurance.

As the children grow in the family the participation in the community becomes broader. Not only are there memberships through clubs, religious organizations, and community organizations, but the children have contact through the school and through clubs of their own that broaden the base in the community. The children are pleasant and well behaved, and while they may make mistakes, they are never delinquent. Each child does well in school and each child is popular in his own way among his peers. And each child has the opportunity and expectations of going through college. As the children grow older, they develop interests of their own. They may earn money for themselves, but not because they need it. They can stay dependent upon their parents for as long as they require, provided that they are improving themselves. In fact, the parents are always glad to help in whatever way they can to give their children a good opportunity for a better life.

The external view of the family by the community requires that they be successful. Bad examples and poor marriages embarrass the community, and license on the part of particular individuals may threaten the solidarity of each person's marriage. Lack of success along financial lines may cause burdens to the community, also. A family that has no children may be viewed as less than complete. And children should be well raised because even though poor starts may end well, good starts may end better, and what the community needs is more good citizens.

There may be many exceptions to these values, and mistakes may happen in marriages and in this case they should be terminated in understanding of the mistake. Women, and in some cases the couple, may not wish to have children, and if their time is devoted to a good purpose or a career, this is permissible. Tolerance for deviation is considerable, but only when the deviation is not frequent and leads to other success which is also considered important.

The description could be continued, but the violinist is tiring in his rendition of "Hearts and Flowers."

Rather than analyzing this idealized picture of the American marriage, let us restate the picture in considerably different terms. There are some clinicians who diagnose as "neurotic" what Hadden and Borgatta describe in Reading 7. They claim that to the degree that one holds an unrealistic idealized image of himself, or others, or a relationship such as marriage—to that degree there will be malfunctioning by the person whose images (attitudes) are out of touch with reality. Indeed, Hadden and Borgatta raise the question at the end of the first paragraph when they ask, "what are the consequences and implications of living with a set of ideal images about the family that do not correspond to reality?" Here then is another look at the American ideal marriage.

8 The True Love of John and Mary

Snell Putney and Gail J. Putney

John has definite ideas about what he wants in a wife. To the cultural expectation that she must be exciting, warm, pretty, dainty, and in need of his love and protection, he has added various other potentialities which through circumstances he has alienated from his self-image. All he needs is a target on

Pp. 113–116 "The True Love of John and Mary" from *Normal Neurosis* by Gail J. Putney and Snell Putney. Copyright © 1964 by G. J. Putney and Snell Putney. Reprinted by permission of Harper & Row, Publishers, Inc.

which he can project this idealized image—and Mary dances by. He hears her laugh, and feels a sudden "irresistible attraction." He flings after his impression of a girl the image that he is prepared to love, and is drawn to it. The basic mechanism would have been the same had he fallen gradually in love with the girl next door, but John happens to fall in love at first sight. He maneuvers an introduction, and the romance begins.

A romance is a prime situation in which to enjoy many aspects of the self. It offers an opportunity for being loving and lovable, excited and exciting. It puts John in a mood to enjoy himself, even under circumstances (such as waiting for a bus in the rain) that he would normally have thought miserable. He surprises himself with the ingenuity he uses to find places to take Mary, and things to do. By tradition (and because parties to a romance are usually at a stage in life when other responsibilities are not too burdensome) many pleasant activities are virtually set aside for those in love. In the context of the romance, John seizes the opportunity to enjoy aspects of himself that he has rarely experienced. Unrecognized self-discovery is a sizable component in the thrill of any romance. Being American, however, he assumes that it is the girl who thrills him.

Among the activities traditionally reserved for romance is the exploration of sexual capacity. Whether the couple copulate or not, there is a sexual focus in romance. John is not a complete novice to sex, but he expects to find it more rewarding with someone he loves; moreover, Mary corresponds to his particularized conception of a desirable sexual partner.

Like most Americans, John also sexualizes his desire to repossess the alienated qualities which he has projected onto his beloved. The lover wants to make these characteristics a part of himself, to reunite with his alienated potential. But, because he thinks of these things as aspects of his sweetheart, he assumes that his desire is to unite with her—a phrase which in America is a euphemism for sexual relations. Following his culture's definitions and interpretations, John develops a *sexualized* interest in Mary which is quite independent of his biological urgings.

John has projected so much of himself onto Mary that he is miserable without her. He is jealous of anyone else who is close to her, for he wants exclusive and constant possession of the potential he projects onto her.

Mary is in a similar state. She finds and loves in John many qualities which she has alienated from her self-image: poise, wit, forcefulness, self-assurance. She, too, has an Ideal, composed of conventional as well as idiosyncratic projections, of many things she would like to be but is sure she is not. She hangs this image on John and finds that he is wonderful.

Moreover, finding someone who thinks that *she* is wonderful is a balm to ease her self-doubts. As an adjusted American girl, Mary has learned to seek self-acceptance indirectly, through winning approval, admiration, and love from others. John's love for her seems the epitome of acceptance, and Mary clings to it.

Because each wants to be loved, each agrees to love the other (not that the bargain is explicit, of course, but it is understood all the same). Like most lovers, these two form a mutual admiration society, dedicated to indirect self-acceptance. No romance is ever open and candid, for both parties are intent on making and maintaining a good impression. Mary seems a faultless angel to John because he is seeing what he has projected onto her—a view she encourages by seeking to conceal less flattering characteristics and by trying to fit his picture of her. Anything he praises, she seeks to emphasize, and because he compliments her on what he expects to see (independently of reality) she finds herself cultivating new and exciting self-potential.

All of this could lead to self-discovery on Mary's part. As realists have long noted, the appearance and disposition of an unattractive, shrewish girl can be remarkably improved by daily assertions that she is beautiful and sweet tempered. Mary would like to believe the image of herself that she sees reflected in John's eyes. But she knows that she is concealing other facets of herself (perhaps ill-tempered or slovenly proclivities) and, moreover, she finds it hard to believe that the charms John attributes to her are real. Any changes which she does perceive in herself she believes are elicited by John and she fears that if she lost him she *might* turn into a pumpkin. So she clings to him as a prop for a masquerade she hopes will never end. Her self-discovery remains unrecognized.

Mary has yet another reason for wanting to believe that she is in love. Having learned a contradictory set of ideas about sex, she is ambivalent about the sexual nature of the romance. She is uneasy about being sexually aroused and thinks that, if her feeling for John is only infatuation, her awakening sexual interests are dangerous and wrong. But she believes that if her feeling is Love she ought to desire him. Since she does find herself desiring him, she feels she had better be in love, and any questions about the suitability of marriage with John are pushed out of her mind.

John and Mary are in love, and they believe it is neither possible nor desirable to know why. But, as adjusted Americans, they are confident that love and marriage go together, and so they are wed.

Such a characterization of American marriage is difficult to accept. How can a young man who is only recently in love with this fantastic, wonderful girl differentiate the objective girl from his subjective reaction to her? Indeed, can he even see the real person through the rose-colored glasses which allow only those rays to pass which illuminate the imaginary ideal? Perhaps we are asking the impossible of the young man if we expect him at this moment of love to cast aside his ideals in favor of the real. At best, perhaps all that we can hope for is that he has before this moment thought about and analyzed his attitudes and values so that the dating process can cope smoothly with the transition from ideal to real.

Successful dating practice in America will greatly reduce the strains of marriage because the couple will have gained knowledge of the opposite sex, developed interpersonal skills, and as the more serious and intimate stages of dating occur, learned more about their specific future partner. Although many foreigners find the Western system of dating many partners shocking, Robert O. Blood points out that such a system is necessary in our relatively untraditional society.

> The fact that Americans date more than others is no accident; our circumstances demand it. In a simple society almost any marriage partner will do, so mate selection can be casual. In a feudal society the emphasis on vertical relationships means that the bride is more a mother's daughter-in-law than her son's wife, so mate selection becomes highly formalized. In the United States mate selection is neither casual nor formal but highly personalized. Our society is complex and highly differentiated. Not only is it stratified into social classes, but within each class there are differences in temperament, tastes, and values from person to person. As a result, potential marital combinations differ in compatibility.
>
> To some extent individual differences exist in every society, but Americans are less prepared to ignore them. In many countries, clashes between husband and wife are settled automatically by the rule of male dominance. Divergent recreational interests do not matter where leisure is not supposed to be spent together. Contrastingly, American patterns of shared decision-making and joint recreation require careful pairing. Dating provides an opportunity for trial-and-error selection. In our affluent, consumption-oriented society so much is expected of marriage that consummate skill in personal interaction is required to fulfill those expectations. Dating also provides opportunities to develop marital skills. So, in more ways than one, the American system of dating is a necessary foundation for our system of marriage.[1]

One theory of dating views it as a double funnel with the later stage of "going steady" leading into marriage. "The double-funnel theory holds that in our culture marriage is best viewed as the ultimate step in a funnel of commitments which start with the very casual commitment to spend an evening together and end with the commitment to spend a life together. The other funnel in the double-funnel theory is the funnel of intimacy. This funnel ranges from casual hand holding to a full and continuing sexual relationship."[2]

"In general, the boy is assigned the role of moving the relationship down the intimacy funnel and the girl is expected to press for movement down the commitment funnel. Reciprocally, the girl is generally expected to regulate movement down the intimacy funnel and the boy regulates movement down the commitment funnel."[3]

As couples move through the double funnel of commitment and intimacy toward marriage, the dating process hopefully facilitates an increasingly realistic appraisal of the relationship. If dating does not facilitate the transition from ideal to real, John and Mary will awake one morning after they are married, look at one another, and ask in some disbelief, "is this the person I married? He has changed so." Has he really changed or is his spouse truly looking at him for the first time without the rose-colored glasses? If and when such a time comes (termed "the honeymoon is over" period by your author), it signifies the real beginning of marital building and growth for the young couple that does have realistic self-knowledge. For John and Mary, however, it may mean the beginning of a new search for the correct mate, one that will meet the ideal and won't change. When the idealized image is strongly held, then belief that the partner has changed gives reason for leaving the spouse and taking up the search again. It is clear that the person who clings to his idealized images is doomed to failure since there is little chance of finding a human being that will coincide, upon realistic examination, with the entire, idealized image. John Robert Clark has a pithy description of this occurrence:

> In learning how to love a plain human being today, as during the romantic movement, what we usually want unconsciously is a fancy human being having no flaws. When the mental picture we have of someone we love is colored by wishes of childhood we may love the picture rather than the real person behind it. Naturally, we are disappointed in the person we love if he does not conform to our picture. Since this kind of disappointment has no doubt happened to us before, one might suppose we would then tear up the picture and start all over. On the contrary, we keep the picture and tear up the person. Small wonder that divorce courts are full of couples who never gave themselves a chance to know the real person behind the pictures in their lives.[4]

On the other hand, for our realistic couple, the end of the honeymoon signifies the beginning of an exciting and challenging period, one of coming to know well and intimately another human being.

Let us now examine more carefully love and the institution of marriage in modern America. Keeping in mind the ideals, a more critical analysis is now in order, after which we can examine some alternate systems for comparison. Although Greenfield's ideas are not based upon research, his analysis of love is timely and thought-provoking.

9 Love and Marriage in Modern America: A Functional Analysis

Sidney M. Greenfield

'*Voi, che cose e amor?*' asked Cherubino in Mozart's *Marriage of Figaro.* "Tell me, you know, what is this thing, love?" Cherubino was still a beardless adolescent and did not know the answer, but he took it for granted that there was one. So have most other people, and many of them have tried to give it, but the most noteworthy feature about all their answers is how thoroughly they disagree. Sometimes, it seems, they cannot be referring to the same phenomenon, or even to related ones. After a while one wonders whether there is something wrong with the question itself, or whether perhaps it employs a word of no fixed meaning and can have no answer.[1]

Love, wrote Theodor Reik, "is one of the most overworked words in our vocabulary. There is hardly a field of human activity in which the word is not worked to death."[2] The literature on the subject, to say the least, is voluminous. However, "if it is true that science is the topography of ignorance," as Oliver Wendell Holmes once said, "then the region of love is a vast white spot."[3]

Most of what we know of love comes from the pens of poets, dramatists, novelists, and philosophers. What they have to say, however, is so variable, idiosyncratic, and full of contradictions that, in sum, it adds relatively little to our understanding of the subject.

Psychologists also have written about love. Most of what they have to say, however, is an elaboration upon, or modification of, Freud's notion that love is "aim inhibited sex."[4] Furthermore, most of their attention has been focused on therapy and counseling, and here they tend to be one with the numerous sociologists and marriage counselors who have done work on the subject. The vast majority of these students and therapists, as Goode has recently stated, have "commented on the importance of romantic love in America and its lesser importance in other societies, and have disparaged it as a poor basis for marriage, or as immaturity."[5] Although they have helped us to specify and describe what love in the United States is—in the ethnographic sense—they have done very little in the way of analyzing their observations and contributing to our understanding of love. Instead, they have devoted their efforts to exposing the evils of romantic love and preaching against its practice.

"Love and Marriage in Modern America: A Functional Analysis" by Sidney M. Greenfield, appearing in *Sociological Quarterly,* vol. 6, no. 4, Autumn 1965. Reprinted by permission of The Sociological Quarterly.

The present paper is an attempt to apply modern sociological thinking to the analysis of the descriptive materials that have been accumulated on the subject of romantic love. In this sense then it is offered as a partial contribution to the understanding of a general phenomenon of love. More specifically, however, it is offered as an analysis of the place of love in modern American society. Following the lead of the family sociologists and marriage counselors, love will be treated not in the philosopher's or poet's sense of a "sweeping experience," not in the psychologist's sense of a universal physical power, and not in the sociologist's sense of a universal attribute of man. Instead, love shall be looked upon as a part of society, as a distinctive pattern of social behavior —as a specific culture trait. Thus we shall take the word to mean a given behavioral complex that exists in a specifiable social context. In this sense, our approach is ethnographic and synchronic. In this paper, therefore, the term love will be used to refer to a specific cultural trait that has been described in modern American society. Whether or not it exists in other societies—or in all human societies—in the same or a modified form is a matter to be demonstrated ethnographically and not assumed *a priori.*

The most abundant descriptive material available on the behavioral pattern called love comes from observations made in the contemporary United States — but restricted primarily to members of the middle class. Thus we shall limit our analysis to this segment of our own society and leave comparisons for another time.

Love, or romantic love, as it is called in the literature, is a behavioral complex composed of a series of specific features or elements. In the first place, it is a pattern that characterizes the behavior of adolescent and adult members of the middle class engaged in the quest of a mate.[6] Such individuals generally act in a distinctive way—distinctive with respect to the way in which individuals not in quest of a mate behave in the same society. In general, middle-class Americans are extremely sober and rational. These same people, however, when they are "in love" tend to be anything but.

Emotion, as opposed to reason, may be taken as characteristic of the thoughts and acts of a person in love; reason is believed to dominate at all other times. The quality of the emotions may be characterized best by a word such as "flighty." Phrases such as "walking on air, floating on cloud nine," and so forth, are used to describe both the feelings and the behavior of someone in love. The theatrical extreme, for example, has been stated by the heroine of a once popular musical comedy when she sang: "I'm as corny as Kansas in August, as high as a kite on the fourth of July. If you'll excuse an expression I use, I'm in love. . . ."

The song writer obviously overstated the case as dramatists often do to emphasize what is commonplace to their audience. Most Americans do not go around singing of their love as one might imagine after watching their movies and theater. However, they do tend to behave in a manner that by their normal standard may be considered flighty and irrational.

In the more exceptional cases, ungovernable impulses are overtly indulged. At times, the person in love can scarcely think of anything but his beloved. A great tenderness is experienced by the lover along with *extreme delusions as to the nature of the loved person.* On rare occasions all else but love seems to cease to matter to the lover; the emotion of the experience is all-consuming. As a French author once put it, one ceases to live when the loved person is absent, and begins again only when he or she is present once more.

Another aspect of the pattern is that one falls in love not by design and conscious choice, but according to some accident of fate over which the victim has no control. Of course it is a well known fact that individuals are taught to fall in love. Whether or not the pattern is learned, however, the significant factor is that individuals come to believe that love can and does strike at almost any time and in any place, and that when it does, the parties involved are helpless victims: they lose control, so to speak, over themselves, their actions and their reason, and they tend to behave emotionally and irrationally.

Directly related to this is the idea that there is one person, or lover for each man and woman in the society. Thus, if and when the paths of these two "right for each other" parties cross, they are helpless and must succumb to the "forces of the Universe."

The recent increase in the incidence of divorce has in no way challenged this belief. At most the pattern has been altered slightly so that there is now one "right one" at a time.

That the entire syndrome is atypical for the society may be seen in the inability of the individual to help falling in love. The general American belief is that man is able to master and control his environment. But in the realm of love, he is the victim of forces even stronger than himself.

Along with the idea of a "right one," goes the over idealization of the loved one. Once he or she is found, and the lovers succumb to their destiny, the real features of the loved one's character become lost in the emotional irrationality that dominates behavior. Love is said to be blind and the lovers are blinded to the faults of their new found mates.

Overriding everything is the belief that love is a panacea. Love is believed to "conquer all" and once it is experienced everything is expected to be better than it was before. One consequence of this is that it is both good and desirable to fall in love.

For middle-class Americans the expected climax of a love affair is marriage. "The sentiment of love," write Waller and Hill, "is the heart of . . . the family. In our culture, people customarily get married because they are in love; indeed it seems preposterous to us that anyone should marry for any other reason."[7]

The syndrome of features that constitutes the pattern, or culture trait, that has come to be called romantic love in American society then may be summarized as follows:

1. Two diligent, hard working, rational adolescents or adults of the opposite sex meet, most probably by accident, and find each other to be personally and physically attractive.

2. They soon come to realize that they are "right for each other."

3. They then fall victims to forces beyond their control, and fall in love.

4. They then begin—at least for a short time—to behave in a flighty, irrational manner that is at variance with the way in which they formerly conducted themselves.

5. Finally, believing that love is a panacea and that the future holds only goodness for them, they marry and form a new nuclear family.

At this point we may note that sexual behavior in middle-class America, in general, is directly related to the romantic love complex. Sex, in the ideal, is restricted to people who are in love and then its practice is generally postponed until after marriage. Thus sexual gratification is linked to and becomes the culmination of the syndrome just described. In terms of ideal patterns we may state that sexual activity is to be engaged in only by people who are married to each other. We know, however, that the incidence of premarital and extramarital sexual behavior is relatively high, and is on the increase. It appears that in spite of this sex is still linked to the romantic love complex in that, by and large, middle-class couples who engage in premarital or extramarital sexual activity invariably believe—at the time—and behave as if they are in love with their illicit partners. Thus it appears that the tie between sex and love is strong though the restriction of sex to marriage is weakening.

Though the pattern is quite clear, most middle-class Americans, as Hunt reminds us, "are firmly of two minds about it all—simultaneously hardheaded and idealistic, uncouth and tender, libidinous and puritanical; they believe implicitly in every tenet of romantic love, and yet know perfectly well that things don't really work out that way."[8] As with other culture traits, however, individuals, to a greater or lesser degree, do tend to approximate the ideal presented above.

The behavior and sentiments associated with romantic love appear to be at odds with what may be taken to be the general characteristics of American society. People in love are flighty and irrational in contrast with the sober rationality that generally prevails.

Students of non-Western societies tend to agree that the pattern just described for the United States is non-existent, or at best very rare in the non-

Western world.[9] The most quoted statement, probably because it is extreme, was made by Linton:

> All societies recognize that there are occasional violent emotional attachments between persons of opposite sex, but our present American culture is practically the only one which has attempted to capitalize these and make them the basis for marriage. Most groups regard them as unfortunate and point out the victims of such attachments as horrible examples. Their rarity in most societies suggests that they are psychological abnormalities to which our own culture has attached an extraordinary value just as other cultures have attached extreme values to other abnormalities. The hero of the modern American movie is always a romantic lover just as the hero of the old Arab epic is always an epileptic. A cynic might suspect that in any ordinary population the percentage of individuals with a capacity for romantic love of the Hollywood type was about as large as that of persons able to throw genuine epileptic fits. However, given a little social encouragement, either one can be adequately imitated without the performer admitting even to himself that the performance is not genuine.[10]

In addition to being both cross-culturally infrequent and atypical in comparison with the general range of behavior in American society—and possibly abnormal—the trait also has been considered pathological. As Truxal and Merrill put it: "The state of being romantically in love exhibits many characteristics of certain pathological conditions known as trance or dissociation phenomena."[11]

But to middle-class Americans, falling in love is not only the right thing to do, it is a panacea, and right and good for its own sake. As Hunt indicates: "At no time in history has so large a proportion of humanity rated love so highly, thought about it so much, or displayed such an insatiable appetite for word about it."[12] As a sympathetic observer (De Sales) once remarked, this "appears to be the only country in the world where love is a national problem."[13] In no other country do people devote so much of their time and energy to a conscious attempt to experience love—atypical, abnormal, and pathological though it may be.

It is at this point that sociologists and marriage counselors generally begin to point out that this is not a good way to begin a relationship as important as marriage. They warn that the euphoria of love generally begins to wane after the first few months. Then the parties gradually return to their more normal way of thinking, feeling, and behaving. With the return of their more rational and sober perspective, however, the promised best of all worlds often begins to crumble as the actual characteristics of the chosen mate are noticed for the first time. Then, in an increasing number of cases, the newly formed family moves along the road of strife, conflict, and eventual separation and divorce.

True as this may be, romantic love has persisted in American society and, as we have already indicated, is as strong, or stronger today than it ever has been.*

The remainder of Greenfield's lengthy article deals with what he thinks to be the reasons for the existence and strength of the romantic love complex in contemporary American society. Basically he hypothesizes that the formation of nuclear families is the basis for the successful functioning of the American economic system.

To conclude, then, the function of romantic love in American society appears to be to motivate individuals—where there is no other means of motivating them—to occupy the positions husband-father and wife-mother and form nuclear families that are essential not only for reproduction and socialization but also to maintain the existing arrangements for distributing and consuming goods and services and, in general, to keep the social system in proper working order and thus maintaining it as a going concern.

Most essays about "love" follow a pattern similar to Greenfield; they are reasoned arguments and opinions of the author. After all, how can we subject "love" to the scientific laboratory? Elaine Walster, an experimental social psychologist, believes, however, that objective research can be done on love, despite popular disbelief. She argues that passionate love is a distinct emotional state. A person will experience love only if (1) he/she is physiologically aroused and (2) concludes that love is the appropriate label for his/her aroused feelings.

---

*Before concluding we may note that in American society there are actual restrictions in the general pattern of romantic love. In theory, anyone is permitted to fall in love with anyone else. In fact, however, as Goode (*op. cit.*) has pointed out, falling in love has been structured so that lovers actually select each other not at random but from within specific cultural categories that have been defined as structural isolates. That is, not only is it right to fall in love, but it is "more right" to fall in love with and to marry someone who is a member of the same ethnic, racial, religious educational, age, socioeconomic, etc., category as you are. This structuring of love not only gets people to marry and to occupy the positions husband-father and wife-mother, but also helps to maintain the structure of the society in accord with the categories.

10 "What Is This Thing Called Love?"   Elaine Walster

Interpersonal attraction and companionate love seem like sensible phenomena. One can predict quite well how much a person will like another, if he knows to what extent the other rewards or punishes the person. Reward has so predictable an impact on liking that Byrne[1] could with confidence propose an exact correspondence between reinforcement and liking: ("Attraction towards X is a positive linear function of the proportion of positive reinforcements received from X or expected from X.") Data support their formulation.

Sometimes passionate love seems to operate in a sensible fashion. Some practical people have been known to fall in love with those beautiful, wise, entertaining, and kind people who offer affection or material rewards to them. Generally, however, passionate love does not seem to fit so neatly into the reinforcement paradigm. Individuals do *not* always feel passionate about the person who provides the most rewards with the greatest consistency. Passion sometimes develops under conditions that would seem more likely to provoke aggression and hatred than love. For example, reinforcement theorists argue that "we like those who like us and reject those who dislike us." Yet individuals experience intense love for those who have rejected them.

> A woman discovers her husband is seeing another. The pain and suffering the jealous wife experiences at this discovery cause her to realize how much she loves her husband.
>
> Lovers pine away for the girls who spurn their affection. For example, a recent Associated Press release reports the desperate excuse of an Italian lover who kidnapped his former sweetheart: " 'The fact that she rejected me only made me want and love her more,' he tearfully explained."

Reinforcement theorists tell us that "frustration always breeds aggression." Yet, inhibited sexuality is assumed to be the foundation of romantic feelings. Freud even argued that:

> Some obstacle is necessary to swell the tide of libido to its height; and at all periods of history whenever natural barriers in the way of satisfaction have not sufficed, mankind has erected conventional ones in order to enjoy love.[2]

The observation that passionate love flourishes in settings which would seem to thwart its development has always been puzzling to social scientists. Poets attribute such inexplicable phenomena to the essential illogic of love. Scientists, who refuse to acknowledge that anything is inexplicable, do not have such an easy way out.

Happily, we believe that a theoretical framework exists which makes the "illogical" phenomena of passionate love explicable and predictable.

Schachter's Two-Component Theory

On the basis of an ingenious series of experiments, Schachter[3] proposed a paradigm for understanding human emotional response. He argues that in order for a person to experience true emotion, two factors must coexist: 1) The individual must be physiologically aroused, and 2) It must be reasonable to interpret his stirred-up state in emotional terms. Schachter argued that neither physiological arousal nor appropriate cognitions *alone* is sufficient to produce an emotional experience.

It is possible to manipulate an individual's physiological arousal artifically. A drug, adrenalin, exists whose effects mimic the discharge of the sympathetic nervous system. Shortly after one receives an injection of adrenalin, systolic blood pressure increases markedly, heart rate increases somewhat, cutaneous blood flow decreases, muscle and cerebral blood flow increase, blood sugar and lactic acid concentration increase, and respiration rate increases slightly. The individual who has been injected with adrenalin experiences palpitation, tremor, and sometimes flushing and accelerated breathing. These reactions are identical to the physiological reactions which accompany a variety of natural emotional states.

An injection of adrenalin will not, by itself, however, engender an emotional response in a person. When an individual is injected with adrenalin and asked to introspect, he will report either no emotional response or, at best, report feeling "as if" he might be experiencing some emotion:[4] Individuals make statements such as "I feel *as if* I were afraid." The person who has been injected with adrenalin perceives that something is not quite authentic about his reactions. Something is missing.

Schachter argues that what is missing is an appropriate label for the physiological reactions one is experiencing. If one could lead the drugged individual to attribute his stirred-up state to some emotion-arousing event (rather than attributing it to the injection of adrenalin which he received), Schachter argues that he would experience a "true" emotion.

The researcher who wishes to test the notion that physiological arousal and appropriate cognitions are separate and indispensable components of a true emotional experience, is faced with the challenging task of separately manipulating these two components. In a classic study, Schachter and Singer[5] conceived of a way to do just that. Volunteers were recruited for an experiment which the experimenters claimed was designed to investigate the effects of a new vitamin compound, Suproxin, on vision.

Manipulating Physiological Arousal: Volunteers were injected with a substance which was identified as Suproxin. Actually, one half of the students were injected with epinephrine (½ cc of a 1:1000 solution of Winthrop Laboratory's Suprarenin). Such an injection causes the intense physiological reactions described earlier. One half received a placebo (½ cc of saline solution).

Manipulating an Appropriate Explanation: Schachter wished to lead some of the volunteers to correctly attribute their physiological state to a nonemotional cause (the injection). He wished to lead others to attribute their stirred-up state to an emotional cause.

Thus, in one condition (the *Non-Emotional Attribution* condition), individuals were given a complete explanation of how the shot would affect them. They were warned that in 15 to 20 minutes the injection of "Suproxin" would cause palpitation, tremor, etc. Presumably, when students began to experience these symptoms, they could properly attribute their stirred-up state to the shot and would *not* attribute their excitement to the activities in which they were engaging at the time the adrenalin began to take effect.

In the *Emotional Attribution* conditions, things were arranged to *discharge* students from attributing their stirred-up state to the shot. One group of volunteers was given no information about possible side effects of the shot. A second group of volunteers was deliberately misled as to the potential side effects of the shot. It was assumed that volunteers who received either no information or incorrect information would be unlikely to attribute their tremors and palpitations to the shot. After all, these symptoms took 20 minutes to develop. Instead, the authors hoped that volunteers would attribute their arousal to whatever they happened to be doing when the drug took effect. The authors then arranged things so that what volunteers "happened to be doing" was participating in either a gay, happy, social interaction or participating in a tense, explosive interaction.

If the subject had been assigned to the *Euphoria* condition, his fellow student (who was actually a confederate) had been trained to generate excitement while they waited 20 minutes for the experiment to begin. As soon as the experimenter left the room, the confederate began "acting up." He shot paper wads into the wastebasket, built a paper tower which he sent crashing to the floor and generally kidded around.

In the *Anger* setting, the confederate had been trained to make the subject angry. The confederate first complained about the experimental procedures. He became especially indignant on encountering the questionnaire they had been asked to fill out (and which admittedly asked stupid and offensive questions). Finally, the confederate slammed his questionnaire to the floor and stomped out.

The authors assessed subject's emotional reactions to the confederate's behavior in two ways. Observers stationed behind a one-way mirror assessed to what extent the subject caught the stooge's euphoric or angry mood; secondly, subjects were asked to describe their moods and to estimate how euphoric and angry they felt.

Schachter and Singer predicted that those subjects who had received an adrenalin injection would have stronger emotional reactions than would subjects who had received a placebo or had received an adrenalin injection but had been warned of exactly what physiological changes they should expect. The data supported these hypotheses. The experiment thus supported the contention that both physiological arousal and appropriate cognitions are indispensable components of a true emotional experience.

The Two-Component Theory and Passionate Love

The discovery that almost any sort of intense physiological arousal—if properly interpreted—will precipitate an emotional experience has intriguing implications. We were particularly intrigued by the possibility that Schachter's "two-component" theory might help explain a heretofore inexplicable phenomenon—passionate love.

As long as researchers were busily absorbed in figuring out how passionate love could be integrated into the reinforcement paradigm, we made little progress. The observation that negative experiences often lead to increased evaluation remained inexplicable.

A sudden insight solved our dilemma. Two components are necessary for a passionate experience: arousal and appropriate cognitions. Perhaps negative experiences do not increase love by somehow improving one's evaluation of the other (beneficially altering his cognitions). Perhaps negative experiences are effective in inducing love because they intensify the second component— arousal.

We would suggest that perhaps it does not really matter how one produces an agitated state in an individual. Stimuli that usually produce sexual arousal, gratitude, anxiety, guilt, loneliness, hatred, jealousy, or confusion may all increase one's physiological arousal, and thus increase the intensity of his emotional experience. As long as one attributes his agitated state to passion, he should experience true passionate love. As soon as he ceases to attribute his tumultuous feelings to passion, love should die.

Does any evidence exist to support our contention? Some early observers noticed that any form of strong emotional arousal breeds love (although not, of course, interpreting this relationship in Schachterian terms). Finck, an early psychologist, concluded:

Love can only be excited by strong and vivid emotion, and it is almost immaterial whether these emotions are agreeable or disagreeable. The Cid wooed the proud heart of Diana Ximene, whose father he had slain, by shooting one after another of her pet pigeons. Such persons as arouse in us only weak emotions or none at all, are obviously least likely to incline us toward them. . . . Our aversion is most likely to be bestowed on individuals who, as the phrase goes, are neither 'warm' nor 'cold'; whereas impulsive, choleric people, though they may readily offend us, are just as capable of making us warmly attached to them. (p. 240)[6]

Unfortunately, experimental evidence does not yet exist to support the contention that almost any form of high arousal, if properly labeled, will deepen passion. There are, however, a few studies designed to test other hypotheses, which provide some minimal support for our contention.*

Since it was the juxtaposition of misery and ecstasy in romantic love that we initially found so perplexing, let us first examine the relation between negative experiences and love.

Unpleasant Emotional States: Facilitators of Passion?

That negative reinforcements produce strong emotional reactions in all animals is not in doubt. There is some evidence that under the right conditions such unpleasant, but arousing, states as fear, rejection, and frustration do enhance romantic passion.

Fear: A Facilitator of Passion   Frightening a person is a very good way of producing intense psychological arousal for a substantial period of time.

An intriguing study of Brehm et al.[7] demonstrates that a frightened man is a romantic man. Brehm et al. tested the hypothesis that "a person's attraction to another would be multiplied by prior arousal from an irrelevant event." In this experiment, some men were led to believe that they would soon receive three "pretty stiff" electrical shocks. Half of the men, "Threat" subjects, were allowed to retain this erroneous expectation throughout the experiment. Half of the men, "Threat-Relief," were frightened and then, sometime later, were told that the experimenter had made an error; they had been assigned to the control group and would receive no shock. The remainder of the men were assigned to a control group, in which the possibility of their receiving shock was not even mentioned.

Men were then introduced to a young co-ed, and asked how much they liked her.

The Threat subjects who expected to be shocked in the future should be quite frightened at the time they meet the girl. The Threat-Relief subjects who had just learned they would not be shocked should be experiencing vast relief when they meet the girl. Both the frightened and the frightened-relieved men should be more aroused than are men in the control group. Brehm predicted, as we would, that Threat and Threat-Relief subjects would like the girl more

---

*These studies are only "minimally supportive" because the authors investigate only liking, not passionate loving—a phenomenon we have argued is unique. Whether or not the same results would occur in a romantic context must yet be determined.

than would control subjects. Brehm's expectations were confirmed; threatened men experienced more liking for the girl (and did not differ in their liking) than did control group men, who had never been frightened. An irrelevant frightening event, then, does seem to facilitate attraction.

Rejection: An Antecedent of Passion   Rejection is always disturbing. And generally when a person is rejected he has a strong emotional reaction. Usually he experiences embarrassment, pain, or anger. Although it is probably most reasonable for a rejected person to label his agitation in this way, if our hypothesis is correct, it should be possible, under the right conditions, to induce a rejected individual to label his emotional response as "love" as well as "hate."

Some slight evidence that passionate love *or* hate may emerge from rejection comes from several laboratory experiments designed to test other hypotheses.[8,9]

Let us consider one of these experiments and the way a Schachterian might reinterpret these data.

The experiment of Jacobs et al. was designed to determine how changes in the self-esteem of college students affected their receptivity to love and affection. First, students took a number of personality tests (the *MMPI*, Rorschach, etc.). A few weeks later, a psychologist returned an analysis of his personality to each student. Half of the students were given a flattering personality report. The reports stressed their sensitivity, honesty, originality, and freedom of outlook. (Undoubtedly this flattering personality report confirmed many of the wonderful things the students already thought about themselves.) Half of the students received an insulting personality report. The report stressed their immaturity, weak personality, conventionality, and lack of leadership ability. This critical report was naturally most upsetting for students.

Soon after receiving their analyses, the males got acquainted individually with a young female college student (actually, this girl was an experimental confederate). Half of the time the girl treated the boy in a warm, affectionate, and accepting way. Under such conditions, the men who had received the critical personality evaluation were far more attracted to her than were their more confident counterparts. (Presumably, the previous irrelevant arousal engendered by rejection facilitated the subsequent development of affection.)

Half of the time the girl was cold and rejecting. Under these conditions, a dramatic reversal occurred; the previously rejected men disliked the girl more than did their more confident counterparts. (Presumably, under these conditions, the low self-esteem individual's agitation was transformed to hatred.)

An irrelevant, painful event, then, can incite various strong emotional reactions toward others. Depending on how he labels his feelings, the individual may experience either intense attraction or intense hostility.

Frustration and Challenge: Facilitators of Passion   Socrates, Ovid, Terence, the Kama Sutra and "Dear Abby" are all in agreement about one thing: the person whose affection is easily won will inspire less passion than the person whose affection is hard to win.

Vassilikos[10] poetically elucidated the principle that frustration fuels passion while continual gratification dims it:

> Once upon a time there was a little fish who was a bird from the waist up and who was madly in love with a little bird who was a fish from the waist up. So the Fish-Bird kept saying to the Bird-Fish: "Oh, why were we created so that we can never live together? You in the wind and I in the wave. What a pity for both of us." And the Bird-Fish would answer: "No, what luck for both of us. This way we'll always be in love because we'll always be separated." (p. 131)

Some provisional evidence that the hard-to-get person may engender unusual passion in the eventually successful suitor comes from Aronson and Linder.[11] These authors tested the hypothesis that: "A gain in esteem is a more potent reward than invariant esteem." They predicted that a person would be better liked if his positive regard was difficult to acquire than if it was easily had.

This hypothesis was tested in the following way: Subjects were required to converse with a confederate (who appeared to be another naive subject) over a series of seven meetings. After each meeting, the subject discovered (secretly) how her conversation partner felt about her. How the confederate "felt" was systematically varied. In one condition the girl expressed a negative impression of the subject after their first meetings. (She described the subject as being a dull conversationalist, a rather ordinary person, not very intelligent, as probably not having many friends, etc.) Only after the partners had become well acquainted did she begin expressing favorable opinions of the subject. In the remaining conditions, from the first, the confederate expressed only positive opinions about the subject.

As Aronson and Linder predicted, subjects liked the confederate whose affection was hard to win better than they liked the confederate whose high opinion was readily obtained.

The preceding evidence is consistent with our suggestion that under the right conditions, a hard-to-get girl should generate more passion than the constantly rewarding girl. The aloof girl's challenge may excite the suitor; her momentary rejection may shake his self-esteem. In both cases, such arousal may intensify the suitor's feelings toward her.

The preceding analysis lends some credence to the argument that the juxtaposition of agony and ecstasy in passionate love is not entirely accidental. (The original meaning of "passion" was, in fact, "agony"—for example, as in Christ's passion.) Loneliness, deprivation, frustration, hatred, and insecurity may in fact supplement a person's romantic experiences. Passion requires physiological arousal, and all of the preceding states are certainly arousing.

Pleasant Emotional States: Facilitators of Passion?

We would like to make it clear that, theoretically, passion need not include a negative component. The positive reinforcements of discovery, excitement, companionship, and playful-joy can generate as intense an arousal as that stirred by fear, frustration, or rejection. For example, in many autobiographical accounts, entirely joyful (albeit brief) passionate encounters are described.[12]

Sexual Gratification: A Facilitator of Passion   Sexual experiences can be enormously rewarding and enormously arousing. Masters and Johnson[13] point out that sexual intercourse induces hyperventilation, tachycardia, and marked increases in blood pressure. And, religious advisors, school counselors, and psychoanalysts to the contrary—sexual gratification has undoubtedly generated as much passionate love as has sexual continence.

Valins[14] demonstrated that even the erroneous belief that another has excited one (sexually or aesthetically) will facilitate attraction. Valins recruited male college students for a study of males' physiological reactions to sexual stimuli. The sexual stimuli he utilized were ten semi-nude *Playboy* photographs. The subjects were told that while they scrutinized these photographs, their heart rate would be amplified and recorded. They were led to believe that their heart rates altered markedly to some of the slides but that they had no reaction at all to others. (Valins assumed that the subjects would interpret an alteration in heart rate as sexual enthusiasm.)

The subjects' liking for the "arousing" and "nonarousing" slides was then assessed in three ways. Regardless of the measure used, the men markedly preferred the pin-ups they thought had aroused them to those that had not affected their heart rate. 1) They were asked to rate how "attractive or appealing" each pin-up was. They preferred the pin-ups they believed were arousing to all others. 2) They were offered a pin-up in remuneration for participating in the experiment. They chose the arousing pin-ups more often than the nonarousing ones. 3) Finally, they were interviewed a month later (in a totally different context) and they still markedly preferred the arousing pin-ups to the others.

Need Satisfaction: A Facilitator of Passion   Although psychologists tend to focus almost exclusively on the contribution of sex to love, other rewards can have an equally important emotional impact. People have a wide variety of needs, and at any stage of life many of one's needs must remain unsatisfied. When any important unsatisfied need is recognized or met, the emotional response which accompanies such reinforcement could provide fuel for passion. To the adolescent boy who has been humored, coddled, and babied at home, the girl who finally recognizes his masculinity may be an over-powering joy. The good, steady, reliable, hard-working father may be captivated when an alert lady recognizes that he has the potential to be a playful and reckless lover.

To the person who has been deprived of such rewards, an intelligent, artistic, witty, beautiful, athletic, or playful companion may prove a passionate and absorbing joy.

Labeling

We are proposing a two-factor theory of passionate love. Yet the preceding discussion has focused almost exclusively on one factor. We have concentrated on demonstrating that physiological arousal is a crucial component of passionate love, and that fear, pain, and frustration as well as discovery and delight may contribute to the passionate experience.

We should now at least remind the reader that according to our theory an individual will be incapable of experiencing "love" unless he's prepared to define his feelings in that way.

Cultural Encouragement of Love

In America, it is expected that everyone will eventually fall in love. Individuals are encouraged to interpret many emotional as well as sexual feelings as love.

Individuals are often encouraged to interpret certain confused or mixed feelings as love, because our culture insists that certain reactions are acceptable if one is madly in love. For example, the delightful experience of sexual intercourse can be frankly labeled as "sexual fun" by a man. Such an interpretation of what she is experiencing is probably less acceptable to his partner. She (and her parents) are undoubtedly happier if she attributes her abandoned behavior to love.

Margaret Mead interprets jealousy in one way:

> Jealousy is not a barometer by which the depth of love may be read. It merely records the degree of the lover's insecurity. It is a negative, miserable state of feeling, having its origin in a sense of insecurity and inferiority.[15]

Jealous people, however, usually interpret their jealous reactions in quite another way; jealous feelings are taken as evidence of passionate love rather than inferiority. Thus, in this culture, a jealous man is a loving man rather than an embarrassed man.

Thus, whether or not an individual is susceptible to "falling in love" should depend on the expectations of his culture and his reference groups.

Individual Expectations

An individual's own expectations should also determine how likely he is to experience love.

The individual who thinks of himself as a nonromantic person should fall in love less often than should an individual who assumes that love is inevitable. The nonromantic may experience the same feelings that the romantic does, but he will code them differently.

Similarly, individuals who feel they are unlovable should have a difficult time finding love. Individuals convey their expectations in very subtle ways to others, and these expectations influence the way one's partner labels *his* reactions. The insecure girl who complains to her boyfriend: "You don't love me, you just think you do. If you loved me you wouldn't treat me this way," and then itemizes evidence of his neglect, may, by automatically interpreting her boyfriend's actions in a damaging way, affect an alteration in his feelings for her. Alternately, a girl with a great deal of self-confidence may (by her unconscious guidance) induce a normally unreceptive gentleman to label his feelings for her as love.

Because "love" is so difficult to define, because it has so many meanings, because we all think we understand it, one's individual beliefs about "love" are a mixture of fact and fantasy. John F. Crosby, a professor at Indiana University, lists a number of myths about sex and love that he feels are held by many Americans. Before reading his article, mark the following statements true or false.

_____ A marriage relationship should fulfill all psychological and interpersonal human needs.

_____ Sex is the same as love.

_____ Love is the same as sex.

_____ Sex is always what it appears to be.

_____ Values are a moralistic hangover, repressive and oppressive in nature.

_____ Romantic love is prosexual.

_____ Conflict is bad; marital conflict is worse.

_____ Communication dissolves all conflict.

_____ Love and hate are opposites.

_____ Man (homo sapiens) by nature is a monogamous creature.

_____ Man by nature is a polygamous creature.

_____ Sexual compatibility prior to marriage is a reasonable guarantee of marital success.

_____ Painless divorce procedures would be a good thing for marriage.

_____ Strict divorce procedures are necessary if marriage is to survive.

_____ The family is in a state of breakdown and decay.

_____ If women would stay where they belong, there wouldn't be so many family problems.

Now read Crosby's article and compare your answers to his.

11 A Marriage Wake: John Crosby
Myths That Die Hard

Myth	A marriage relationship should fulfill all psychological and interpersonal human needs.
Response	False. No single relationship can possibly fulfill the varied and diverse range of human needs. Monogamy makes possible a security-giving dyadic relationship. While the most basic human needs are partially met within the marriage, there need be no limit to "philos" and "agape" relationships beyond the dyad. If the marriage is reasonably stable and secure, both partners may find meaning and fulfillment in many other activities and relationships, both complementing and supplementing the marital relationship.
Myth	Sex is the same as love.
Response	False. Sex is part of erotic love but not necessarily a part of philos or agape. Sexual love per se is purely physical release. If erotic love (eros) is understood in its noncontaminated, historical sense, it is highly charged with passion, tenderness, the desire to give and to create. In any normative sense sex does not

include the totality of the love experience and therefore we are not justified in equating sex with love.

Myth   Love is the same as sex.

Response   False. Except in the case of sexual (libidinous) love. By definition, libidinous love is the physical release of tension created by the libido. For those who accept libidinous love as an end in and of itself, love is the same as sex. However, only this extremely narrow definition of love can qualify to be equated with the experience of sex.

Myth   Sex is always what it appears to be.

Response   False. Sex is not always sexual. Sexual activity is often the most vulnerable carrier for free-floating anxiety. Sometimes it is an expression of anger, resentment, and hostility, or it may be an acting-out behavior through which the individual acts out his deepest feelings and impulses. Thus, sexual desire may be the "cover" for insecurity and a compulsive need for affection.

Myth   Values are a moralistic hangover, repressive and oppressive in nature.

Response   False. A fair and unbiased reading of the histories of Eastern and Western civilization, together with testimony of the existential psychologists, would seem to indicate that when man can define purpose and meaning for himself, with or without reference to duty or supernatural phenomena, he is happier and more self-fulfilled than those who fail to define the meaning and purpose of their existence for themselves. Meaning and purpose presuppose values and a value structure. What needs to be laid bare is the "moralistic" claim based on unquestioning acceptance of custom, tradition, dogma, taboo, and preachments rather than on enlightened reason and learning through human experience. Values which are freely chosen and embraced without coercion are neither repressive nor oppressive.

Myth   Romantic love is prosexual.

Response   False. Romantic love is blatantly antisexual, for sex is considered only as an inconsequential by-product of the idealized love relationship rather than as a genuine human experience in its own right. While sexual or libidinous love omits eros, philos, and agape, romantic love emphasizes an idealized form of philos and agape, spiritualizes eros, and denies the libido.

Myth   Conflict is bad; marital conflict is worse.

Response   False. Conflict is a fact of life; it is neither good nor bad in itself. The denial of conflict may take the form of suppression and repression of anger, hostility, and resentment, thus also reducing positive feelings of love. The ability to face conflict creatively and honestly must be learned. The effect of dealing honestly and forthrightly with conflict is an important prerequisite for keeping alive and vital the positive feelings of love, affection, fidelity, and commitment.

Myth   Communication dissolves all conflict.

Response   False. Excellent communication between two people who are not afraid of facing conflict and who are reasonably mature and creative in their ways of resolving conflict may not be sufficient to resolve the conflict. Not all conflicts can be resolved, even by compromise. Yet the conflict need not be dangerous as long as it is not repressed, denied, or avoided. One mark of maturity is learning to accept the things that we cannot change, even after resolute and honest efforts at compromise. Disappointment may be uncomfortable, but it need not be devastating: Aron Krich has commented that "By denying disappointment, all we do is shut out our awareness of the real cause of our pain."[1] The belief that there should never be disappointment in marriage is a corollary of the belief that all conflict should be resolved. These two beliefs are the result of unrealistic expectations.

Myth   Love and hate are opposites.

Response   False. The opposite of love and hate is indifference. A person in a state of indifference (sometimes described as having "fallen out of love" or "love is dead") is unable to experience either positive feelings of love and affection or negative feelings of anger, resentment, hostility, and hatred. This then, is the worst state of all, for it portends the death of meaning in the relationship. The negative feelings can only be understood in the light of the preexisting positive feelings. Love and hate are dynamically related; since love is an emotion that deeply affects the human

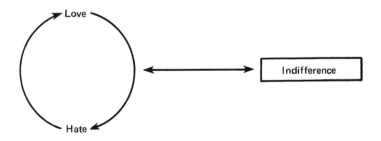

Fig. 1   The Opposite of Love and Hate Is Indifference

psyche, it is unrealistic to think that there is no possibility of love in resentment or resentment in love.

Myth   Man (Homo sapiens) by nature is a monogamous creature. Man by nature is a polygamous creature.

Response   Neither belief has ever been established. Early societies were essentially isolated from each other, and their marriage patterns were monogamous and polygamous. In polygamous societies the method of subsistence combined with the desire for a low or high birth rate so that in hunting, fishing, food-gathering, and nomadic societies polyandry was more likely since it kept the birth rate down. In polygynous societies, one may expect to find an agricultural subsistence and a higher birth rate. Whether or not monogamy or polygamy is the "natural" thing cannot be resolved by looking at the animal world, for the wolf and the tiny gerbil are monogamous, while many other species are not. The appeal to morality depends entirely on the mores of the society in which the appeal is made. In some instances, a man would be considered lax in his duty if he had only one wife. The appeal to religious authority depends on the religious tradition to which one appeals. The appeal to libidinous drives and desires for justification for multiple mates may reveal more about man's psyche than about his libido. The traditions, customs, and mores of a given society together with one's own sense of value and meaning would appear to be the more accurate predictors of "man's essential nature."

Myth   Sexual compatibility prior to marriage is a reasonable guarantee of marital success.

Response   False. It is a reasonable guarantee that prior to marriage the couple is sexually compatible—nothing else. Marriage counselors have reported numerous instances in which premarital sexual compatibility did not guarantee marital compatibility. The sexual relationship is affected by many variables, including finances, child discipline, individual autonomy, degree of fulfillment, and general level of marital satisfaction. A few marriages may have an adequate sexual relationship despite the fact that the marital relationship as a whole is poor. The question becomes a chicken and egg proposition: Does a good sexual relationship create a viable marital relationship or does the total marital relationship make possible an enjoyable sexual relationship? Whichever way, one thing is established. The sexual relationship is inseparable from the total marital relationship; each affects and is affected by the other.

Myth   (a) Painless divorce procedures would be a good thing for the institution of marriage. (b) Strict divorce prodedures are necessary if the institution of marriage is to survive.

Response   False on both counts. Strict divorce procedures are unrealistic, punitive, and dehumanizing because they reduce the couple and their children to the state of prisoners of each other and the system. Human growth and self-actualization can hardly be the result of such a state of being. Extremely liberal divorce laws may do the family structure an equal injustice. If divorce is reduced to a mere ritual the couple may never come to terms with the possibility for human growth and actualization implicit in the facing of conflict. Conflict resolution is not an easy thing, as we have seen; conflict resolution requires a looking into oneself which is usually an uncomfortable and threatening experience. Consequently, many people not only unconsciously repress conflict, they also consciously avoid it or run away from it. The option to exit from marriage is important but if the exit is too easy and attractive the marriage will be dissolved without either partner having to face himself, the other, or the dynamics of their interpersonal situation. Perhaps our society will one day evolve into a position in which divorce is serious but not cruel and punitive, not an easy avenue of escape, and neither dehumanizing nor void of commitment and trust over time.

Myth   The family is in a state of breakdown and decay.

Response   False. Which family? Whose family? Moralists and politicians seem to relish this theme. The evidence to support it is little different from the evidence used by Socrates and Aritstotle circa 400 B.C. A companion myth is "the youth are going to the dogs." In recent years the family in the United States has undergone changes in life style, leisure-time pursuits, mobility, method of communication, and intergenerational relationships. As the function of the rural, economically self-sufficient, three-generation stereotype of the past has changed, so has the structure of the family changed. Is this to be defined as breakdown? Divorce rates are higher than in previous decades. Does this mean that more marriages are failing or that more failing marriages are admitting the failure and doing away with the pretense? The family, in one variation or another, has survived for several thousand years. There is little question that it will continue to survive, perhaps evolving and changing, with variations in function and then structure. Man has a basic need for close, affectionate primary relationships. There are few places in American society where a person may afford the luxury of being totally himself, accepting of and accepted by those he loves and who love him, sharing the joys and sorrows, the accomplishments and the failures of everyday life. No society or group within a society has succeeded over a period of time to effectively replace the family as the primary socialization unit for the young. Even the kibbutzim are variations of family structure. As rigid stereotypes, customs, and traditions break down, the family will be increasingly free to explore new variations and new modes of expression. The family at its best is an emotional base of operations for parents and children, who need the security of being wanted, loved, and needed. From this base, family members can venture forth into the world.

Myth   If women would stay where they belong, there wouldn't be so many family problems.

Response False. This is scapegoating par excellence! People who are terribly threatened by change would like to endow the past with sanctity and righteousness. The status of the female in any culture is a vital clue to the economic, marital, and familial patterns of that culture. When women were challenged with maintaining the household and assisting their spouses with management of the farm or other family enterprise there was ample opportunity for her self-fulfillment. Not so today. The female has every right to expect total equality as a human being —equal rights, privileges, responsibilities, and pleasure. There is much to be said for the position that a self-actualizing woman with many diverse interests or employed in some meaningful (to her) capacity can attain and maintain a higher quality of interaction and relationship with her husband and her children. Role reversal may be threatening to the male, but there are absolutely no a priori or preordained role specifications that hold for all societies. Beyond the biological fact that the female carries the fetus for nine months and then gives birth, there is little today which physiologically or biologically limits the sphere of the female.

Section 3

The Romantic Ideal
Ethnic, Cultural, and Class Differences

Since the majority of readers will have been reared within the United States, it may be helpful to step outside of the American culture and examine values and attitudes surrounding marriage in other societies. The variations of courtship and marriage patterns are myriad (one wife or monogamy, multiple wives or polygyny, arranged marriage, marriage for love, etc.), but the important thing to remember is that all cultures have rules, and to the degree that a system works, it is correct and natural to that culture. Thus South India's Todas' preferences for cross-cousin marriages are as correct to them as is the Manus of New Guinea's taboo against such marriages. Neither is more natural or unnatural than the other. In the book, *The Family in Various Cultures,* Queen and Habenstein conclude that since there is such variance among family patterns "no single form need be regarded as inevitable or more 'natural' than any other." They further state, "we assume that all forms of domestic institutions are in process, having grown out of something different and tending to become still different. But there is no acceptable evidence of a single, uniform series of stages through which the developing family has passed and must pass."[1]

One of the first differences that an American will notice when studying the marital customs of other cultures is that there are many reasons for marriage besides romantic "love." Although romantic love has had a long history in many cultures, it is only recently that "love" has become the only popularly accepted basis for marriage. Acceptance of "love" as the *only* legitimate reason for marriage is indigenous to America, although the idea has been growing throughout much of the world, especially since World War II and the assumption of broader world leadership by the United States.

Morton Hunt, in tracing the history of love from the ancient Greeks to the present day, ascribes the invention of love to the Greeks, ". . . . they also invented love, gave it two names—'eros' (carnal love) and 'agape' (spiritual love) and elaborated upon both its theory and its practice."

Love has never since divested itself of its Greek trappings. Cupid (Eros) and his arrows are a Greek conceit; Sappho drew up a formal symptomatology of lovesickness which has been faithfully adhered to by lovers for twenty-five centuries; Platonic love, that long-discussed and marvelously misapplied term, originated with Plato's own attempts to build incorporeal metaphysics out of the desires of the flesh; and a whole set of familiar love tales emerged from Greek sources— Odysseus and Penelope, Daphnis and Chloe, Cupid and Psyche, Dido and Aeneas, Hero and Leander, and many others. Greek literature of earlier times had been made up chiefly of heroic histories, political diatribes, religious hymns, philosophic inquiries, and the like, but beginning with the Golden Age (about 480 B.C. to 399 B.C.) it became progressively diluted with an ever greater admixture of love lyrics, amorous laments, and protracted romances ending either in bliss or misery. In some of these—even in the briefest epigrams—love sentiments occasionally achieved a quality quite unknown to the primitive people who preceded the flowering Athenian culture:

My soul was on my lips, as I kissed Agathon: It came there (poor soul) longing to cross over to him.

Hunt is quick to point out, however, that love was not considered so much "an ennobling and transforming goal of life," or a basis for marriage, as it was an "amusing pastime and distraction, or sometimes a godsent affliction."[2] This latter theme is found in many cultures. For example, love was considered a grave offense, if acted upon, in ancient Japan. Sugimoto describes this in *Daughter of the Samurai:*

When she was employed in our house, she was very young, and because she was the sister of father's faithful Jiya, she was allowed much freedom. A youthful servant, also of our house, fell in love with her. For young people to become lovers without the sanction of the proper formalities was a grave offense in any class, but in a samurai household it was a black disgrace to the house. The penalty was exile through the water gate—a gate of brush built over a stream and never used except by one of the eta, or outcast class. The departure was public, and the culprits were ever after shunned by everyone. The penalty was unspeakably cruel, but in the old days severe measures were used as a preventative of lawbreaking.[3]

In this case the law broken was that of a couple "falling in love" without the proper sanctions. Indeed the proper sanctions seldom had anything to do with "love."

Marriage in many cultures has been and still is based upon other than romantic love considerations. Economic and/or social status is often an important basis for marriage. The Hindu of India have always placed responsibility for finding a suitable mate on the parents or older relatives. Criteria by which this potential mate was judged included economic status, caste, religion, family, and physical appearance.

The importance of economic considerations may be appreciated by investigating the bride-price contractual marriage found in many parts of Africa.

The bride-price is not originally for the purchase of the wife's person. It has been rather recompense to her kin for the children she is expected to bear and who will reinforce the husband's group. The wife's people can and do employ the wealth so acquired to pay for a wife from another group for one of their young men, to restore the balance. At the same time, the fact that wealth came to them in virtue of the first marriage enlists their interest to maintain it in face of disturbance; and since claim for repayment is baded on the wife's default, not simply on any kind of breakdown, their interest is both in discouraging her from misbehavior, and defending her against mere aspersions. The bride-price too is security for her well-being once she has left her family group.

Thus among the cattle-herding tribes the bride-price consists of a recognized number of cattle. All the husband's kinsmen who contribute to make up that number have claims on the bride, and so an interest in maintaining her position among them. If the husband behaved in such a way as to break the union, and they were unable to restrain him, they had to permit her to return to her people without receiving back the bride-price; but she could not take her children. If the marriage were dissolved through the fault of the wife, her kinsfolk had to return the number of cattle they had received but were allowed to retain a proportion if there were children left with the father.[4]

The bride-price arrangement represents a strong economic influence guiding marital patterns.

European history, on the other hand, is replete with examples of marriage for power motives. The proper marriage for the king's daughter was obviously one that served to strengthen the monarchy. A Hungarian king, Matthias Corvinus (1458–1490) enunciated the policy, "Bella gerant allii, tu felix Austria nube." (Other nations wage war, you, happy Austria, do better by marrying.)

One example of the success of this policy started with Maximilian I, a Hapsburg who was Holy Roman Emperor (1493–1519). He married Mary, the orphaned daughter of Charles the Bold, Duke of Burgundy, who held large parts of the Netherlands. Philip, Maximilian's son, married the daughter of Ferdinand and Isabella of Spain. These two marriages secured vast territory for Maximilian's grandson, Charles V. In 1519 he became King of Spain, King of the Netherlands, Holy Roman Emperor, ruler of the Austrian lands, and the wearer of many other crowns. Thus, the securing of power was a valid function of marriage in the past.

Companionship, intellectual rapport, and convenience are other valid purposes for marriage, yet the American culture limits such considerations and favors only one—love. This limited basis for marriage, as mentioned earlier, is gaining acceptance in other cultures as they confront westernizing influences.

Bride-price arrangements, marrying for power motives and all kinds of socially arranged marriages are indeed just that, socially arranged to support the ideals of the larger social system. The family *is* a social institution. The relationship between the family and the society is reciprocal; each affects the other. Thus an individualistic social ethic such as found in America supports a small nuclear individualistic family system. Single family dwellings are sought, privacy becomes a family watchword, in-laws and the elderly are kept outside of the nuclear family, and community interaction is minimized. The family teaches their children the value of individualism. The family acts as an individualistic unit within the larger society, and the individual family members tend to "do their own thing" rather than the family "thing."

Americans often discuss why alienation has become so widely expressed in our society. Yet, it seems clear that for society to exalt individualism there will also be feelings of loneliness and alienation. To be individual means that ties to family, friends, and the larger community are weaker and more tenuous. And without such ties loneliness and feelings of unrelatedness arise.

And what of a social system that stresses collectivism and community good as opposed to individualism? In this case we will find a different family system. Although information is scarce, the recent relaxation in Chinese-American relations has allowed some study of the family system evolving under communist rule in China. What we find is a much different set of goals and ideals sought within the family setting.

12 The Modern Chinese Communist Family

Ruth Sidel

The organization of life in China's neighborhoods can perhaps best be viewed as a total community support system, one fostered and maintained by the residents of the neighborhoods themselves. As life in the Fengsheng Neighborhood demonstrates, the people of China's cities have a myriad of ways in which they can interact: within their courtyard, where residents talk informally, communally clean the courtyard, plant and prune the greenery, admire one another's children, and discuss the latest political events; within their study group, where people read together, discuss politics, evaluate their own and others' attitudes and contributions, and are in turn evaluated; within the residents' committee, in which members are encouraged to help one another and to come together in large numbers for common purposes such as the Great Patriotic Sanitation Movement; within the neighborhood, where people work cooperatively to provide preschool care, to provide work for the unemployed in local factories, and to provide health care; and finally within the place of work, which provides not only study groups but a larger central focus, an avenue to contributing to the society, a parallel system of providing human services, and a setting for warm social relationships.

This total structure is characterized first by intimacy. People live and work together very closely and know each other well. The concept of privacy seems to be quite different in China, where an individual's personal life, his health, and his work performance are all viewed as being in the public domain, since they all affect the role he plays and the contribution he makes to society. The very structure of work and of residential communities, even the physical structure of the courtyards built within walls, serve to enhance this intimacy.

The second notable characteristic, one closely tied to the first and in fact made possible by such close relationships, is control. Just as one's personal affairs are a subject of concern for one's associates, so must one's antisocial ideas and deeds be a subject of concern. It was due to just such community concern and the exercise of community (even if "community" means the entire country) control that the Chinese have accomplished what is in the eyes of some Westerners an astonishing feat—the eradication of drug addiction and of venereal disease. But for a community to be able to exercise such control, the people must be willing to grant the necessary authority. The view, for example, that the individual has a right to choose a course of action that seems to harm only himself is not accepted in China. Whatever happens to each individual affects the entire society; there are no victimless crimes.

According to one observer of the Chinese legal system:

> Most people do not commit serious crimes without warning. Such actions are a part and perhaps the culmination of an entire pattern of dissatisfaction, unhappiness, or confusion. ... The Chinese, through the small groups, treat these symptoms of unhappiness and possible deviation as soon as they appear. The effort is to solve problems before they get entirely out of control, somewhat like treating a physical disease.
>
> As a person begins to express improper thoughts or deviant tendencies, others will try to "help" him. This takes the form of criticizing the incorrect actions and explaining what would be correct. It also involves discovering and curing the root causes of the problem. For example, a person might be sloppy in his work and consequently damage production. He is criticized for his carelessness, but also he is given additional technical training to improve his skills. Moreover, other aspects of his life are examined to find the root causes of his difficulties. Perhaps an unhappy marriage is adversely affecting his work; if so, the factory group must find means of "helping" his family life.[1]

Thus the functioning of the entire person is seen as the concern of the community in which he lives and works, and that community is responsible for helping him, through criticism, support, and if necessary, through modifying his environment. This amount of peer or societal control would, no doubt, be intolerable to many in the West, but it seems to be accepted, by and large, by the Chinese, and indeed it seems to stem at least in part from their past. The individual's right to self-determination, to personal growth, or even to self-destruction has never been revered in China as it is in the West.

A third characteristic of life in China's neighborhoods and places of work is the number of warm relationships an individual is likely to have. In addition to the marital relationship and the parent-child relationship, an adult may well have a warm relationship with his/her parents, neighbors, friends, and co-workers. This phenomenon is at least a partial explanation of the seeming acceptance on the part of married couples of their living and working in different cities. One is not so completely dependent on one's spouse; there are others with whom one interacts with warmth and mutual dependence.

In conjunction with the multiplicity of warm relationships, people have the opportunity to play a variety of roles at every stage of life. With one's child one can be nurturing; with one's parents one can be nurtured. A member of a residents' committee can at one time help a neighbor; at another time she may herself be the one who is helped. In the factory a group leader can be both the one who is criticized and the critic; a shop foreman can be teacher and student. A student may at one moment be the pupil and the next moment be teaching another student. An elderly person can both help his neighbors and be helped by others. One characteristic does not rigidly define the individual. A person who has a chronic illness and needs constant help may be a group leader; the young teach the old as in the "Each One Teach One" efforts of the 1950's; the intellectuals go to the countryside to learn from the poor and often illiterate peasants. People are not artificially locked into their roles in the way so many people in our society are because of both the limited variety of relationships and the limits that class and status place on the individual.

. . .

In part what makes it possible for people in China to play various roles within their communities is a strong element of deprofessionalization. Human services are provided at the lowest level of organization largely by nonprofessionals recruited from the communities in which they live. Local health workers are trained for brief periods of time in the hope of eliminating the alienation that occurs during extended educational experiences and in the hope of decreasing the distance between the helper and the helped. Most social services are provided by residents with no training but with a knack for dealing with others' problems. Marital disputes, interfamilial disputes, welfare problems, and problems of the aged are all handled by indigenous leaders in the residents' committees and in the neighborhoods or in the places of work. The elderly themselves are used extensively in these roles, thereby drawing on their traditional respected role within the community, their experience and talent, their ability to compare the "bitter past" to the present, and another great asset, their free time. The Chinese do not want to waste any talent; it is one of their greatest strengths that a meaningful way to contribute is found for people at all ages and levels of accomplishment—from the five-year-olds folding boxes in the kindergarten to the elderly group leaders helping their neighbors to solve their differences. This feeling of being needed, of fulfilling a function beyond the scope of one's own needs, gives people both a sense of self-worth and a sense of connection with the wider environment. Furthermore, structuring a society in which most people have a meaningful function reduces the sense of alienation that so characterizes our era.

Connected with the utilization of talent at all levels and with the deprofessionalization, whenever possible, of health and welfare services is the companion result—demystification. If primary health care at the local level can be provided by Red Medical Workers who were formerly housewives and who have had only three to six months of training, then what can be so mystical, so special, so technical and difficult to grasp, about medical care? If people are urged at every level to participate in community health and in their own health care—even patients in psychiatric hospitals are told their diagnoses and exhorted to work with the psychiatric personnel to understand the causes of the disease—then medicine can no longer be viewed as a magical art/science with rituals that can be performed only by specially anointed priests. Mao urges everyone to participate, to taste the pear, and in that way to understand the pear. If one's elderly untrained neighbor down the street, a friend whom one has known for years, who speaks the same language, belongs to the same economic class, holds similar values, and lives in the same life-style, does marital counseling in the residents' committee, how mysterious and unfathomable could marital counseling be?

Concomitant with demystification is the peculiarly Chinese emphasis on self-reliance, a self-reliance that is collective in nature. A job, food, a roof, and basic medical care are guaranteed, but in addition the individual citizen within his local collective is encouraged to initiate ideas, to innovate, to work together with others to improve his environment. Thus a neighborhood factory must exist on its meager income at first, its employees earning a minimal salary, until step by step the income increases and subsequently salaries increase. The nursery-kindergarten begins with a few children and fewer teachers, supported only by parental fees and by the local neighborhood, and it gradually develops into a larger, smoothly functioning institution. The emphasis is on decentralization, on encouraging those at the local level to build their facilities themselves with minimal support from the city, the province, or the central government. Clearly the focus on self-reliance and local autonomy has been developed and fostered in large measure because of economic conditions, but it has also been fostered for political reasons. Neighborhood residents encouraged to develop their own satellite factories and local health stations, and peasants in the countryside urged to follow the example of the famous Tachai Production Brigade and develop their communes through "hard work" and "self-reliance," must, in order to work effectively, be aware of the political and economic goals of the society, must be knowledgeable about local political and economic conditions, must be able to work within a group to determine priorities and methods, and, in sum, must be active participants in the society. And that, clearly, is the Chinese goal—to encourage as many of the nearly 800,000,000 Chinese as possible to become active participants.

One of the central problems or contradictions of this approach is that special-interest groups and their goals sometimes get short shrift. The process of women's liberation is an excellent example of conflicting goals within China's development. The role of women in China has undergone a revolutionary transformation since 1949. The central government has taken active steps to guarantee women basic human rights. The 1950 Marriage Law abolished arranged marriages, outlawed paying any price in money or goods for a wife, outlawed polygamy, concubines, and child marriage, and guaranteed the right of divorce to the wife as well as to the husband. The central government has also had a strong equal-pay-for-equal-work policy.

However, the continuation and extension of that liberation has been slowed by many factors: the continued existence of "feudal ideology" on the part of women themselves, men, and the elderly, who still have substantial influence; the lack of sufficient jobs for all women in the rural as well as the urban areas;

and the economic and political policy of encouraging decentralization and self-reliance. A commune, for example, in addition to a basic concern about the rights of women, must also be concerned with maximizing crop production, developing small industries, providing educational and health services, developing political leadership, and a host of other issues.

. . .

The Chinese refer to this spirit as "revolutionary optimism," a concept that "the Chinese people are part of the revolution, a revolution which will ultimately be victorious. No matter what the difficulties, the individual will have a bright future."[2] The physically or emotionally ill patient is urged to obtain treatment and to overcome his problems not only for his own sake but also for the sake of the revolution. A couple involved in a marital dispute is urged to "unite" for the sake of the revolution. Students are exhorted to study for the revolution. The individual is urged to subordinate his own feelings to the larger cause. As one observer has written of the Chinese revolutionary view of the new man: "Losing his own individual identity, he partakes of the greater spirit of the group and thereby achieves a spiritual transformation."[3]

Taking part in the greater spirit of the group, the belief in goals beyond one's own personal happiness and well-being and even beyond the happiness and well-being of one's family, can make many difficult, hard-to-bear aspects of life not only tolerable but possibly even meaningful. Many Chinese workers and peasants, of course, do highly repetitive work, and educated men and women spend a certain proportion of their time doing manual labor, but such work takes on an added dimension, a new and very different meaning, if it is viewed as part of a cooperative striving to reach a greater goal, a goal one fervently believes in.

The contrast is striking between the sense of commitment, of cooperation, of relatedness, evident in China's neighborhoods and the picture of American society vividly described by Philip Slater. He claims that "Americans have voluntarily created and voluntarily maintained a society which increasingly frustrates and aggravates" three basic human desires—"the desire for *community*," "the desire for *engagement*," and "the desire for *dependence*."[4] The question that must be raised is, What is the relevance of the organization of China's cities to us in the West? What is the relevance of Red Medical Workers, neighborhood hospitals, residents' committees with locally selected leadership, small satellite factories, study groups, and small children singing about Chairman Mao? What can we learn from a culture whose cities have lent a sense of community for centuries by virtue of the traditional architecture and city planning? What can we learn from the urban organization of a society whose revolutionary values stress collectivity and cooperation rather than individualism and competition? What can our postindustrial, media-barraged communities, whose residents often relate more intensively to television programs and personalities than to life around them, learn from the technologically underdeveloped Chinese society in which neighborhood life and daily work are still intensely meaningful?

Although technology has simplified our lives enormously, it is also a primary cause of our isolation. We may be a long way from washing our clothes in a stream, as do some Chinese women, simultaneously exchanging news and personal advice with the other women of the village, but we are also moving away from the local laundromat or the apartment laundry room where one can get a sense of those who live nearby. Not only do our washers and dryers make it possible to do our laundry in isolation, but our telephones and televisions, while on the one hand putting us in touch with others, on the other hand separate us by keeping us within our homes. Even our kitchen appliances encourage less and less communication within the family. (Ralph Keyes, in his aptly titled book *We, the Lonely People: Searching for Community,* quotes a mother talking about the generation gap: "I'm gonna tell you what brought on the whole thing—dishwashers. That's right, dishwashers. I got to know my kids better, they told me more, when we washed dishes together. One would wash, another rinse, and a third dry. We'd fight but we'd also talk. Now that we have a dishwasher, there's no regular time when we get to know each other."[5])

The hope, of course, was that with more technology, with more conveniences, we would be freed from physical labor and have more time to "communicate," to "relate meaningfully to one another." But we are learning that perhaps communication takes place around shared activity, mundane, everyday activity such as commuting to work together, making dinner, or doing the dishes. It is extremely difficult for people to talk about what is on their minds without a warm-up period, without structure around which to talk, without shared experiences. And yet we seek greater and greater privacy, privacy that will inevitably diminish the number and depth of our human relationships.

We seek a private house, a private means of transportation, a private garden, a private laundry, self-service stores, and do-it-yourself skills of every kind. An enormous technology seems to have set itself the task of making it unnecessary for one human being ever to ask anything of another in the course of going about his daily business. Even within the family Americans are unique in their feeling that each member should have a separate room, and even a separate telephone, television, and car, when economically possible. We seek more and more privacy, and feel more and more alienated and lonely when we get it.[6]

What can we learn from the Chinese as we try to build bridges to one another, to form a new sense of community? We can learn that we need not rely solely on professionals in order to care for one another, that ordinary untrained people can reach out if permitted and encouraged to do so, and that they can help to provide health care, emotional support, physical attention, and above all the feeling that someone cares. We can learn that giving is as important, perhaps, as any other human need and that by providing mechanisms for people to give to one another we humanize all of us.

It is clear from this description of modern Chinese society that the family and the society blend into one another. The Chinese husband, wife or child is a part of their immediate family but, in addition, each is participating in the larger community in very meaningful and personal ways. Their obligation is not only to themselves and their immediate family, but they are also committed to the larger community in which and by which their individual family exists. Thus the family has many ties to the community from which to draw support. For example:

. . .

"If a couple is quarreling, a member of the residents' committee will go to the home and advise the couple to unite. Sometimes even children of eight or nine will come to the residents' committee to ask for help. Whoever is available will go. We will talk separately with the husband and with the wife and then all talk together. If the children are at home, they will attend, and if older people live in the home, they may attend, too."

If the marital problems persist and the couple wish to request a divorce, they must go to see a "cadre of basic state power" in the Administrative Office of the Ching Nian commune. This cadre is a man about forty years old without any special training but one who has a "good knowledge of the Chinese Marriage Law and of party policy." According to members of the committee, this cadre has "more experience with this kind of work" and "is good with other people's problems." He will first ask the couple their reason for wanting a divorce; he will then "try his best to advise them to unite, not to separate." He will talk with members of their working units and consult with members of their residents' committee. He will then meet with the marital partners separately, then together—often three to five times and sometimes even as many as ten times.

If the couple still wish a divorce, they will then simply obtain a certificate from this same cadre. Out of 9,100 families in the Ching Nian commune from January to September, 1972, seventeen couples requested divorces. Six couples were "united," and the remaining eleven, whose "characters and feelings were different," received divorces.

Similarly, if a couple wish to marry, they go to the Administrative Office of the commune. After they are asked their age and if either has been married before, they are issued a certificate that states that they are married. Representatives from both the residents' committee and the commune stressed that if all is in compliance with the Chinese Marriage Law, they always give the certificate. Since part of the current massive birth-control efforts include urging young women to delay marriage until they are twenty-four to twenty-six, and men until they are twenty-six to twenty-nine, the question was raised about what action the Administrative Office would take if a boy of twenty-two and a girl of nineteen wished to marry. The response was that they would urge them to wait but that if the couple insisted, they would receive their marriage certificate. They elaborated by saying that most women living in the Ching Nian Lu commune marry around the age of twenty-three and most men around twenty-four or twenty-five.

Although the residents' committee is heavily involved in helping residents when such help is needed, the expectation seems to be that families will take care of one another, within the context of full employment (for men, at least), decent housing, at least a minimum income, and essentials kept at artificially low prices. Members of the committees do not rush to help with each crisis; it seemed, rather, that families were expected to work out their own problems but that these committee members were available when they were needed. While China is a society where many basic necessities are guaranteed, it is simultaneously a society that places a heavy responsibility on the individual to work out his own problems whenever possible, to help family, friends, and neighbors with their problems, and to be informed about and contribute to that society.

The reader may have noted that almost nothing is said about the personal relationship between the husband and wife. In reading the various material on Chinese Communist family life seeking the most enlightening article for this reader, your author found little if any reference to personal aspects of the man and woman's relationship. In numerous cases, the man worked in another city, visiting home only occasionally. In all of the personal reports given by family members, the talk was always of the community and the state and the work done by family members. It is difficult to know just exactly what this lack of emphasis on the personal relationships in the family means. Since information is difficult to come by, it may simply mean that the Chinese are much more interested in propagandizing for the state, presenting what they want to be, rather than all the things that may be. It is obvious that the relationship of the family to the larger community is much more important than it is here in the United States. However, the reader will have to withhold judgment as to the depth and quality of the personal relationships within the Chinese Communist family until such a time as communications between our countries are free and open.

Lest the reader believe that the characteristics of the Chinese family that have been described are all new and unique to the modern communist era, it is important to remember that the Chinese family historically had educational, political, and economic responsibilities. Because China is so vast and in earlier times so rural, the majority of the population lived in the country, often out of touch with any governmental agency. During many centuries control was vested in the eldest male family member. There simply weren't enough government officials to go around. Thus, unquestioning obedience to and respect for elders were the major means of control and policing. Historically, the Chinese family was a large extended clan and it was this much larger group over which the elders presided.

Another family system that displays a much larger number of ties than found in the nuclear family is the American Hopi Indian family. The Hopi family's ties are to a large number of relatives rather than to a state community as in the case of the modern Chinese. The Hopis number only about four thousand today. They live on three adjoining mesas in the desert region of northern Arizona. Actually they live in the midst of the large Navajo Indian reservation, yet they have maintained their own family traditions.

13 The Matrilineal Hopi Indian Family

Stuart A. Queen and Robert W. Habenstein

Monogamy to the exclusion of all other forms is the characteristic marriage institution of the Hopi. Husband, wife, and children make up the nuclear group which becomes a unit in the larger extended family. Inasmuch as rules of matrilineal descent and matrilocal residence are observed, the Hopi household is distinguished, according to one authority, by " . . . the fact that a mature woman, her daughters, and occasionally her granddaughters, occupy a common residence through life and bring up their children under the same roof."[1] This description may obscure somewhat the role of the nuclear family, to be discussed later. On the other hand, we should not overlook the fact that the most significant nonresidential kinship unit is a group of blood relatives traced through the female line, which owns most of the property including the home, which owns and operates the ceremonials, and which is the basis of kin groupings larger than the family. In our terminology this grouping is called the matri-sib.[2]

The matri-sibs carry with them other features, two of which may be mentioned here. Each has its totemic counterpart: bear, lizard, eagle, or other animal. And all matri-sibs are gathered into a handful of constellations or superorders which we call phratries.*

*The phratry is exogamic; thus marriage cannot take place between matri-sibmates within the same phratry, and, as we shall see, the phratry constitutes an important ceremonial unit of the Hopi.

Terminology and Kinship Orientation

The family and household are the Hopi institutions in which the individual forms those associations and learns those patterns of reciprocal behavior which become the prototypes of most of his later associations and behavior in the society at large.

The kinship terminology reflects this fact. One calls one's own mother, her sisters, and all women of her generation in the matri-sib by the single term "mother." One's mother's brother and all males of his generation in the matri-sib are called "mother's brother." Mother's or father's father and all males of their generation in the matri-sib are called "grandfather." Mother's or father's mother and any old women of their generation in the matri-sib are called "grandmother." All men and women of one's own generation and matri-sib are called "brother" and "sister." All men and women in one's father's generation and matri-sib are "father's brother" and "father's sister." All children of men in one's own matri-sib are "brother's child." All children of women of one's own matri-sib are "sister's child."

As noted, each matri-sib is part of a larger exogamous unit, the phratry, and kinship terms and obligations are extended to cover one's own phratry and the phratry of one's father. The same terminology and behavior are likewise extended to the phratry of one's ceremonial father, and, if one has been cured of a serious illness, to the phratry of the medicine man who cured him. The result is that one finds himself related to about one half of the members of his village. Naturally, not all of these connections are of equal importance. Titiev has listed them in descending order of importance as follows:

1. Limited family, consisting of own parents, brothers, and sisters.
2. Mother's sisters and their children.
3. Other members of own household.
4. Other members of own clan.
5. Father's household.
6. Other members of own phratry.
7. Other members of father's clan-phratry.
8. Ceremonial father's clan-phratry.
9. Doctor father's clan-phratry.[3]

Marriage is actually or theoretically forbidden within the first seven categories but permitted within the last two.

The reciprocal behavior which goes with these kin relations determines many of the attitudes and activities of the Hopi. A brief description of several of these patterns will throw light on the family life of the Hopi as well as on the way in which the familial pattern itself is projected into society as a whole.

1) Husband-Wife

The most important factor in this pattern is the relative position of the husband and wife in the household. The husband is a guest in his wife's household, his closest connections being with his mother's household. The wife, on the other hand, remains in the house in which she has been reared, and in the event of a family quarrel is backed by a solid wall of kin. Perhaps as a result of this difference in position the Hopi husband will often act toward his wife with seeming formality if not brusqueness. In general, however, the bond between husband and wife is variable and depends largely on the characters of the individuals concerned.

2) Father-Son

There is a much closer connection between father and son here than one might expect in a matrilineal society. The sexual division of labor tends to strengthen this bond, for the boy receives from his father much of his instruction in herding, farming, and weaving. Also, jural authority is divided with the boy's uncle, thus permitting easier relations between father and son. In childhood years the bond is less intimate but even then the father makes toys for the child. After the Kachina initiation, described below, and until marriage, the bond is very close and is characterized by mutual consideration for each other's welfare. When a man dies, his son buries him and inherits, directly, much of his father's property. This close tie between father and son does not extend to classificatory fathers; they are, however, treated with friendliness and react in turn by bestowing gifts and attention on their "sons." In general one might say that the bond between real son and father derives its character less from any ideal pattern to be applied to all "fathers" than from a natural affection which is to be expected where contact and cooperation are close and intimate and where the exercise of authority and the disciplining of the son does not rest solely with the male parent.

3) Mother's Brother-Sister's Son

This is the reciprocal relation which should most influence a boy's life according to the classic idea of a matrilineal society. Actually the real father takes over much of the role one might expect the mother's brother to play. The mother's brother is the disciplinarian, and his authority is drawn from his position as the male member of the mother's generation who is in one's own sib and lineage. He carefully supervises the boy's upbringing so that the boy may some day be a reliable worker, and in doing so he often resorts to drastic means, putting the nephew through a series of trials and deprivations. At the boy's marriage he is the chief person consulted in the choice of a mate, and often after the marriage he instructs the couple in their future duties as man and wife. This is not to say that the bond between uncle and nephew is a harsh one. Often great affection is shown on both sides; it is certainly not reduced by the consideration that it is from his maternal uncle that the boy expects to inherit ceremonial and sib offices.

4) Mother-Daughter

This reciprocal relation is one of the closest and warmest to be found in Hopi society, for the ties which bind mother and daughter persist throughout life. The mother teaches the daughter all the things she will need to know as a full-fledged member of society—how to grind corn, cook, take care of children, make baskets and pottery, and how to behave toward strangers, relatives, and mates. In addition to the functional relationship there is a great deal of love and respect shown between mother and daughter.

5) Father-Daughter

The father actually has few duties to perform for his daughter and vice versa. The bond between them is primarily one of affection, but even this is not so warm as that between mother and daughter.

6) Brother-Sister

This is a very close reciprocal relation and one that contains a great deal of affection. There are no taboos on association between them, and they play together until the sexual division of labor separates them. Even after this there is close cooperation between brothers and sisters, and after marriage they become to each other's children "mother's brother" and "father's sister" respectively.

These six reciprocal relations are only a few of the many that the Hopi observe, yet they tend to draw, in miniature, a picture of the many bonds the Hopi individual has and to show the nature of these bonds in governing almost the whole of his behavior. They also illustrate the fact that, although his matrilineal relations in the household play a considerable role in the individual's experience and education, the nuclear family—mother, father, and children—are also a close-knit group sharing obligations, privileges, and affections.

The Family Cycle

Mate Selection

Courtship among the Hopi is informal. A girl who has undergone the important rites of adolescence, usually performed between the ages of sixteen and twenty, is ready to receive suitors, although she will probably not marry until she is seventeen or older. Boys of twelve or thirteen are also ready for courtship, for they begin at this time to sleep in the men's ceremonial house, the *kiva,* instead of at home, and thus have the opportunity for nocturnal assignations.

The stage is set, then, for the custom of *dumaiya,* in the observance of which the boys, partly disguised, pay visits by night to girls of their choice. They usually spend the night, but leave before daybreak to avoid detection by the girls' parents. If, however, a couple is exposed, no serious punishment follows. The parents are well aware of such visits, and, although they do not give them their open sanction, they allow them if the boy is a proper marriage prospect. Indeed, a girl of marriageable age usually has several lovers. Eventually she is likely to find herself pregnant. In this event she names the favorite among her lovers as her choice, and a match is arranged between the families and households involved. As a result, of course, no boy will visit by night a girl he is unwilling to marry.

There are several other occasions on which the choice of a mate may be made. In former days it was customary to give an informal picnic on the day following an important ritual. In preparation for this occasion the girls prepared *somiviki,* or "maiden's cake," to supplement the rabbits and other small animals provided by the boys. If a girl had decided on a youth as a future mate, she would extend an invitation to him to accompany her to the picnic and would present him with a loaf of *qömi,* a bread made of sweet cornmeal, in lieu of *somiviki.* Since such a gift was tantamount to an engagement, boys accepted invitations to picnics only from girls they were willing to marry. The picnics also served as occasions on which nocturnal assignations could be arranged.

Qömi might also be presented to a youth during the bean dance ceremony in the *kiva.* On this occasion it was customary for unmarried girls to hand out *somiviki* to the performers as each passed from the *kiva* on conclusion of the dance; sometimes a loaf of *qömi* was substituted for *somiviki* and had to be accepted for fear of offending the giver. Such a proposal was not accepted as binding however, since the loaf could be discarded or given to the father of the Kachinas. In this event the girl would soon learn that her proposal had been rejected.

The form of courtship most frequently described for the Hopi, however, is that in which, when the girls grind corn during the night in a chamber separate from the parents' sleeping room, prospective suitors come to engage in small talk with them and perhaps to propose marriage or even to arrange for a nocturnal assignation.

Certainly, in view of this information and in spite of statements to the contrary, which have been made by many authors, the Hopi do not seem to place a high value on virginity and apparently do not consider it a requisite for marriage.

However, the prospective bride and groom must observe several restrictions if they are to make a marriage sanctioned by society. The principal prohibition is against marriage within the nuclear family, extending to the members of one's phratry. This rule applies not only to one's own phratry, but also to that of one's father, although in the latter instance the taboo is not so strict. In addition it is considered improper for a girl or boy to marry someone previously married. The violator of this taboo is punished, according to Hopi belief, by being forced to carry a heavily loaded basket on the journey to the underworld after death. Finally, the prospective bride and groom are expected to be temperamentally congenial. Outside of these restrictions there is great freedom of choice, and marriage for love is certainly not unknown.

Once the decision to marry is made by the young couple, the boy goes in the evening after supper to the girl's house and there states his intentions to her parents. If he is acceptable, he is told to go home and tell his parents about it. The girl then grinds cornmeal or makes bread, and carries it to the house of her prospective groom. At this time the mother of the boy may refuse the bread or meal, in which case the match is usually broken off. If, however, the food is accepted, it is given by the mother to her brothers and to her husband's clansmen, and the wedding plans go forward.

After this event the girl returns home to grind more meal with the help of her kinswomen, while the boy fetches water and chops wood for his mother. The girl is preparing for her formal bridal visit to the boy's home, and he is completing his last chores for his mother.

In the evening after these chores are completed, the bride dresses in her manta beads and her wedding blanket. Accompanied by the boy, who carries the meal she has ground, she walks barefoot to his house. There she presents the meal to her prospective mother-in-law and settles down for a temporary three-day stay before the wedding. During this period the young couple may see each other, but they must observe sexual continence.

On each of the three days preceding the marriage the bride rises early and grinds cornmeal for her mother-in-law. During this period she is partially restricted in her behavior as she has been and will be during other crisis periods in her life, e.g., at puberty or confinement. She eats, however, with other members of the family, takes part in the conversations, and is not subject to such taboos as being forbidden to eat salt or meat or having to scratch herself with a stick.

At some time during the three-day period the groom's house is visited, or "attacked," by his paternal aunts, who break in on the bride and shower her with invective and often with mud. They accuse her of laziness, inefficiency, and stupidity. The boy's mother and her clanswomen protect the girl and insist that the accusations are unfounded. In spite of appearances all this is carried off in a good-humored way, and finally the aunts leave, having stolen the wood their nephew had brought his mother. The wood is used to bake *piki,* which is given to the mother, and thus all damages are paid for.

On the morning of the fourth day the marriage is consummated. On this occasion the girl's relatives wash the boy's hair and bathe him, while the boy's relatives do the same for the girl. At Old Oraibi[4] the heads of the newlyweds are merely washed together in a basin and their hair is twined together as a symbol of their union. As soon as their hair is dry the couple follow a path of cornmeal sprinkled by the boy's mother to the eastern edge of the mesa, where prayers are made to the sun.

The couple may now sleep together as man and wife, but they remain at the boy's mother's house until the girl's wedding garments are complete. These garments are woven by the groom, his male relatives, and any men in the village who wish to participate. On occasions when various parts of the work are finished the groom's family holds a feast to pay the workers, the necessary food for the feast being supplied by his relatives. The garments themselves consist of a large belt, two all-white wedding robes, a white wedding robe with red stripes at top and bottom, white buckskin leggings and moccasins, a string for tying the hair, and a reed mat in which to wrap the entire outfit.

After the job is completed—a matter of about two weeks—the bride dresses in her new clothes and returns home, where she is received by her mother and her female relatives. She is accompanied on this journey by her husband's relatives, who make a final exchange of gifts with her mother's household. During the evening the groom appears at his mother-in-law's home and spends the night. The next day he fetches wood for her and from then on is a permanent resident in her house—unless a divorce sends him packing.

During the winter and indeed until the following July, the bride may not attend a dance. At the *Niman* dance in July, however, she finally attends a ceremonial. Her appearance at this time is supposed to ensure rain and a happy married life. Perhaps, however, the wish to show off her wedding robes is as powerful a motive. After this appearance the robes are put away until that time when they will serve as a shroud, since these garments will be necessary for the trip through the underworld.

Nearly all Hopi marry, for without marriage it is difficult to play a full adult role in the society. This fact perhaps emphasizes the role of the conjugal group as a real functioning unit. Indeed, in recent years more and more of these marriage groups are setting up households for themselves, and the old matrilineal household is in danger of disappearing entirely. As long, however, as the extended household exists, the conjugal family can form, break through divorce, and reform without disturbing the household overmuch.

.   .   .

Disjunctions

The incidence of divorce has been rather high among the Hopi, possibly one out of three marriages ending in divorce—nearly comparable to the rate for other Americans today. Titiev reports an even distribution of divorce among the various sibs and phratries, noting that "loose marriage ties and frequent adultery are long-standing Hopi traits."[5] One basis of the "loose marriage ties" is the lack of authority of the husband in the matrilineal family.

The mechanics of divorce are very simple. The husband merely goes home to his mother's house. The initiative, however, may be taken by either wife or husband. The wife seeking to terminate her marriage places the husband's belongings outside the door of the dwelling. The children remain with their mother and are cared for and educated by the household group in the absence of a real father.

Family Controls

To the Hopi the universe of man, animals, plants, supernatural things, and natural phenomena functions as an ordered, interrelated system whose essential principle is reciprocity. It is a unified system operating according to principles known only to themselves. The whole is set in motion and controlled through man's activities and volition, for although there are nonhuman elements which operate mechanically in the universe, without man's will, expressed in ritual and psychical acts and states, the universe would cease to function.

The underworld of the dead and the upperworld of the living stand in vital conjunction with a reciprocal and complementary relationship existing between the living and the dead. The spirits of the dead are for the most part benign and helpful. For example they may take the shape of clouds and bring life-giving rain to Hopiland.

The thoroughgoing ceremonialism of the Hopi with the traditional dances, festivals, and rituals, of which the well-popularized snake dance is but one, give meaning and coherence to Hopi behavior, institutions, and culture.

Hopi symbols expressed in art and artifact articulate a system of implicit concepts, attitudes, and values which are meaningful, consistent, and harmonious.[6] Seen as a body of norms or ethical prescriptions this system has appropriately been termed the "Hopi way."[7]

The subjective or personal side of the Hopi way as reflected in personality and character of the individual emphasizes cooperation, unselfishness, modesty, and nonaggressiveness. The Hopi is expected to cultivate the "good heart," and not to feel anger, sadness, or worry, but to be tranquil and of good will.[8]

It should not be assumed that the integrated world view of the Hopi and its reflection in Hopi character automatically produces a culture unruffled by dissension or deviant behavior. Hopi argue, quarrel, show some anxiety, and often stray from the public norms of the tribe. But insofar as individuals are involved, the controls are usually adequate to the task. There are no competing religious doctrines or secular ideologies to challenge the Hopi way. When a village becomes divided over an issue—a rare occurrence—the solution is for the discontented to establish a separate community elsewhere on the mesa.

The Hopi family is an agency of social control acting in part for the larger kinship unit, the matri-sib. The latter, as noted, is part of the phratry system,

yet the locus of strength resides with the matri-sib. The emphasis on ma-
trilineality is balanced to some degree by the leadership males exert in ceremo-
nies and their male-centered activities within the *kiva*.

The generation of social cohesion among the Hopi is produced primarily by
ceremonial activities. By participating, with "good heart," the members, their
emotions excited by the color, rhythm, and sensuousness of the rites with their
dramatic overtones, develop a deepening sense of the meaningfulness and
importance of their religio-ethical beliefs. And to the extent that such meaningfulness is achieved, the Hopi balance by internalization—the development of
conscience—and "inner control" the norms and prescriptions that make up
tribal doctrine.

Functions of the Hopi Family

In many ways the Hopi family reinforces or correlates its activities with other
forms of social organization; conversely, as in the case of the Kachinas, the
religious or spiritual world is directly invoked to reinforce family discipline
and training. But in most day-to-day interaction the parents, wife's brother,
and other kindred, through reward and punishment, through ordering and
forbidding, perform the educative and orientational functions.

The nuclear family provides a regularized sexual outlet for its members.
Sexual matters are considerably less tabooed among the Hopi than among
other groups and societies, our own included. Yet the external marriage controls are not rigid or inflexible. The relative ease with which marriages are
terminated suggests that sexual satisfaction and companionship may comprise
the major functions of the Hopi nuclear family, while child care, sustenance,
protection, and some aspects of discipline may be shared with or relinquished
to the household and matri-sib.

Close ties, nevertheless, exist between father and son and mother and daughter. The role of the uncle as disciplinarian and the reward-punishment functions of the Kachinas relieve the parents of some of the strain occasioned in
the socialization of children and permit bonds of comradeship and affection
to develop. The functions of the nuclear family, then, are for the most part
shared, shared in such manner as to distribute responsibility through the
primary marriage units: the household, kindred, and matri-sib.

Both the Chinese and Hopi families reflect cultures that differ greatly from
mainstream American cultures. However, even other Western industrialized
societies also differ from the United States in the values and mores that
guide marital behavior. Sweden is often invoked as an example of sexual
enlightenment. Such a conclusion seldom illuminates the Swedish values
and behavior patterns. For example, premarital sexual experience appears
freer in Sweden than in the United States. Yet the conclusion that such

behavior constitutes promiscuous behavior cannot be supported. The modal age of marriage for women in Sweden is 23.3 years while in the United States it is 20 years. An additional three years of life and experience will certainly serve to raise the cumulative percentage of women having experienced sexual relations. Ira L. Reiss, in his book *Premarital Sexual Standards in America* (1960), reported the following:

A few years back, I asked a male Swedish student of mine about the sexual standards in his country as compared to our own. This student told me what many Swedish people have said—the American female is much freer with her sexual favors in all respects except intercourse. The Swedish female will not usually indulge in "heavy petting" unless she is seriously affectionately involved and therefore intends to have intercourse; otherwise, she feels, such behavior is far too intimate. The American female pets with much more freedom, and yet she stops short of actual coitus. To this Swedish student, sex in America is too much of a "tease"—too much apart from the rest of life—but it is more restricted for people who are seriously involved with one another. In this sense, one might say that although American women are more virginal than Swedish women, they are still more promiscuous sexually.

While many statistics seem to support the Swedish position that compulsory sex education is valuable in producing wholesome sexual behavior, the question of sex education is still vigorously debated even in Sweden. On the positive side, sex offenses are practically negligible in Sweden. Less than one percent of the offenses against the Penal Code of Sweden were sex offenses. Only 432 offenses involved rape, and although Sweden's population is small (eight million) this is still a surprisingly low figure. On the negative side, there is considerable concern by officials over rising venereal infection. During 1965, 23,928 cases of gonorrhea were registered which represented a five percent gain over 1964 although the population is relatively stable. The majority of venereal infection is among the young. A pilot study in a VD clinic in Uppsala revealed the average age for women to be 17.2 and for men 18.3 years. The Swedish National Board of Health stated:

Despite all our efforts to educate the young people through lectures, brochures and other means, they just don't seem to care. They have blind faith in penicillin and many of them even think its 'tough' to take a risk by deliberately refraining from using condoms or by carelessly selecting their sexual partners.

Sweden's government leads the way in trying to equalize sex roles. In 1920, Sweden initiated the first democratic family laws in the world. Equal roles and mutual rights and responsibilities for husband and wife were prescribed by the law. The husband's guardianship over his wife was revoked, and both marriage partners now assume financial obligations to support one another as well as their children. Housework is regarded as a financial contribution. In the mid-1960s Sweden made it possible for husbands as well as wives to secure leaves of absence from work in order to remain home and attend children if there is a definite need. Women have the option of retaining their maiden names if they desire. In certain cases husbands may assume their wives' names.

Within the schools real efforts are being made to do away with traditional sex roles. Boys now take courses such as sewing and child care while girls learn mechanics and other pursuits thought of as exclusively masculine in the past. Radicals in the sex-role debate advocate rearing boys and girls in exactly the same way, collective supervision of children, and a work situation in which either mother or father can remain home during the first three years of a child's life.

Basically, the state has assumed greater responsibility for children. Not only are illegitimate children accepted, but many parenting functions are assumed by the state in child care centers. The government has also pushed the schools toward more extensive sex education aimed at destroying stereotypic sex roles.

Recently the Royal Commission on Sex Education ordered a large-scale survey of Swedish sexual behavior. They wanted to know the effects on Swedish life of—

improved and easily available contraceptives,
laws promoting equality of the sexes,
and the school sex education programs.

They found that sex relations were starting younger (median age 16.9 years for those now 21 to 25) and more partners are involved. Despite this, they did not find evidence of diminished commitment to the sex partner, whether married or not. Freer premarital sex has apparently not led to more extramarital sex as Kinsey suggested it did here in the United States. The overwhelming majority of Swedes felt that promiscuity is wrong and that you don't hurt a good relationship.

It remains to be seen just what these changes will mean to Swedish family life of the future. At this time it does not appear that fewer sexual restrictions are destroying the Swedish family.[1,2]

A small homogenous country such as Sweden can systematically work to change attitudes toward sexuality and marriage more easily than can a country with a large and diverse population such as the United States. It is difficult, if not impossible, to reach consensus on such topics in America.

America is often referred to as a "melting pot" culture because people of so many and diverse backgrounds settled here. There is considerable question as to how well certain of these groups have been assimilated. The Negro and Mexican-American minority groups have, in many ways, created their own marital values and mores. Not only is there a distinction in such values among racial and national groups, there are distinct differences among classes in the United States. Both Kinsey's study of the male and his study of the female demonstrated class differentiation about marriage and sex. In order to understand better the American system governing these aspects of life, it is necessary to investigate both class differences and minority group differences.

The following reading compares lower-economic groups cross-culturally. Again the reader will gain insights into various subcultures' attitudes toward sexuality. In this case, however, the insights concern the lower-economic classes. The four cultures discussed by Rainwater are the Mexican, Puerto Rican, English, and American.

14 Marital Sexuality in Four Cultures of Poverty

Lee Rainwater

Sexual Life and Interpersonal Intimacy: Class Patterns

Oscar Lewis has asserted that "Poverty becomes a dynamic factor which affects participation in the larger national culture and creates a subculture of its own. One can speak of a culture of the poor, for it has its own modalities and distinctive social and psychological consequences for its members . . . (it) cuts across regional, rural-urban and even national boundaries." He sees similarities between his own findings about the Mexican poor and findings of others in Puerto Rico, England, and the United States. This paper deals with such similarities in one area of interpersonal relationships, namely, in the attitudes and role behaviors which characterize the sexual relationships of lower-class husbands and wives in these four countries. This paper seeks to demonstrate that, in spite of important differences in the cultural forms of these four areas, there are a number of striking similarities in the ways husband and wives act sexually and in the ways they regard their actions. The concern is thus not with the simplest level of sexual description—"Who has intercourse with whom, how and how often?"—but with the meanings these experiences have for their participants and for the assimilation of heterosexual with other family roles.

Lee Rainwater, "Marital Sexuality in Four Cultures of Poverty," *Journal of Marriage and Family,* November 1964. Copyright 1964 by National Council on Family Relations. Reprinted by permission.

The central sexual norm: "Sex is a man's pleasure and a woman's duty."
That sexual relations exist for the pleasure of the man and that enjoyment for
the woman is either optional or disapproved is specifically noted in each of
these four cultures. Women are believed either not to have sexual desires at
all or to have much weaker sexual needs, needs which do not readily come to
the fore without stimulation from a man. In Tepoztlan, " . . . women who are
passionate and 'need' men are referred to as *loca* (crazy) . . . ,"[2] in the other
three areas, women are likely to be regarded as immoral if they show too much
interest in sexual relations with their husbands. In Gorer's study of English
character,[3] one set of questionnaire items deals with the nature of women's
sexuality. Gorer reports that the poor were more likely than the more affluent
to agree that women "don't care much about the physical side of sex" and
"don't have such an animal nature as men" and to disagree that women enjoy
sex as much or more than men.

Man's nature demands sexual experience; he cannot be happy without it;
and if he is not satisfied at home, it is understandable that he looks elsewhere.
That the wife might look elsewhere is a common fantasy of men in these areas,
but neither men nor women so often say that dissatisfaction with sexual
relations is likely to lead the wife to stray. The husband's anxiety that his wife's
"unnatural" impulses could lead her to look for a lover, however, is often given
as a reason for not stimulating her too much or developing her sensual capacities through long or elaborated lovemaking.[4] Stycos notes that Puerto Rican
men expect much more elaborated sexual experiences in their relations with
prostitutes or other "bad" women.[5]

In all four areas, it is not considered appropriate for parents to devote
attention to the sexual education of their children. Boys may be encouraged,
either overtly or covertly, to acquire sexual experience. This seems most fully
institutionalized in Puerto Rico.[6] Elsewhere, the boy seems to be left more to
his own devices. In any case, there is recognition that boys will acquire a fair
amount of knowledge about sexual relations and that they probably will have
intercourse with available women. In Puerto Rico and Tepoztlan, these women
are seen as very much in the status of prostitutes or "loose women," and the
boy feels he must be careful about approaching a more respectable girl. These
lines seem more blurred in England and the United States—in these countries,
in the context of group or individual dating, boys seem to feel freer about
forcing their attentions and less vulnerable to repercussions from the girl's
family.[7] The Latin pattern of sharp separation of "loose women" and the
virginal fiancée seems a highly vulnerable one in any case and quickly breaks
down under the pressures of urbanization in a lower-class environment.[8]

Girls, on the other hand, are supposed not to learn of sexual relations either
by conversation or experience. Mothers in all four cultures do not discuss sex
with their daughters and usually do not even discuss menstruation with them.

The daughter is left very much on her own in this area, with only emergency attention from the mother—e.g., when the girl proves unable to cope with the trauma of onset of menses or begins to seem too involved with boys. Later, women will say that they were completely unprepared for sexual relations in marriage, that no one had ever told them about this, and that they had only the vaguest idea of what this shrouded part of their marital responsibility involved. Girls tend to be trained to a prudish modesty in relation to their bodies (even though they may also elaborate their dress or state of undress to attract boys)—in England, for example, Spinley notes that girls will not undress in front of each other or their mothers.[9] Modesty in the two Latin cultures is, of course, highly elaborated.

The sexual stimulation that comes in all of these cultures from the close living together of children and adults is apparently systematically repressed as the child grows older. The sexual interests stimulated by these and other experiences are deflected for the boys onto objects defined as legitimate marks (loose women, careless girls, prostitutes, etc.) and for the girls are simply pushed out of awareness with a kind of hysterical defense (hysterical because of the fact that later women seem to protest their ignorance too much).

In these cultures, therefore, marriage is hardly made attractive from the point of view of providing sexual gratification. The girls are taught to fear sex and most often seem to learn to regard it in terms of the non-erotic gratifications it may offer. The boys learn that they may expect fuller sexual experiences from other, less respectable objects, and in some group (Puerto Rico most overtly[10]), because of their identification of the wife as a "second mother," men have very potent reasons for not regarding the wife hopefully as a sexual object. Yet both boys and girls know that they will marry; the girls are anxious to do so, and the boys feign resistance more than maintain it.

For the girls, the transition to the married state often takes place via a period of high susceptibility to romantic love. The girl becomes involved with notions of falling in love with a man—this being but vaguely defined in her mind and oriented to an idealized conception of love and marriage. Stycos sees this as a "psychological mechanism intervening between . . . rebellion (against the cloistered life imposed by parents) and elopement, providing the dynamism by which this radical move can be made."[11] Spinley notes that girls fall in love more with love than with their particular boy friends.[12] Arnold Green has described a similar pattern for a lower-class Polish group in the United States.[13] Lewis notes that participation in courtship is one of the main gratifications of the adolescent period, albeit one flavored with many risks.[14] The girl is both pushed toward marriage by her desire to get away from home (where demands for work and/or support tend to be made increasingly as she gets older) and *pulled* in that direction by her knowledge that the only appropriate role for a woman in her culture is that of wife and mother, that if she does not marry soon she runs the risk of being regarded as an immoral, "loose" woman or a ridiculous old maid.

For the young man, too, marriage looms large as representing the final transition to adult status. In Tepoztlan, only married men may hold responsible positions; without marriage one is still tied to one's own father. In Puerto Rico, the situation is similar, and in addition, one cannot be considered truly masculine until one has fathered children, preferably sons. If one is to establish himself as an independent adult, he needs a woman to wash and cook and take care of him as his mother would. Sex, too, plays a part in the man's desire for marriage. Because in reality women of easy virtue are not as available as the norm has it, the man may want to be married to have sexual relations whenever he wants—as one American said, "It's nice to have it ready for me when I get home." Also, some American men express the desire to have a woman whom they know is "safe" and "clean," i.e., does not have a venereal disease.

But the assertion of independent adult status which marriage represents in these groups meets with considerable opposition from parents, more so for the girl than for the young man. Lewis notes that in the mid-forties as many as 50 per cent of unions took place by elopement,[15] and Stycos indicates a similarly high percentage for Puerto Rico.[16] Because girls are not cloistered in the United States and England as they are in these Latin cultures, clear-cut elopement is not so much the pattern, but feigned surprise and anger are common parental responses, and it is not unusual for a premarital pregnancy to be used as a final argument to the parents to accept the marriage of their daughter to a man whom they like to feel is "not good enough for her." The wife in particular, then, is launched into marriage during a period of overt strain in her relations with her parents. Although later relationships with relatives may come to be central to her integration socially, during this period she is often more "alone" than at any other time in her life.

The "honeymoon trauma." The adjustment to sexual relations is observed to be difficult for many women in all four groups. Stycos notes that in a majority of cases, the wedding night was traumatic for the woman, with trembling, weeping, and speechlessness being frequently reported.[17] Several women were so frightened that they managed to delay the first intercourse for several days. Lewis reports a similar pattern for Tepoztlan,[18] although he feels that the less sheltered girls of today are less likely to be so resistant. Lewis also notes that the fact that couples often start their marriage sleeping in the same room with the husband's family imposes additional constraints. Slater and Woodside indicate that many of their English lower-class women reported unpleasant wedding nights but claimed to have overcome their initial fear and repugnance,[19] a pattern also noted in the United States.[20] It should be noted that the wife's modesty and reticence are not necessarily disapproved by her new husband; he may value them as an indication that she is still a virgin and that she is not "oversexed." Even so, he is confronted with a problem: while he does not wish his wife to be desirous independent of his initiation, he does need her cooperation, and he does not like to be made to feel guilty by her protests and fright.

Individual behavior and the norm. The effect of early socialization processes and later experiences, then, seems to be to establish the husband as the one to whom sexual relations are really important and the wife as the unwilling vehicle for his gratification. Given this cultural statement of the nature of men and women, what are the actual patterns of sexual gratification in these four cultures? For Tepoztlan, Lewis reports only what is presumably the majority pattern: " . . . much of the women's expressed attitudes toward sexual relations with their husbands dwell upon its negative aspects and reveal feelings of self-righteousness which border on martyrdom. Women speak of submitting to their husbands' 'abuse' because it is their obligation to do so."[21] For the husband's part, he reports, "Husbands do not expect their wives to be sexually demanding or passionate, nor are these viewed as desirable traits in a wife. Husbands do not complain if their wives are not eager for or do not enjoy sexual intercourse. . . . Some husbands deliberately refrain from arousing their wives sexually, because they do not want them to 'get to like it too much.' . . . Few husbands give attention to the question of their wives' sexual satisfaction. In general, sexual play is a technique men reserve for the seduction of other women." (Furthermore, a passionate wife may be considered a victim of black magic.) Perhaps some wives of Tepoztlan do enjoy sexual relations with their husbands, and the husbands do not object, but Lewis apparently did not find this pattern frequent enough to warrant comment.[22]

Stycos reports a similar pattern for Puerto Rico: most women say they do not enjoy sexual relations; for them, sex is a duty and their emotional stance a continuation of the premarital rejection of sex as an appropriate interest for a woman.[23] Women report a sense of disgust and revulsion about this necessary role, or they communicate a sense of detachment and minor irritation. Some women say they deceive the husband into believing that they enjoy sexual relations somewhat—perhaps to keep them from feeling too guilty, perhaps to allay any suspicion that they have a lover. The woman in this case seeks a balance of apparent enjoyment and reticence in which she communicates to her husband that her interest is solely due to her love for him, that her enjoyment is secondary to his right. Women use various excuses to cut down the frequency of intercourse—they feign sleep, or illness, argue about the danger of becoming pregnant, welcome menstruation, seek to prolong postpartum abstinence—but they feel that such a course is risky because it may make the husband violent or suspect infidelity. Stycos also notes that over one-third of the women in his sample indicated real enjoyment of sexual relations, but he does not discuss how these women differ from the majority who to some extent reject sexual relations.

The patterns described by Stycos for Puerto Rico are also apparent in data from lower-class American families currently being studied by the author.[24] Table 1 presents a tabulation of wives' attitudes toward sexual relations with their husbands for 195 middle- and lower-class women. The women's responses were categorized into three gross patterns: *highly accepting of sexuality* (referring to positive statements of interest in, desire for, and enjoyment of sexual relations with the husband and explicit or implicit indications that sexual relations were highly significant in the marital relationship), *moderately accepting of sexuality* (referring to positive statements about sexual relations with the husband, but without glowing testimony to the importance of, or gratification in, sexual relations, and often with an effort to place sexuality in proper perspective in relation to other activities and gratifications in marriage), and *lack of acceptance of sexuality* (in which the wife indicates that sexual relations are for the husband's gratification, not hers). In the middle class (no significant differences between upper-middles and lower-middles), only 14 percent of the women indicate lack of acceptance of sexuality; in the upper-lower class, this proportion rises to 31 percent and in the lower-lower class, 54 per cent of the women do not show acceptance of themselves as sexually interested and do not indicate enjoyment of sexual relations. The women who do not find sexual relations enjoyable range in their attitude toward the necessity to have intercourse: a good many try to neutralize the unpleasantness they feel, others are overtly hostile to the husband about his demands, but the latter pattern seems a difficult one to maintain since it has ready repercussions on the marital relationship, and generally the women fear their husbands will stray or desert them. Some of these women report with pride that they never directly refuse their husbands, although they use the same devices reported by Stycos to reduce the frequency of their husband's demands. (One device reported by these women but not mentioned by Stycos is precipitating an argument with the husband so that he will go out to a tavern.)

TABLE 1   Social Class and Wife's Enjoyment of Sexual Relations

	Middle Class (58)	Upper-Lower Class (68)	Lower-Lower Class (69)
Highly accepting: very positive statements about enjoyment	50%	53%	20%
Moderately accepting: enjoyment not emphasized	36	16	26
Lack of acceptance: avoidant or rejecting attitudes expressed	14	31	54
	100%	100%	100%

For England, Spinley reports only that the most common pattern is for sex to be only the man's pleasure,[25] but Slater and Woodside supply some idea of the frequency of the wife's enjoyment of sexual relations. They report that only a minority of women find real gratification in sexual relations and that about half indicate that they do not participate of their own wish.[26]

Women in all of these areas sometimes justify holding back from emotional participation in sexual relations by saying that they are less likely to become pregnant if they do not have orgasm. This is perhaps related to the general tendency, observed in the English and American reports at least, for the sexual relationship to become less and less involved, more automatic, after the first few years of marriage. There is not only a decrease in frequency, but also a tendency to relegate intercourse more and more to the category of satisfying the husband's biological need, and for whatever sense of mutuality has existed to wither. Several American women who reject sex comment that earlier in marriage they had sometimes enjoyed intercourse but that now, with many children and other preoccupations, would just as soon do without it. Slater and Woodside also note that the longer-married women tend to be the more dissatisfied.[27]

Kinsey's data on educational level and sexual behavior are by and large congruent with the patterns outlined here.[28] He finds that although men of lower educational status are much more likely than men with more education to have premarital relations, women of this status are less likely to do so. He finds that for women, erotic arousal from any source is less common at the lower educational levels, that fewer of these women have ever reached orgasm, and that the frequency for those who do is lower. For men, he reports that foreplay techniques are less elaborated at the lower educational levels, most strikingly so with respect to oral techniques. In positional variations in intercourse, the lower educational levels show somewhat less versatility, but more interesting is the fact that the difference between lower and higher educational levels increases with age because variations among lower status men drop away rapidly with age, while the drop among more educated men is much less. The same pattern characterizes nudity in marital coitus.

One final aspect of marital sexuality can be considered: the prevalence of extramarital relations. As noted, the sexual norms of all of these cultures or subcultures treat extramarital relations on the part of men as understandable, sometimes as to be expected, while such relations by wives are strongly disapproved. Kinsey finds that men of below college level are more likely than others to have extramarital relations, but the lowest educational level is not the most frequent participant in such relationships. Also, the differential between college and grammar-school-only men disappears with age (by the 36–40 age period, college-level men show a slightly higher incidence than those in grammar-school levels). Extramarital intercourse, except in the early married years, does not seem as highly class-bound as does premarital intercourse. Since no comparable data are available for the other three societies, it can only be said that extramarital relations by the husband—so long as there is no marked interference with the life of the couple—are not heavily condemned. Indeed, in Puerto Rico and Tepoztlan, at least, they are to be expected.

For women, considerable unclarity exists in the reports for all four areas. It is known that the partners for erring husbands are usually prostitutes or single, separated, or widowed women, but this is not always the case. It is not clear who the married women who participate in these affairs are, or whether they do so out of sexual desire or from other motives—to get even with the husband, to receive attention and presents from another man because the husband ignores them, or what. Kinsey's data indicate clearly that few lower-status women have extramarital relations and that the proportion is lower than among more educated women, especially for marriages of longer duration. It seems likely that in these lower-class groups, the concern about the wife's extramarital relations is more a manifestation of the husband's concern over her taking revenge for his domination than a prevalent pattern of deviance which he must realistically guard against.

Cultures mold the expression of sexual drives, the manifestations of male potency and female receptivity, in varied ways to conform to the requirements of particular social and cultural systems. Each individual in the system responds sexually not only, or even primarily, in terms of sexual drive, but in terms of the interpersonal implications which such action has.[29] What, then, are the characteristics of the social systems and processes of socialization to which the patterns of sexual behavior and attitudes outlined above represent accommodations?

In all of these lower-class subcultures, there is a pattern of highly segregated conjugal role relationships. Men and women do not have many joint relationships; the separation of man's work and woman's work is sharp, as is the separation of man's and woman's play. Stycos indicates that half of the women in his sample do not report common activities with their husbands outside the home, and many of the remaining cases report only infrequent or limited outside activities[30]; a similar pattern seems characteristic of Tepoztlan[31]; and in both groups, the necessity for respect toward the husband reduces joint activities. This has been the traditional pattern in England and the United States, although trends toward less segregation are observable.

The low value placed on mutuality in sexual relations can be seen, then, as in part an extension of a more generalized pattern of separateness in the marital relationship. It is not difficult to understand that husbands and wives do not think of sexual relations as a way of relating intimately when they have so few other reasons for doing so. The sole segregation of which the pattern of sexual relationships seems a part has as one consequence a considerable difficulty in communication between husbands and wives on matters not clearly defined in terms of traditional expectations. It is difficult for such couples to cope with problems which require mutual accommodation and empathy. This has been noted as one reason couples in these groups are not able to practice birth control effectively[32] and seems also to be involved in the distance husbands and wives feel with respect to sexual relations.

In these groups, then, husbands and wives tend to be fairly isolated from each other. They do not seem to be dependent on each other emotionally, though each performs important services for the other. In the traditional social systems of these groups, social integration is somewhat separate for the husband and wife. Each participates in relatively closed social networks to which he can look for a sense of stability and continuity in his life.[33] For women, social relations often are organized about relations with kin, the woman regards herself as most importantly a person embedded in a network of kin extending upward to maternal figures and downward to her children. The importance of "Mum" for the English lower class has been noted by many observers, and Mum in turn is the center of a network of kin and neighbors which absorbs many of the emotional demands of the wife.[34] In Tepoztlan, the young wife traditionally orients herself to her husband's mother or to her own at a later date. The tie with the grandmother also seems important emotionally. In the United States, this pattern of kin relating is not so sharply defined as in other areas, but some evidence exists that lower-class people maintain kin relationships more fully than do middle-class people.[35] It is not clear from the Puerto Rican data how much wives orient themselves to kin networks, but it is clear that whatever their social relationships, these do not depend on joint relating by the couple to others.[36]

The husband's social network is not as dependent on kindred as that of the wife, although his too tends to be closed in the sense that the men he relates to tend also to relate to each other. His status in the home, and among the wife's kin network, tends to be tangential. Though he may be defined as the final authority, by default he usually has less influence on what goes on from day to day than his wife or the maternal figure to whom she looks for guidance. His important social relationships are outside the home, with other men—some of whom may be relatives, others not. His performance as a husband and father is more influenced by the standards they set than by his wife's desires, just as her behavior is more influenced by the standards and expectations of her kin-based network.

What all of this suggests, in short, is that in a system characterized by closed social networks, the impact in the direction of highly segregated conjugal roles makes close and mutually gratifying sexual relations difficult because neither party is accustomed to relating intimately to the other. Further, a close sexual relationship has no particular social function in such a system since the role performances of husband and wife are organized on a separate basis, and no great contribution is made by a relationship in which they might sharpen their ability for cooperation and mutual regulation.[37] It is possible that in such a system, a high degree of intimacy in the marital relationship would be antagonistic to the system since it might conflict with the demands of others.[38]

However, not all lower-class couples can be said to be caught up in closed social networks of the kind just discussed. Where residence is neolocal and geographical movement breaks up both kin and lifelong community relationships, the lower-class couple finds itself either isolated or participating in loose social networks in which there is not so great an opportunity for relationships with others to take up the emotional slack of a segregated relationship between husband and wife. In these situations, there is a tendency for husband and wife to be thrown more on each other for meaningful standards and emotional support, a push in the direction of joint organization and joint role relationships.[39] The impact of such a disruption of previous social networks is probably greatest on the wife. Since she does not have the work situation as a ready base for forming a new network of relationships, her network probably remains denuded for a longer period of time. This is apparent in some of the United States data[40] and can be inferred for Puerto Rico. In this situation, the stage is set for sexual relations to assume a more important role in the couple's relationship. The wife wishes her husband to be more affectionate and to spend more time with her. She may try to overcome her resistance to sex. The outcome will depend on the husband's ability to adapt to the new situation, in which his sexual need is not the sole factor, and in which he is expected to moderate his demandingness in the service of a mutually gratifying relationship. The relationship becomes one in which, as one American woman said, "He takes and I give, but I take, too." Given the cultural norms to which such couples have been socialized, however, such a delicate accommodation is not easily achieved.[41]

The socialization experiences of husbands and wives, of course, provide the motivational basis for the role behaviors discussed above and account for some of the resistance to change which individuals show when the network of relationships changes.[42] As has been noted, girls growing up are not encouraged to internalize a role as interested sexual partner, but are taught instead a complex of modesty, reticence, and rejection of sexual interests which continues into marriage. Girls are not rewarded, either prospectively or after marriage, by the significant others in their social networks for tendencies in the direction of passionate wife. Instead, the direction of proffered goals is toward functioning as a mother to children and husband, and perhaps continuing as daughter to a maternal figure. Although during late adolescence the girl may break from his pattern via romance and elopement, she finds that her greatest security comes from a return to the fold (if it is available). Finally, since her father has not been an integrated part of the household during her childhood, she has never developed the early psychic basis for a close relationship with a man which could be transferred to her husband. (Or the relationship with the father has come to have incestuous overtones which make a transfer difficult.)

The socialization experiences of the boy make greater allowance for a sexual role, but primarily in a narcissistic way. The boy learns to regard sex as a kind of eliminative pleasure for himself, and there is little emphasis on the sexual relationship as a social relationship. The aggressive component in sex is strongly emphasized, in the form of seduction and fantasies of raping, fantasies which in England[43] and the United States[44] are sometimes acted out in sham fashion as part of individual or group "dating" behavior. The masculinity of the *macho* pattern in the Latin cultures incorporates an aggressive pride in relations with men and with women; with respect to women, it stresses both having many partners and being insistent on taking one's own pleasure in each relationship. In the English and American lower class, there is no comparable name for this pattern, but the behavior encouraged is very similar. This exaggerated masculinity may be viewed as an overcompensation for the difficulty the boy has in developing a masculine identity. His early life is spent much in the company of women; he tends to identify more with his mother than with his father since the latter is not much in the home and tends not to interact closely with his children.[45] The heavy emphasis on man's pleasure and indifference to the woman serves to ward off feelings of inadequacy stemming both from past difficulties in identification and present marginal status in the family.[46] Given this vulnerability in his sense of masculine competence, it is not difficult to understand that the husband in these groups does not want to complicate his functioning as a sexual partner by having to take into account, or by stimulating, his wife's needs and demands. Nor does he want to feel that he has to compete with other men to keep her affections.

Thus, even though the current social situation may encourage joint role organization and greater dependence of husband and wife on each other, the legacy of socialization directed toward a system in which man and women orient themselves to different social networks and sharply segregated conjugal roles makes change difficult, and reduces the frequency with which couples develop sexual relations involving mutual gratification.

Summary

This paper began with an examination of similarities in the patterns of marital sexuality in four "cultures of the poor," all part of, or strongly dominated by, the over-all Western European culture. It was shown that among the lower classes of certain communities in Mexico, Puerto Rico, England, and the United States, there are significant similarities in the sentiments expressed by husbands and wives concerning sexual experiences and in their expectations about sexual role performances by the two marital partners. The paper has concluded with an explanatory hypothesis which seems adequate to account for the data from these four cultures, but which perhaps has wider applicability. It will occur to the reader, for example, that middle-class marriage according to the "Victorian" model was and is similarly marked by a lack of mutuality in sexual relations; in place of mutuality, a variety of repressive and mistress-lover patterns have developed. A more general hypothesis can be advanced which very likely is relevant to these situations also. This is that *in societies where there is a high degree of segregation in the role relationships of husbands and wives, the couple will tend not to develop a close sexual relationship, and the wife will not look upon sexual relations with her husband as sexually gratifying* (although she may desire such relations signifying the continuing stability of the relationship). This leaves open the question of whether in other cultures having such a role segregation pattern, the wife may commonly seek other relationships for sexual gratification, as on Truk, nor does it take into account the complexities introduced in societies in which polygamy is common. Should such a hypothesis have wider validity, it would represent an additional step toward understanding patterns of sexual relations in different societies as more than anthropological *curiosa.*

One minority group in the United States which has maintained somewhat different values and mores regarding marriage is the Mexican-American population. Despite living in the United States, they have been able to maintain some of the characteristics of the native Mexican family. There are over five million Mexican-Americans, most of whom live in the Southwestern states of Texas, New Mexico, Arizona, Colorado, and California. There are over one million living in Los Angeles County alone which makes it the capital. In addition, there are another four million people of Spanish descent such as Puerto Ricans, Cubans, and South Americans living in the United States.

Just as with the black and oriental populations, Mexican-Americans historically have been denied access to the American mainstream due to limited job opportunities. Basically, they have been used in the agricultural sector of the economy. Because of the poverty and lack of economic opportunities in Mexico, job-starved Mexican nationals have looked northward. Even at lower wages than paid Anglos for the same work, the wages are so much higher than in Mexico, that a large, eager illegal labor pool is available. American agriculture has been quick to utilize this inexpensive pool. These alien laborers are especially upsetting to the legal Mexican-American population since wages are forced down and jobs reduced by their presence. Recently a "wet line" (border patrols and checks) was established by agricultural unions trying to control illegal entry. The legality of such vigilante patrols is questionable, but they do indicate the great concern felt by Mexican-Americans over illegal Mexican laborers.

Nathan Murillo lists eight major cultural values that tend to set the Mexican-American family apart from the familar Anglo-Saxon Protestant ethic.

1. Material objects are usually seen as necessities and not ends in themselves.
2. Work is viewed as necessary for survival but not as a value in itself.
3. Higher value is assigned to activities other than work in the Mexican culture.
4. It is much more valuable to experience things directly through intellectual awareness and through emotional experience than indirectly through past accomplishments and the accumulation of wealth.
5. The time frame between Mexican-Americans and Protestant-ethic Americans is quite different.
6. The Anglo is taught to value openness, frankness, and directness, while the traditional Latin approach is to use diplomacy and tactfulness when communicating with another individual.
7. The Anglo-American style of kidding can be offensive to the Mexican-American who interprets and reacts negatively.
8. The Mexican-American has a penchant towards utilizing his full "range of psychological senses to experience things about him . . . to touch, taste, smell, feel or be close to an object or person on which his attention is focused.[47]

An understanding of the Mexican family system is of value when studying the Mexican-American family. The following reading first discusses at great length the theoretical problems that face the investigator and then launches into a discussion of the findings of Mexican research. Although methodological problems are of the utmost importance to the sociologist, our purposes are better served by focusing on the research findings rather than on the theoretical arguments. First, the topic of male-female relations, which lies at the base of the entire system of family relations will be discussed. Then each of the role relationships within the family will be taken up: husband-wife, father-son, father-daughter, mother-son, mother-daughter, brother-sister, brother-brother, sister-sister. Some of the relationships will be discussed in more detail than others because of the availability of more material and of their greater contribution to family dynamics. Dr. Peñalosa is a Professor of Sociology at California State College, San Bernardino.

15 Mexican Family Roles

Fernando Peñalosa

Male-Female Relations

In social life a Mexican man's marital status is of little practical importance, as a man carries on virtually the same sort of social life after marriage as he did before—and one in which the women have little part. The woman's position on the other hand is completely tied in with her marital status, and her behavior rigidly circumscribed by it. Yet the demands which are made upon the husband at home give him little rest from his outside worries. He has of course more and greater responsibilities than the woman, both at home and at work. This situation takes its toll in the men's mental health. Psychologists report that neurotic symptoms are more widespread among men than women, and the principal area of disturbance appears to be the family.[1]

Male-female relations are based on strongly held beliefs in the superiority (biological, intellectual, and social) of the male. The female is clearly valued less, despite the various circumstances in which she is placed on a pedestal by males. In effect ambivalently rejected by the male-oriented culture, she identifies with the children. This she is able to do because she had already assumed feminine identification with her own self-denying and submissive mother, as a result of the close mother-daughter relationship.

Sharing in the cultural ambivalence, the son may feel both veneration for and resentment against his mother. He may in later years pour out this resentment by devaluing, depreciating, and humiliating his wife or mistress. According to González Pineda:

> Thus begins the cycle of converting her into another saintly, good, self-denying and revered mother of the following generation, while he is converted into another hateful and hated father.[2]

The reference is to neurotic versions of this pattern, but the intergenerational process is clear.

This ambivalence of the men toward women takes another form in their division of women into "good" and "bad." "Good" women are the mother, wife, daughters, and sisters who are supposed to be disinterested in sex, and "bad" women are those less respectable women whom one can take as mistresses or otherwise enjoy sexually. One's own mother, not infrequently equated with the Virgin Mary, is supposedly a sexless creature, and by extension so is the wife. The husband believes he must be careful not to arouse his

Fernando Peñalosa, "Mexican Family Roles," *Journal of Marriage and the Family,* November 1968. Copyright 1968 by National Council on Family Relations. Reprinted by permission.

wife too much lest she take an active interest in sex, with the consequent danger of becoming a "bad" woman. This fear is expressed symbolically with frequency in Mexican films, plays, and novels, with the bad-good girl theme; that is, an ostensibly "good" girl or woman actually turns out to be "bad." This is the opposite of the common theme in American motion pictures where the ostensibly "bad" girl is actually "good."[3] Whether "good" or "bad," the most consistent characteristic of the ambivalent male-female relationship appears to be the basic lack of respect and consideration of the man toward the woman. The man is said openly or covertly to value the woman primarily as merchandise rather than as a person, because he takes into consideration what she has cost him financially and in other ways.[4] Woman's virtue is glorified at the same time that prostitution is legalized by men and widely patronized by them. The ambivalence combines a constant preoccupation with the opposite sex with a not always patent but acute and exaggerated disdain for them.

The nature of male-female relationships in Mexican society is the outcome of a lengthy and consistent socialization process. The male begins to learn his role very early in childhood. The ideal of manliness despises elegance, beauty, or sentimentality and fosters a hard attitude toward life. The girl for her part early learns to be submissive and to cultivate the feminine charms. Any signs of feminization are severely repressed in the boy, as are attempts at self-assertiveness on the part of the girl.

With the arrival of adolescence, the boy is expected to show signs of virility by acting or at least talking in the sexual sphere. The boy sets out at one and the same time to seek two girls: a "good" girl, one of the type he can idealize and eventually marry, and a "bad" girl, one he can immediately exploit for sexual purposes. He is expected to play the role of Don Juan from now on, and the measure of his manliness will be primarily in terms of sexual exploits and only secondarily in terms of strength or daring.

At the same time the adolescent and young adult girl is going through the most satisfying period of her life, when the all-powerful male submits to her "as slave to queen" as the local rhetoric has it. She is the goal of romantically speaking and serenading suitors, and she enjoys her position on the pedestal. She will later on enjoy a similar adulation on the part of her children when she has become a mother.

No discussion of Mexican male-female relations could be considered even partially adequate without some mention at least of *machismo*. This is that much-publicized Mexican trait of manliness, in which the man constantly tries to express and constantly looks for signs in others that his manliness is being recognized. One frequently expressed notion is that *machismo* is a manifestation of orality. A great deal of Mexican "manly" behavior consists merely of verbal, that is, oral, behavior. Significantly also, when the man is faced with frustration in his attempts at demonstrating his manliness, he may regress and seek consolation in alcohol.

The behavior related to *machismo* has been the result of the deprival of a constant and secure masculine identification. The latter is also sought in the male's social relationships, which tend to be all-male in character. After working hours the typical Mexican joins his friends and carries on with them a life that differs little if at all from that which he practiced before he was married.

The role complementary to that of the *macho* or male is of course that of the *hembra* or female. These are reciprocal roles in that the culture pattern calls for the motives and expectations of one role to be matched by the motives and expectations of the other, and behavior in one role calls forth the corresponding behavior in the other. Each is then able to predict, with a considerable degree of accuracy the effect of one's behavior on the other, and he behaves accordingly. Bermúdez has introduced the term *hembrismo* to stand for the feminine counterpart of *machismo*.[5] *Hembrismo* is considered to be an amplification of the characteristics ordinarily considered as feminine, that is, weakness, passive attitude toward the male, and inertia. Bermúdez claims that *hembrismo* is the product of ineptitude and egotism on the part of the woman. For example, a woman would stay with a faithless husband either because of the desire to maintain her social position or because she would be unable to support herself, rather than out of devotion to the family and her role in it.

Basic male-female attitudes and relationships are of course the core of the husband-wife relationship and hence crucial to an understanding of the entire system of role relationships within the family constellation. Before these relationships are taken up here, a word is necessary concerning how widespread in Mexican society are the patterns about to be discussed. In the first place, there appears to be general agreement that family structure and psychological characteristics of the lower class on the one hand and the upper class on the other are basically the same.[6] The main difference appears to reside in the fact that, in the lower class, motivations are less carefully concealed and expressions of aggression more open. In the upper class the unconscious motives behind attitudes are difficult to discover without deep psychological study.

The authoritarian Mexican family structure as here described is probably found in its most typical form among the middle-class people of the provinces and among middle-class Mexico City families of provincial origin. In the provinces the lower class seeks to emulate this form. In the metropolitan areas, particularly Mexico City, American influence is strong in the upper and middle classes. There are, on the other hand, strong currents of family disintegration in the lowest economic levels characterized by the so-called culture of poverty. It should also be emphasized that the relationships described here refer to the nuclear family only. The extended family in Mexico is apparently a thing of the past and is not discussed in the literature; nor are fictive family relationships, such as ceremonial godparenthood (*campadrazgo*), dealt with here. Keeping these structures in mind, we now turn to a discussion of family role relationships.

Family Role Relationships

There is a dramatic change when the male-female relationship changes from that of wooer-wooed to that of husband-wife. In the local phrasing, after the honeymoon the slave becomes the king. Furthermore the idealistic side of his ambivalent attitude toward women is now more likely to be channeled toward his mother than toward his wife. Not only does the wife cease to be an object of idealism, but neither is she considered as a sexual object in the full sense. The male believes that sex ought to be practiced differently with the wife than with the mistress. In any case he deals with his wife as he saw his father treat his mother. Since in Mexico there are few symbolic means of expressing masculinity other than *machismo,* he will necessarily emphasize the latter. He remains, ideally, sole breadwinner and absolute master of his household.

Woman's place is definitely in the home, first in that of her father, then in that of her husband. Any work outside the home obviously reduces not only the woman's financial dependence on the men but also the amount of time she can spend attending to their needs. This principle is most fully maintained in the conservative middle- and upper-class families. It is least fully maintained in modern families at the upper and middle levels; and in both the provincial and the metropolitan lower class, because of the economic necessity of having the women work.

Generally the husband carries out his family obligations as he sees fit. Any demand by the wife for masculine responsibility by the man may be perceived by the latter as a demand for submission to her. Similarly any request for assistance with the children or in housework is regarded as an affront to his dignity. Although the family thus may become a battle ground of egos, in the last analysis both husband and wife find what they are seeking: the wife finds security and the husband finds the satisfaction of his impulses.[7]

This complementary resolution of the potential husband-wife conflict is less satisfactory among families at the lowest socioeconomic levels in the cities because of the great instability of such families. In fact, some authors have questioned whether such domestic units are properly called families at all. These unions, sanctioned by neither church nor state, are frequently transitory. The woman may have several children, each by a different father. The father may have several different "families" in different parts of the city or at different times. And yet the social psychological structure appears to be the same as among the less disorganized families.

> There is a common sentiment of abusive domination of the women by the men; and of the unconditional submission toward men by the women.[8]

The search for men to support them economically appears to be merely the woman's pretext for conceiving more children and hence being able to continue in the role of self-denying mother.

Before entering into a systematic discussion of parent-child and sibling relationships, brief attention will be paid to certain additional aspects of the socialization process as it proceeds in the Mexican family. It cannot be gainsaid that Mexican children are greatly loved by their parents. Yet there is a frequent use of deception whenever this is convenient for the parents. The child is severely punished for lying, but when the parent is discovered by the child to have been lying, the parent makes use of an irrational affirmation of authority. It is not unusual for children to be beaten, especially by a dissatisfied and bitter wife unable to strike her husband. As the children are socialized they begin to emulate, as best they can, the respective parental roles. Eventually they become rivals of their parents, the boy from the point of view of the father's social position and girl from the point of view of the mother's biological functioning.

As far as the various family role memberships are concerned, the important criteria are generation and sex and, with reference to siblings, order of birth as well. Although each of the relationships has some unique characteristics of its own, other characteristics are shared with some of the other relationships. Furthermore the different relationships are mutually interdependent and, as a totality, form the social system which constitutes the Mexican family structure.

The father-son relationship is generally a distant but respectful one. At times it verges on the severe. At a very early age the boy begins to identify with a "very powerful, severe, superperfect, idealized father."[9] With the increasing age of the child, the father not only plays less with him but also does not replace the play with shared interests and activities. The strong image begins to fade in time and by adolescence has vanished even though the father's word remains law. His adult behavior will be largely a manifestation of an attempt to create in himself the image formerly held of the father. He can find security only in repeating the behavior of his father in the treatment of his own wife and children.

During adolescence the boy also begins his estrangement from religion. This is in effect a rebellion against the mother, the person who has imparted the moral and religious values now rejected, but also against the father who cannot be opposed openly. The young man does however begin to reject the authority of the priest, a sort of symbolic father.

As in so many other cultures, the peer group becomes all important in adolescence, particularly for the Mexican boy in his search for male identity. But contrary to what may be more usual elsewhere, the peer group relationships of youth continue virtually unchanged after marriage.[10] The Mexican man's social world is a man's world. He spends a great deal of his effort and money in making his social position stand out in the world of males. The underlying dynamism here seems to be the much-commented-upon inferiority complex of the Mexican male, the other side of the *machismo* coin. It would seem almost as if Alfred Adler had devised his theories especially for the purpose of understanding the Mexican personality. Ramos, as mentioned above, ascribed this phenomenon to historic causes. It can however perhaps best be understood in terms of the father-son relationship: the son's feeling of utter powerlessness before the father and the impossibility of relating to and identifying with him. In other words the explanation is to be sought in the values which are at the very base of various aspects of the Mexican family.

With reference to the father-daughter relationship, the father is not ordinarily quite so distant nor so severe. This is partly because the daughter is not expected to emulate him in any way, nor is she at all a threat to his male status. The attitude of the father toward the daughter is rather a protective and possessive one. He wishes to feel secure in the knowledge that the females in his household will not challenge his dominance. For example, great jealousy or at least a large measure of incomprehension may be directed toward the daughters' suitors. While the latter point is frequently stressed in the literature, relatively little attention has otherwise been given to the father-daughter relationship. This is apparently because this particular relationship, of the four parental-child relationships, is the least productive of conflict and tension and hence is of less interest to students of the Mexican family.

The mother-son relationship, as in all cultures, is particularly crucial in the Mexican family. Writers are in agreement with the notion that during the first year of life, at least, the relationship is one of intense closeness and pampering, which favors certain narcissistic tendencies in the child. This relationship is probably also the source of Mexican orality. The Mexican man manifests "an extraordinary need to be nourished, to receive from others, to depend."[11] The Mexican's constant need to talk has also been frequently noted. The existence of a mother-child relationship with great oral satisfactions has apparently led to tendencies for a number of areas of behavior to become fixed at that level. The widespread prevarication to be found in the society, for example, seems to be orally related; it is a defense in the sense that the man is constantly afraid of being feminine and the woman of not being loved.[12]

In early childhood the mother is not only close but also dominant to the point that the son can identify easily with her. But the close relationship is interrupted by the birth of the next child, to whom the closeness will now be manifested, while the older child finds himself deprived of some of the most significant aspects of this most important relationship. When he grows up and has a son of his own, he is reminded of the time he was displaced by the younger brother, and this affects his relationship with his own son. The effect of the break in the relationship depends on whether the displaced child is a boy or girl. While after the first year the daughter is brought up with increasing severity, the son generally enjoys fewer and fewer limitations and much more tolerance for his behavior.

As the years pass, the mother helps the boy in his striving for independence. She is more permissive so that he will be more of a man as Mexicans conceive of that role. More aggression is permitted when he is little. When he is older, she allows him to go out alone and come home late, something not at all permitted to the girl. His peccadilloes are ordinarily overlooked. Since the mother sees another *macho* in the making, however, her attitude towards the boy is ambivalent. Similarly the boy develops an ambivalent attitude toward the mother. The boy both reveres and feels hostility toward her. The latter feelings derive not only from the notion that the mother has not provided him with an effective father, but also because she "abandoned" him in his early childhood.

The subconscious longing for the mother is said to be expressed in adulthood not infrequently in alcoholism and in the phenomenon of *guadalupanismo* (highly emotional, devout veneration of the Virgin of Guadalupe).[13] One possibility is that the aggressive impulses of the male derive from an attempt to displace his reaction against his guilt feelings for harboring hostility against the mother. Another aspect is that when he was young he resented his father's infidelities to his mother. Now as a man he hopes to be unfaithful with complete impunity from others and from his own conscience as he proceeds to treat his wife as his father did his mother.

The mother-daughter relationship is undoubtedly the closest of the four child-parent relationships. This is because of the close identification between the two roles. In the first year of life, the mother ordinarily cares for and feeds the daughter with even more attention than she does the son. The mother perceives a reflection of herself in her daughter and begins to live through her. Because of the close relationship prevailing between mother and daughter on both emotional and household chore levels—a situation utterly without parallel in the father-son relationship—the daughter ordinarily manages a full identification with the mother.

After the first year the daughter is brought up with somewhat more severity than the son. Sphincter training is required earlier in girls and the reactions of modesty, manners, and cleanliness are taught sooner and more insistently to the girl than to the boy. Infantile masturbation is more harshly and more violently punished in the girl.

During the second year the little girl begins to be taught to be submissive to men. The daughter acquires feminine qualities as a consequence of the submission which is expected of her. The mother teaches the daughter to distrust men at the same time that she is learning to wait on her father and to care for and pamper her brothers. Little girls learn early to assume responsibilities and tasks, especially those that are particularly maternal in character, such as taking care of smaller siblings. The eldest daughter particularly is likely to assume maternal roles. The mother ordinarily wishes to be dependent upon the daughters as soon as possible.

At the same time that the daughter is taught about the untrustworthiness of men, she is also being taught that she is incapable of defending her own emotional and sexual integrity and of living in accordance with the moral standards taught her. Only the mother is perfect, it is implied.

It is not at all unusual that, when the daughter comes to have children of her own, the mother attempts to direct the socialization of the grandchildren, maintaining that the daughter is unable properly to care for them. The grandmother thus seeks to retain the only relationship in which she found security and which age now denies her, namely, motherhood. In any case, the mother-daughter relationship is the closest and longest lasting of the family relationships after the marriage of the children. Furthermore, sister-sister relations after marriage are strongly oriented toward the mother.

Brother-brother relations and sister-sister relations in the Mexican family are similar in that deference of younger to older is taught and respect among siblings is expected. One's behavior must be especially circumspect in the presence of one's siblings; there must be no looseness of act or word, particularly in the sexual area. After marriage sister-sister relationships (which typically are extended to include the mother) tend to be closer and longer lasting than brother-brother relationships. As a result, close relations between brothers-in-law are not infrequent.

. . .

Conclusion

A number of implications suggest themselves in the light of the preceding. For example, it is not to be expected that such family patterns will remain unaffected by current social trends sweeping Mexico. A number of influences currently affecting the Mexican family are worthy of mention. Family patterns are being modified in the direction of greater stability with the upward mobility increasingly characterizing Mexican society as it becomes more and more industrialized and lower-class persons move up into the middle class. On the other hand, the rapid urbanization process seems to be promoting the opposite, particularly in the rapidly growing "culture of poverty." Influences in the direction of the weakening of tradition stem partly also from the popular media of communication which portray Western, especially American, patterns of behavior so at variance with the authoritarian-patriarchal forms considered the norm in Mexico. Knowledge of and interest in American ways is keen, and while many of these ways are deplored, others are emulated and admired— at least in the more mobile segments in the population.

An expanding economy and society are now providing more opportunities for personal expression and growth and thus also more situations for the development of self-esteem, particularly for the men. In the previously static society, there were many fewer opportunities, and mere subsistence was a problem for many. The patriarchal society was an understandably based on the absolute economic dependence of the family on the father. With an expanding and modernizing economy, there are increasing opportunities for women to gain advanced education and employment outside the home and for young men to achieve social positions higher than those of their fathers.

It would be expected therefore that, in the more modernized, industrialized, and urbanized United States, the Mexican family is likewise undergoing attenuations of the traditional patriarchal, authoritarian family. In order to ascertain the degrees of change of the family pattern among Mexican-Americans, an ambitious research program would be required. Minimally, any such research would have to sample the various social class, regional, and urban-rural variations. Smaller scale research could focus perhaps on only one or two of the variants, but results could not be extrapolated to other variants. It is hoped that the frame of reference presented in this paper may serve as at least one perspective and baseline from which studies might be made of the Mexican-American family.

The Mexican-American family pattern may undergo change as the community becomes more integrated into the middle-class American mainstream. In such a case the family structure will resemble more closely the nuclear family pattern.

The Negro family has become the center of focus for many investigators especially since the Office of Policy Planning and Research, U.S. Department of Labor, issued *The Negro Family: The Case for National Action,* popularly known as the "Moynihan Report" in March, 1965. According to this report, "At the heart of the deterioration of the fabric of Negro society is the deterioration of the Negro family":

> There is considerable evidence that the Negro community is in fact dividing between a stable middle-class group that is steadily growing stronger and more successful, and an increasingly disorganized and disadvantaged lower-class group. There are indications, for example, that the middle-class Negro family puts a higher premium on family stability and the conserving of family resources than does the white middle-class family. . . .
>
> There are two main points to be noted in this context: First, the emergence and increasing visibility of a Negro middle-class may beguile the nation into supposing that the circumstances of the remainder of the Negro community are equally prosperous, whereas just the opposite is true at present, and is likely to continue so.
>
> Second, the lumping of all Negroes together in one statistical measurement very probably conceals the extent of the disorganization among the lower-class group. If conditions are improving for one and deteriorating for the other, the resultant statistical averages might show no change. Further the statistics on the Negro family and most

other subjects treated in this paper refer only to a specific point in time. They are a vertical measure of the situation at a given moment. They do not measure the experience of individuals over time. Thus the average monthly unemployment rate for Negro males for 1964 is recorded at 9%. But during 1964, some 29% of Negro males were unemployed at one time or another. Similarly, for example, if 36% of Negro children are living in broken homes at any specific moment, it is likely that a far higher proportion of Negro children find themselves in that situation at one time or another in their lives.

This view is disputed by some Negro leaders who feel that deterioration of Negro society caused by the discrimination of the white majority has lead to the disorganization of the Negro family.

It should be noted that there is often confusion between class and race characteristics. Most of the traits attributable to the black urban family are really traits found in any lower-economic-class family, not just black families.

Disorganization within the black family appears greater than it really may be because the lower-class black family tends to be compared to the middle-class rather than lower-class white family. Middle-class black families are similar to middle-class white families. Lower-class black families are similar to lower-class families of any race. Of course the black family does have unique traits aside from the general class traits, due to its African heritage, alienation from the white society, and economic deprivation.

Some critics of black family research say that if we were to look at black family life-styles objectively, we would find that its culture is not a poor imitation of its white counterpart but a fully developed life-style of its own! Be that as it may, the black family is different in many ways from the mainstream white middle-class family. If there are weaknesses in the black family, regardless of the reasons, strengthening these weaknesses should facilitate and improve black life in the United States.

The following reading represents a thorough review of our knowledge of the black family. Of necessity the first part of the article is devoted to tracing the history of the American Negro, for this history has in many ways determined the unique characteristics of the American Negro family. Stuart A. Queen has served as chairman of the Sociology Department at the University of Kansas and is Professor Emeritus at Washington University. Robert W. Habenstein is currently a Sociology professor at the University of Missouri.

16 The Contemporary Black American Family

Stuart A. Queen and
Robert W. Habenstein

The following chapter deals with the varying forms or profiles of the American black family, seen first historically and then currently. Necessarily, the historical development will be brief and intended to serve only as a backdrop to assist in the understanding of modern development. Without some reference to its history, one cannot fully comprehend the present social, cultural, and political developments in the American black community. On the other hand, an attempted full explanation that merely rakes up the ashes of the past would be equally inadequate.

Because blacks are now proportionately more urban than the majority whites, and because it will be in urban life that their acculturation and/or differentiation will be increasingly significant, we will focus on black families who reside in, but do not necessarily come from, essentially urban settings.

Historical Backdrop

Blacks today make up between eleven and twelve percent of the population of the United States and constitute the nation's largest and most visible minority group. Their introduction to America in 1619 was not as slaves but as servants. Foreign in their folkways and mores, different in color, the Africans were not assimilated easily into the white colonial society. It eventually became both psychologically and economically expedient to give them slave status. Through the first half of the seventeenth century the English colonists, who, in contrast to the Spanish and Portuguese, had little or no experience with institutionalized slavery, fashioned a system of their own.[1] Slaves were defined as something less than human and consequently not to be taken into or given the protection of the colonists' social, political, and religious institutions. Instead they were incorporated into the economy as property on the same basis as livestock, their value set by their utility. By the end of the seventeenth century, the institution of slavery was an accomplished fact in Virginia, Maryland, and the Carolinas, and Georgia followed a half century later. Although slavery spread through the middle colonies and into New England, it was not economically profitable. The slave codes were progressively less harsh from south to north, and slavery became less attractive to northern colonists than was the slave trade itself.

The bulk of the slaves and the predominance of the slave economy were then in the southern colonies. The plantation system, with its large number of field hands cultivating extensive agricultural holdings, cast slavery into a mold that persisted for well over two centuries in the South. Slaves as chattels could be utilized rationally without regard for human or social bonds and sentiments. The majority of the males were used in the fields, domiciled separately and moved about as they were needed. Only under special circumstances—as house servants or artisans—were they permitted to take wives and to establish families. In such cases the opportunity for personal contact and the establishing of personal bonds between master and slave could take place—always within, however, the limits set forth by the widely separated statuses.

Whatever social organization may have prevailed in their native Africa, whatever family arrangements, forms, and usages found in the mores of the preexistent cultures, these were stripped from, or eventually lost, to the blacks brought to America. Dispersion of social groups, separation of husbands from wives and families, a callous disregard for kindred relationships, all but destroyed the African cultural and social heritage. The memories of such heritage dimmed with the passing centuries.[2] The sporadic appearance of pan-African movements in the United States, however, indicates they have not been completely extinguished.

The status of the male slave suffered more than that of the female. In nearly two and a half centuries of slavery the black male could expect less consideration by whites as a human being, less social status, less responsibility, more alienation from white society, more violent treatment, and a more demeaning appraisal of his personality. Black-white sexual involvements were proscribed, but when they did occur, the punishment for black male-white female sexual relations was much greater than for those in which white males had relationships with black females. Thus the mixing of races that occurred during the period of slavery was predominantly at the initiative of the white male.

The upshot of the differential treatment of the black male slave was the establishment of a social role, reinforced often by personality type,[3] that made for economic, social, and personal instability. It is this legacy of slavery that overshadows the development of the contemporary black family. As a historico-cultural force it operates to undermine the development of male black ego-strength and to hinder the development of a form of family organization in which the father's role can be clearly identified and stand as a model in the socialization of his children.[4]

Obviously the status of the black female slave never fell so low as that of her male counterpart. Neverthless, she was the victim of a deliberate imbalance, inasmuch as young vigorous males were preferred by plantation owners and as long as the importation of slaves was permitted were imported disproportionately. The unnatural imbalance in the black male and female populations continued until the middle of the nineteenth century. Thus among nearly all slaves in America, the women were necessarily shared by men—the opposite of the polygynous pattern that prevailed in many African tribal cultures from which slaves were recruited. Marriage for field hands was uneconomical and prohibited, but for house and yard servants and for artisans it was some-times permitted but without legal sanction. Since children were economic assets to the owners, the female slave could look forward to having children in substantial numbers and possibly a succession of mates rather than a perma-nent spouse. Children, then, were frequently born into a family consisting of mother, other siblings, and quite possibly maternal aunts and grandmothers.

Slave mothers might develop strong maternal attachments to their children or grow to be indifferent toward an increasing number of offspring whose fathers were often absent or perhaps unidentifiable. Indeed her own children could well prove to be an added burden to a mother charged with the responsi-bility of the care and nurturing of the white children in the master's house. For the most part, then, their role as breeders, nurses, and household servants put mothers in a strategically better position than male slaves. Further, their sexual exploitation by white owners and their sons introduced a personal relationship that had no counterpart for the black male.

Female slaves, in short, usually found themselves heading families without fathers, often burdened with heavy domestic responsibilities in two families, and with higher performance standards set for them by the white society than for black males. Their coping abilities to adjust were both tested and developed in and by slavery. The net result of more than three centuries of differential treatment, both during and after slavery, has been an overburdening of women with responsibility for the care, socialization, and, if necessary, the subsistence of their families.

Emancipation from slavery was a crisis in the life of the black that tended to destroy his traditional ways of thought and action.[5] Thousands of freedmen found themselves in an unorganized state, set free by decree but without norms or institutions to give continuity and direction to their lives. Those families that had managed to develop stability during slavery held fast, but families loosely held together broke apart. Men wandered about, often looking for family members from whom they had long been separated. Some sought land for farms or work to achieve these goals and a stable family life to sustain the prosperous farm life that they desired. Others formed casual marital and familial attachments, to be severed as they continued to wander.

Wars and economic booms stimulated the northward migration of blacks. Many migrated ahead of their families to find work and get established. Like most immigrants, they settled in the center of cities in areas of minimal services and choice. Families followed to find themselves in an environment that was strange, exacting, and often hostile. Lacking institutional supports, short on communal controls, and suffering chronically from weak economic underpin-ning, the black family faced the grim problem of survival and reorganization. The magnitude of the problem can be appreciated when one recognizes the crises facing a slavery-disorganized people—upheavals caused by mobility, exchange of rural for urban environment, economic survival, the need to gain social acceptance, and to develop a positive self-image.[6] To cope with the vagaries of their social, political, and economic environment, black Americans through the years have developed a variety of forms of family organization. We have distinguished four types: (1) *traditional matriarchal,* (2) *traditional small patriarchal,* (3) *acculturated middle majority* and (4) *adaptive urban matricentric.* The first two are essentially historical in origin; the remainder we have constructed to characterize current profiles of black family organization.[7]

Traditional Matriarchal Black Family

In the matriarchal family the mother, or perhaps, the maternal grandmother and daughter, holds dominant influence over property, authority, and household affairs. The Billingsleys have distinguished three subtypes[8] of the matriarchal family pattern: (1) father absent, (2) a father or series of fathers temporarily present, and (3) father constantly present. In the last case, although the father is present, he usually cannot be the breadwinner or assert parental authority because of his precarious status in the labor market. All three of these subtypes find their roots in traditional black family organization. We have noted that by virtue of his occupational status and restricted personal freedom, the slave husband was at best a sometime husband. After emancipation the achievement of a strong parental role was extremely limited, if not blocked, by his inability to maintain the status of breadwinner for the family. With her acceptance of the dominant role in the family, the female in the mother-centered family came to develop a "keen sense of personal rights,"[9] accompanied by a grim realization that males could not always be trusted to accept normal parental responsibilities. These handicaps are also the legacy of slavery and its aftermath.

Small Patriarchal Black Family

The black sociologist E. Franklin Frazier in his unrivaled study of the black family has traced the development of the patriarchal family from early slave days.[10] Slaves who had won or bought their freedom could also buy freedom for wife and family. Such an act would establish a proprietary interest in their family. To the extent that a plot of farmland was obtainable, or a breadwinning job available, the free or emancipated black could then establish the basic economic flooring for a stable black middle-class family. And, with his economic dominance would come, in Frazier's words, "the downfall of the matriarchate." Thus, in both a rural environment, where the father-headed farm family with all members holding an interest in the successful operation of the farm enterprise was characteristic, and in the urban areas, where the father's job gave him status and authority, a stable patriarchal family could emerge. Both this form and the matriarchal type, then, reflect the adaptability of American blacks to the crises and disjunctions of slavery and emancipation.

Both these types developed over centuries; the remaining two, which are more recent in their origin, build upon and to some extent derive from the older forms. They will be examined in greater detail.

The Acculturated Middle Majority Black Family

Jessie Bernard has traced the institutionalization of marriage among blacks from emancipation to the present. Legislative efforts of the states to legalize marriages and make them a matter of record were reinforced by military authorities, the Freedman's Bureau, the church, and the schools. Marriage sanctioned by these diverse institutions took on a positive value to blacks: as a status symbol, as an evidence of equality with whites, as a source of dignity lent to the alliance by minister and church, and as a joyous occasion in the wedding itself.[11] In Bernard's words:

> Thus, the outside world came increasingly to impinge on the Negro world. With the advent of child-welfare programs and public-health activities, all kinds of documentary proofs of relationships came to be required, and the old casual patterns became anachronistic. People had to prove that they had been born, had married, had borne children, had died. The intrusive hand of the official recorder appeared even in the backwoods, and once-spontaneous—even impulsive—human interrelationships were forced to take on the stern permanence of a written form.[12]

The consequence, in the decades following emancipation, was a reciprocal process: external norms exacted compliance, and the compliant behavior, in turn, became valued and eventually supported by internal or indigenous norms.

When norms are internalized in such a manner that they become associated with the ego, or personality, *acculturation* has occurred. From the standpoint of the group, acculturation implies the incorporation of cultural forms and usages into its areas of strongest collective belief as to what ought to and must be done. For the individual to violate such norms is to invite sanctions from the group, and probably, to engender on his part a feeling of guilt and anxiety.[13] For the majority of black Americans the history of the past century has been presumably a history of acculturation, a gradual process of accepting and internalizing and contributing to the norms of the middle majority of American whites. Secondarily, it has been a history of adaptations, some drawn from slave times, which may have run obliquely or counter to the normative mainstream of our society. Finally, there has been the expressive cultural infusion that has contributed to the making of the modern American life style.

Family Structure

The *acculturated middle-majority* black family accepts monogamy as the proper marriage form; the ideal of a permanent mate is qualified realistically by the recognition that marriages can fail, and the divorce is an acceptable, if regrettable, alternative to a permanently unhappy marriage relationship. The nuclear family group consisting of husband, wife, and children living in their own home and managing domestic affairs without pressure or influence from parents—the primary relationship—represents the ideal in household arrangements. The tendency toward establishing a stable residence conflicts with the desire to leave deteriorated or inferior dwelling areas behind in search of more suitable housing. Thus, when it can be attained, the single dwelling in the suburb or the better-class apartment as far away from the slums as possible remains the residential goal.

The size of the family is likely to be smaller than that found in the adaptive urban matricentric black family. Nevertheless a concern for parents is expressed in a willingness to share the domicile if the parents clearly cannot manage their own housing needs. Both sides of the family will be included in the extension of effective kinship relations, but such bilaterality is not likely to extend to more distant relatives. Close in-laws, grandparents, aunts, uncles, and cousins round out the effective kinship circle. Perhaps most important in household organization by comparison with the adaptive type is the tendency to afford more physical privacy and greater areas of inviolate life space for its members. The family, in a social psychological sense, seeks to close in on itself.

Family Cycle

Mate selection for the acculturated middle majority tends to be achieved at a somewhat later age than for the adaptive group. The process usually begins with casual dating in high school, possibly going steady in the senior year, and marriage only after at least high school education has been completed. For others, the serious going together will take place in college. Also, for a few females the husband will have been met first as a member of the armed forces. A standard pattern seems to be that of dating, going steady, becoming engaged, and being married with considerable ceremony in church, or at least before a minister, with friends and relatives from both sides of the couple present. Black females, in view of a disadvantageous sex ratio, tend to find the process of mate selection complicated. Their image of the ideal mate may emphasize occupational stability, stable personality, and "good prospects." In turn, the male may be selective, and somewhat disposed to seek a mate of light color. Some males seem not to want to marry at all, but in the long run blacks are a more married group than are whites.[14] Although racial intermarriages are proportionately very small in our society, when they do occur they are dominantly between a black male successful in his career and a white female.

A recent study compared black-white marriage in 1960 and 1970. Although racial intermarriage between blacks and whites is still rare, only 51,409 such marriages in 1960 and 64,789 in 1970, there was a fairly large percentage increase. During the 60s there was a 24 percent increase in the number of black-white marriages. A 66 percent increase in the North and West was offset by a 35 percent decline in the South. Moreover, the 62 percent rise in marriages involving a black husband and a white wife was accompanied by a 9 percent decline in marriages involving a white husband and a black wife. During this same time existing black-white marriages suffered a high rate of attrition. Of marriage involving a white husband and black wife contracted in the ten years prior to the 1960 census only 47 percent were still in existence in 1970, and of those involving a black husband and a white wife only 63 percent. In 1970 only 1.2 percent of black males had white wives and only .7 percent of the black females had white husbands.[15]

Traditionally, motherhood has meant more to black women than wifehood, and the maternal role has in most cases entailed heavy responsibility. In the acculturated family, a sharing of responsibility for socialization of the children is present. Children are wanted, but family size is likely to be restricted. Parents project high hopes for their children's futures, expect to provide them educational and cultural advantages they themselves might not have enjoyed, and are willing to plan and make sacrifices on their children's behalf. It is not part of this pattern for the wife's mother, the children's "granny," to become the principal socializing and caretaking female of the household. When mothers work—a higher proportion of black females are in the work force and working than are white females—they often employ paid baby sitters or send their children to day-care schools rather than use parents for the job.

Children are wanted, socialized, presented with definable male models by the father, given emotional support from mothers, and encouraged to achieve. Since education is so highly valued, both sexes are encouraged to absorb all the learning they can. While it is currently the case that black females have more education than males, this imbalance does not reflect an ideal of the acculturated family. In any event, the number of college graduates among blacks is rising at a faster rate than the overall increase in the total nonwhite population.[16] Success models in various walks of life are becoming more available for both sexes and are communicated to the members of the acculturated family in both black and white media.

Both parents are quite likely to be present during their offsprings' infancy and childhood. Bernard has noted that the most common type of black household is one in which there is a male head and his wife, and that most children under fourteen live in families of this type.[17] Although their cultural heritage may have little to offer in support of the arrangement, husbands will assume the instrumental (disciplinarian) role and the wife the affective (emotional support) role. The discipline, however, is not likely to be harsh and both parents may be overindulgent.[18]

In view of the restricted range of opportunity and the discriminatory practices, which have a stronger impact on the black male, the wife may find herself with equal if not better occupational life chances. But, when both husband and wife have a college education or when both are prepared for a business or professional career, husband-wife relations develop on the basis of common interests, congeniality, and mutual respect for the individuality of the other.[19] The result is an added equalitarian dimension to acculturated family organization.

The Adaptive Urban Matricentric Black Family

One associates the acculturated black family with better urban dwelling areas, usually away from the core of the central city, and with the suburbs. Conversely, turning toward the center of the American city, or the center of its black community, one finds a type of black family quite divergent from the acculturated type, a family revealing characteristically different organizational and personal elements. We have already given this family type, or cluster of tendencies, the name *adaptive urban matricentric* black family. To describe this type most clearly we have chosen first to examine its habitat and some of the social processes that have led to its creation.

The Ghettoized Black Community

After emancipation, particularly after the turn of the century, the movement of blacks was to the cities of the South and North. Black communities grew rapidly in size. Yet by World War I they were still a small fraction of the total population, usually well under five percent. For the most part, but not universally by any means (Harlem, for example), black migrants and older black residents were usually restricted in their dwelling areas to the poorer or poorest section of town. Often these areas had been abandoned by European immigrants and their succeeding generations eager to move toward more desirable places of residence. The labor needs and boom atmosphere of industrial cities during World Wars I and II attracted increasing numbers of rural Southern immigrants of both races. More recently, agricultural technology and large-scale farming have pushed small farmers off their lands and diminished the market for unskilled rural labor. In all, some 2.75 million blacks left the South between 1940 and 1960, and by 1964 the black population outside the South had increased five-fold since 1910.[20] Most of the blacks moving north and west have crowded into the slums of some two dozen cities from Boston to San Diego. Increases in the last three decades have been phenomenal. Blacks now comprise at least one quarter of the total population of nearly all major cities; yet most have found dwelling areas restricted to the central city, the areas of decreasing aesthetic, physical, economic, and political quality, areas of high social and personal disorganization as revealed by nearly any index.

"Ghettoization" is the word coined to describe the living arrangements of urban blacks. Disturbingly, the residential segregation of blacks has increased in the past decades. Karl and Alma Taeuber constructed segregation indices for 109 American cities and in comparing these for 1940, 1950, and 1960 found that segregation was increasing or had increased in most metropolises, with older southern cities, hithertofore less segregated, now following the pattern of northern urban black ghettoization.[21] G. Franklin Edwards, black sociologist, notes that the central city *cores* inhabited by blacks are "inferior in terms of housing, quality, recreational facilities, schools and general welfare services."[22] Further, ". . . all of these deficiencies contribute to crime, delinquency, school dropouts, dependency, broken families, excessive deaths, and other conditions which represent the pathology of the ghetto."[23] Of the latter one might specify illegitimacy as a crucial development in light of the substantial increase in black illegitimate births over the past several decades. Possibly one third or more births in black ghettos are of this character.

This rise in illegitimacy must be viewed against the *decreasing* ability of the urban slum black male to maintain steady employment and sustain the role of married head of the household.[24] Unemployment, particularly severe in slum areas, falls most heavily on the unskilled, the young, the high school dropouts. Black urban populations are younger than white and contain potentially more able-bodied workers. Paradoxically, next to "urbanized" American Indians, they contain the highest proportions of unemployed. Insufficient education, lack of employment, underemployment, and, for many, depleted energies and ego stamina needed to cope with the frustrating urban environment are prime factors affecting urban black family organization. This is particularly the case in the inlying cores of metropolitan central cities.

Matricentric Adaptation

The three central factors seen as providing the basis for a mother-centered urban black family are, then: (1) ghettoization, and consequent *isolation* of blacks in central city cores; (2) economic insecurity, partly a function of sluggish national economic growth, partly caused by job discrimination, and partly a consequence of labor-saving technology claiming unskilled and low-skilled black males as heaviest casualties; and (3) a growing disparity between black female and male occupational life chances, with the male having fallen behind.[25]

In the face of these contingencies, the pattern of response by the blacks of the ghetto has been to combine elements of a traditional form of family organization—the matriarchal family—with indigenously developed adaptations. Significantly, this alternative form will exhibit behavioral patterns that are not supported by deeply held norms. The adaptations are essentially external. They represent things people *can* do to get them past daily contingencies and life crises, but not necessarily what, in keeping with general normative prescriptions, they feel they *ought* to do.

Family Structure: Marriage Institution

A fragile monogamy severely compromised by even less permanently institutionalized marital attachments characterizes the marriage institution of the adaptive urban matricentric family. The black female is the pivotal figure; it is she who makes, often has to make, the decision to accept or demand a marriage partner. But, since a shortage of eligible adult and young adult males disposed to marry is also chronic in the core areas of the black urban communities the female may have to settle for less than the best in a mate. Conversely, the male may and can play the field. A tendency for the more economically stable or prosperous urban blacks, as well as for most whites, to avoid involvement with core-area blacks and to permit institutions to grow and develop independently, often tangentially to the mainstream of American culture, has contributed to the distinctiveness of the subculture that is emerging in the central cities.

The tenuous character of the black husband's role leads to the building of the effective household unit around wife, her children, and often her mother. These arrangements are not necessarily defined as ideal; they may often be makeshift. For example, after having been absent for weeks or months a husband will often return home and try again to be the head of the household.[26] But by doing so he may jeopardize his wife's welfare allowance for their dependent children.

Family Structure: Family and Kinship

A modified extended family[27] built around the mother-daughter relationship and usually extending through three generations is the modal form of organization for the adaptive family. The very large matriarchal family with a number of daughters, children, and possibly husbands under one roof, presided over by the wise and authoritative "granny" is infrequently encountered. Neither is the completely isolated nuclear family, with husband, wife, and a few children, separated by choice from kin ties and local attachments, very much in evidence. Rather, when looking across the broadest continuous segment of the family life cycle, on finds in the adaptive family one or more married daughters, sharing with the mother under a common roof the responsibility for support and socialization of the children. The father, in such a family, occasionally present, often itinerant or permanently absent, plays the weakest or most incidental role of all the adult principals. The patronymic is respected but its meaning lies essentially in the respectability conferred on children and not as a device for reinforcing patriarchial authority.

Residence, in the long run, tends to follow the neolocal-matrilocal pattern. Ideally, the first residence of the married couple will be outside the wife's mother's household but not necessarily far from it. Children have great freedom and are encouraged frequently to visit aunts, grandmothers, great-grandmothers. If such relatives are nearby, the pattern of visiting both for children and adults is informal, selective, and, to some extent, haphazard. If they are distant the family itself may make extended visits. Households are, in terms of access and life space, very much open—to relatives, friends, acquaintances, friends of friends, and so forth. Relatives, particularly maternal, introject themselves into the operations of each other's families; older generations feel free, if not obligated, to offer advice to the younger, and not infrequently a child will be sent to live with a maternal aunt or grandmother.

Family Life Cycle: Mate Selection

Marriages in the adaptive urban matricentric black family take place at a somewhat earlier age than for blacks generally. Mate selection is a serious matter, but it is preceded by a number of steps involving peer-group associations. Rainwater found that adolescents tend to become deeply involved in their peer-group societies beginning as early as the age of twelve or thirteen, and they continue to be involved even after first pregnancies and first marriages.[28] Both sexes become heavily committed to peer-group activities and are introduced to a wide range of experiences. Adult black society, in contrast to white, is much less closed to black adolescents. The behavior of the latter "more often represents an identification with the behavior of adults than an attempt to set up group standards and activities that differ from those of adults."[29]

Boys and young men seek to enhance status and self through participation in street games. In verbal contests those male youths who can claim and demonstrate success in gaining sexual favors from and dominance over females are much admired. They are thus ranked according to their success in seduction, and to survive in the peer group they must develop an ability to "make out" in talk, if not physically, with the opposite sex.

The girls, according to Rainwater "are propelled toward boys and men in order to demonstrate their maturity and attractiveness." But not wishing to be taken advantage of or to get into trouble, they approach sex relations ambivalently, and few, if any, are disposed toward outright sexual promiscuity. The boy seeks to build up his "rep" and the girl seeks to limit her sexual relations to as few boys as possible. Competitiveness, aggression, ambivalence, status striving, physical enjoyment, and persuasion all in one way or another enter the picture.

Life Cycle: Pregnancy and Parenthood

The second stage in the formation of families, notes Rainwater, is that of premarital pregnancy.[30] If the girl is fortunate, the step may be avoided. But premature pregnancy is not the catastrophe that it would be for acculturated middle-majority blacks. Parents, who have been cautioning the daughter against such hazards and now find their fears justified, nevertheless know what to do. Usually the girl will continue to live at home and her mother will take the major responsibility for rearing the child—or children. Pregnancy becomes a measure of maturity for the girl, but once the baby is in the care of the grandmother, who may well be only in her middle or late thirties, the unwed mother can resume activities with her peer group.

Inasmuch as it is not necessary to have a man around the house in order to have and rear children, the decision to marry may be considered apart from the necessity to give the child a father. But the designation of the child's father is felt necessary—for the sake of the child. Not to know who one's father is seems "the ultimate in illegitimacy."[31]

For the youth to father a child means the creation of a new bond between himself and the girl. It is asymmetrical, however, in the sense that his claims for affection and fidelity are the more binding. In any event, and as with most groups in the broader society, marriage challenges peer-group loyalties and constitutes a threat to its cohesion.

Marriage, as noted, is approached ambivalently. The security of her own home is appealing to the girl, and the contingencies and uncertainties of setting up an independent household are often intimidating. The long peer-group associations have not socialized either boy or girl sufficiently to permit adult parent roles to be firmly internalized. Past histories of marriages of friends and relatives give little comfort to the couple. And, finally, the young male must face the prospect of uncertain occupational life chances. Thus, marriages are likely to be impulsive; prudent judgment and prolonged consideration, in most cases, would militate against the step. Once married, and on their own, the young couple find it indeed hard to prevent marital disruption.

Life Cycle: Parents at Work

A steady job at good wages in desirable work surroundings is a rarity for black males of the central-city core area. The wife's chances for congenial employment are considerably better. Most wives in the adaptive family work after marriage. Eventually the wife finds herself burdened with increasing responsibilities for household management, socialization, *and* breadwinning. The wife, therefore, is as likely to send her husband away as he is to desert a family that, from the beginning, he was never too confident of heading. Rainwater has found wives showing little respect for husbands who have fallen into unemployment. It is almost a marital maxim that if the husband cannot win bread he cannot take up the house and life space of the wife. If she does not make this plain he nevertheless accepts this as the code of his group. As the husband is increasingly less present in the house, the street and tavern claim more of his time. Philandering, drinking, and getting into scrapes become substitute activities for his former life style, which, though more desired, is now almost impossible to attain. Eventually he appears at home only after drinking; at such times argument and violence become the final elements of discord as the marriage shatters. Or the husband may quietly drop out of the picture and join thousands of other homeless males who are lost to the ongoing society and are often missed by its last and least personally involved representative, the census taker.

Life Cycle: Role of Women

The life cycle for the female who becomes the focal point of the adaptive family type has two prolonged stages. Following a relatively brief and—as much as possible—sheltered childhood, she finds herself involved deeply in her peer group for as long as two decades. Heterosexual association, sexual exploitation, pregnancy, even marriage, figure prominently in this stage, but the overriding consideration is the dominance of peer-group commitment. As she enters the job market and as her children grow up, she finds the mother-manager-breadwinner role demanding more of her time. Her adolescent children ignore her most of the time, and, following her example, enter the street and peer culture well before puberty. Before she has had time to establish and sustain—and be sustained by—the mother role, she faces the pregnancy of her own daughters. Her maternal role has been overlaid by her continued peer-group associations, and, like childhood in comparison with the larger society, is relatively short. But as a woman in her late thirties, she will probably have to face two or three more decades of responsible involvement with daughter's children and even grandchildren.

What must give way is the engrossing outside life of the peer group. Clubs, associations, "sets," the street, cabarets, friends' homes, movie houses, and shops can no longer monopolize her time. By now a mate or several husbands have come and gone. Home life, more time-consuming and engrossing, is made more congenial, with male companions or a "friend" who lives in but does not present the complications of a husband.

Problems of the Two Family Types

Socialization and Identity

Since a primary function of the family is the socialization of the young so that they develop a firm sense of who they are and what they can and perhaps should do in an ongoing society, we might examine the manner in which this problem is met in the two family types.

In the adaptive urban matricentric family, the absence or weak presence of the father hampers the development of the masculine ego. Mothers hold most of the power to award or withhold emotional gratification and often find difficulty in giving equal shares of response and recognition to the male children. In default of a strong father figure, and immersed in an expressive or acting-out subculture, male youth exchange the mother-dominated restricted family life for the peer group, street activities, and the colorful, sometimes violent, tenor of life of the adult world. Both male and female find themselves inside a large world they cannot completely adapt to their needs, a world that frustrates ambition, confidence, respect for others, and ultimately self-respect. Females must adopt a sense of wariness, males of opportunism—to "make out" at any point in time, but with little sense of life continuity. It is thus, as Rainwater observes, such gratifications as the children in the matricentric family can obtain must be procured deviously, and without necessarily adding to one's self-respect.

Yet there *is* survival and at some periods there may be more than precarious existence. The young children, for example, experience a rather casual upbringing—far different from the intense, anxious concern of middle-class parents for their infants. This may have its advantages. At a different level of concern, if the work force continues to absorb more females and reject more males, the coping qualities found in matricentric families may deserve closer study and greater appreciation. Perhaps most impressive is the continued human involvement of adult and aged females in an active, ongoing, family-centered world, and the utilization of makeshift substitute husbands—boyfriends—as old age companions. Thus, what are difficult problems at one stage in the life cycle give way to reasonable adaptations and inventive solutions in another. For a youth-centered, achievement-oriented society, however, the matricentric adaptation to urban black life conditions remains an alternative of dubious continuing value.

The acculturated middle-majority family bears a responsibility for socialization that is difficult to overestimate. The necessary product, a person of firm ego, with a well developed sense of adult role-identification and a strong enough sense of morality and purpose to propel him into leadership for just causes, is defined as worthy and necessary across nearly *all* levels of black society. The peer group, school, and other formal groups may or may not play supportive and integrative roles. Since the institutional realms representing the middle-majority white society have yet to work out appropriate means of adult socialization of the black members who come within them, an even stronger ego identity for the latter may be required. Thus the responsibility is thrust back to the family and other primary agencies. And, it should not be forgotten that the equalitarian impulses of acculturated family members have yet to become organized into a viable system of role differentiation and tension management.

Conversion at Mass Level?

Finally, at the mass-behavior level, there is evidence that with respect to consumption of goods and services economically successful black Americans are moving toward the middle-majority white life style, and giving up rapidly what has been called the Negro market. The newer consumption patterns of blacks, with more stress on life insurance, retirement funds, house purchases, and general upgrading of living standards, suggest a value conversion toward family, home and community status. Although less heralded than other changes in the social world of the black American, these new consumer changes might well mark one of the more important bases for the development of a further acculturated black family.

Nevertheless the evidence for polarization of the two family types remains impressive. Particularly notable is the increasing concentration of poverty in the predominantly black-inhabited central-city cores. The process is marked not only by the migration of more successful blacks toward the perimeters of black residential areas—seeking to expand these—but also by the migration of industry to the city's suburbs and beyond. Since newly located industries are likely to be more automated than those left behind, the number of low-skilled employees needed decreases. Not only do central-city blacks suffer unemployment, but those retaining their jobs must face the prospect of a longer journey to work or moving of their household. And those searching for work, in addition to color discrimination, are further disadvantaged by having to seek work farther and farther from home. These socio-economic-logistic factors operate to isolate further and economically depress those blacks who are already most vulnerable to the vicissitudes of a dynamic society. For many the situation is desperate.

The adaptive urban matricentric family is a fusing amalgam of many social elements. To some extent it contains elements of a *genus of family found wherever there are poverty-stricken people.* It also reflects the adaptation of historical practice to modern exigency. In addition, indigenously developed folkways are obviously present. Finally, the adaptive family draws from, and is immersed in, an expressive church, club, cabaret, and, more recently, protest *mass* black culture. The elements do not combine into an institutionalized family type; rather, they hang together in a dynamic state of quasi-organization, continually subject to the play of economic and social forces. Thus, the adaptive, nonacculturative elements of family organization, in the last analysis, are likely to persist just to the extent that prejudice, discrimination, and economic disadvantage remain the lot of the central-city black.

Section 4

The Family and Its Alternatives

For most middle-class Americans, the term "family" evokes the stereotypic image of a nuclear family consisting of a dominant father, a mother, and several children. Yet there are numerous family structures that exist in the United States as well as varying philosophies of what the ideal family should be.

The extended family, in which several generations live and work together, exists in the United States in rural settings and to some extent among the Mexican-American population. Some members of the younger generation advocate a return to a similar system by establishing communal living groups or group marriages. However, the communal living groups found among contemporary American youth tend to be composed of young persons and perhaps their children, two generations at most. The traditional extended family included all age levels through several generations.

The "hang-loose" ethic of a portion of the American population often encourages freer sexual mores, temporary liaisons, and the establishment of families without legal sanctions, i.e., living together.

The demands made by the more militant women's liberation groups will certainly effect some change in the traditional family power structure as male and female roles change and interchange.

Although the pessimists have long interpreted change in the traditional family structure as a prelude to the disintegration of the family, historians have demonstrated the continuing viability of the family and its ability to exist in many forms and still fulfill its role as a primary institution within a culture. Alvin Toffler in *Future Shock* observes that

> "The family of the future will take on many forms. Some people, no doubt, will continue to marry for life and make a success of it. But we will also see a rash of experimentation with newer arrangements from operative communes, corporate families, and temporary marriage, to legally sanctioned rearing of adoptive children by homosexuals (and single persons)."[1]

The purpose of this section is to consider some of these varying family forms. Despite the mass media's continual discussion of atypical family forms, it should be remembered that the vast majority of Americans live in the traditional nuclear family composed of husband, wife, and children.

There is much concern in America over human rights. The family is the major transmitter of one's basic philosophy of life. Thus one's attitude toward the concept of human rights derives in large part from the family in which he is reared. Despite the outcry of criticism from youth about their parents and the family structure, the families of the 1950's may be remembered as having uniquely produced children that are socially aware, concerned, and active in securing human rights for all. Concerns such as Chisholm's may already have been met by the American family.

... the immensely difficult sensitive tasks of helping the young grow beyond their own families, their own culture, and beyond their own capacity, if they are to ever learn how to see things from the other's point of view. This *must* be done if Americans are to learn to relate properly and in a planned sense, to their environment, to themselves, and to their fellow man, a matter of cultural, personal and social health.[2]

Of course, only with time will we be able to make an accurate judgment as to how free our children really are and how responsible they will be with their new freedom.

It seems appropriate then to start this section by considering human rights and the role of the family in their achievement. Goode's concern in the following article is twofold: the influence of the larger society upon the rights of individual family members, and the influence which family life itself has on human rights in the larger society. He points out that stratification systems have been supported by certain family patterns such as control of mate selection by the elders, bride price, dowry, and proscription against inter-class marriage. Recognition of such forces is one reason why doctrinaire revolutionists are so preoccupied with changes in family patterns.

17 Family Patterns and Human Rights

William J. Goode

Goode asks two questions in this article:

1. What kinds of family patterns are most likely to support full implementation of human rights?
2. What kinds of family patterns would the full implementation of a human rights' program create?

He devotes the first several paragraphs to the problem of human rights as a specific part of social structure, a social subsystem in itself. He points out that stratification systems have been largely supported by family structure in the past and this fact accounts for revolutionary movements attempting to change basic traditional family patterns.

Every rigid stratification system, erecting barriers against the able poor, has relied on a highly controlled family system as its base, whether we look in the past at Tokugawa, Japan, or in the present at India. The family system is the keystone of every stratification system. Very likely, every utopia conceived by man has in imagination changed the existing family system. Every wise man has also said that to transform a society it is necessary to rear the children differently, to socialize them for a new set of role obligations.

Since those who are concerned with human rights are not likely to be in positions of power, and therefore are more likely to view with alarm than to point with pride to accomplishments, it is perhaps useful to assert that at least in this one crucial area of human rights a considerable revolution is taking place. Though the facts noted here are well known to students of social change, and have been documented in great detail elsewhere, it is worth while to summarize some of the areas in which human rights relative to family patterns have been extended over the past half century.[1] Let me simply list the main points of change here.

Mate choice. Prior to the Chinese Revolution of 1911, it is safe to say, most marriages in the world were arranged by the parents of the couple. A high but unknown proportion of the girls who married were given little or no choice because they were married in their early 'teens. Since that time, and at an increasing tempo since the Second World War, young people in every major area of the world have gradually come to have a voice in this important decision.

From "Family Patterns and Human Rights" by William J. Goode which appeared in the *International Social Science Journal,* Volume XVIII, No. 1 (1966). Reproduced by permission of Unesco.

Bride price or dowry. Linked with parental arrangement of marriages in most societies was some type of dowry or bride price. These were not typically purchases, of course, but merely reflected the economic stake of the elders in the alliance between families. As young people have come to make their own choices, they have also begun to reject such exchanges, thereby achieving a greater freedom of choice in their own lives.

Inter-caste and inter-class marriage. Barriers to inter-caste and inter-class marriages have been rooted in custom as well as law. In almost all parts of the world the legal barriers have been eliminated, and custom has been eroded, too, under the impact of the freedom of choice given to young people. That most marriages will continue to be intra-caste and intra-class goes without saying, but the individual has a wider range of alternatives open than a half century ago.

Control by elders and other kin. Most social systems, including those of great nations such as China, India, Japan and the Arab countries, permitted by law and custom a rather wide control by elders over the young. These areas included geographical mobility, occupational choice, the level of education to be achieved, the allocation of income, and the participation in religious rituals, not to mention more trivial matters. Of course, even in the most industrialized of nations the network of kin plays an important role in the lives of married couples, but in most countries the adult now has a greater freedom in choosing which relatives he will support or listen to. In these respects, India remains perhaps most laggard among the great nations. In perhaps no country can young adults ignore their elders without personal cost, but in most they can obtain jobs without the blessing of their elders, and need not remain in tutelage until their elders die.

Inheritance. Although it may be asserted that any inheritance system which permits much property to pass from one generation to the next within the same family gives an advantage to one set of people and thereby restricts the freedom of another set, some steps toward freedom in this area may be noted. In traditional societies, there is little testamentary freedom, since the direction of inheritance is clear and fixed: e.g., equal inheritance among sons in China, primogeniture among *samurai* in Tokugawa, Japan, inheritance by brothers from the brothers of the previous generation in India, and so on. However, the modern civil codes have increasingly granted testamentary freedom. In addition, most of these great societies omitted the female almost altogether. Islam did not, of course, but the girl received a half-share. The newer civil codes have moved steadily toward granting equal inheritance to all children, and widows have come to be recognized even in societies that were once only patrilineal.

Contraception. The right to choose whether one will bear children, or how many, has until recently been granted to only a minority of the world's population. That some will wish to bear many children in order to obey a religious injunction need not be questioned, but equally no advocate of human rights would wish to condemn a couple to having more children than they wish. The threat of over-population has stimulated many campaigns which are gradually opening this area of choice to the peoples of the world. It is also worth mentioning here that this is especially an area in which women have not been permitted any choice, although the burden of children was theirs. Numerous studies have shown that even in areas of high birth rates most women are generally willing, and more than men are, to limit their families.

Abortion. Most countries continue to deny the right of the woman, in the event of an unwanted pregnancy, to end it. This freedom has been most widely granted in the Communist countries and in Japan, with somewhat less tolerance in the Scandinavian nations. Various arguments are currently used to support the prohibition against free choice in this area, although without question open debate about the issue is much more acceptable than a generation ago.

Divorce. It is surely a denial of choice if individuals are forced to remain in a marriage they dislike, and at the present time almost all of the world's population is permitted by law to divorce. In India, brahmins were not permitted to divorce, though some divorce did occur, and lower castes did have that permission. Of course, in India as in other nations permitting no divorce the husband typically had or has other alternatives open to him, such as concubines, second wives, and so on. The Westerner should keep in mind, however, that some nations and cultures did permit divorce before the modern era. Islam traditionally gave the husband great freedom to divorce, and divorce rates were very high among the farmers in Tokugawa and Meiji, Japan. Both of these were patrilineal societies. Matrilineal societies have ordinarily been relatively permissive regarding divorce.

Egalitarianism within the family. Although there is little quantitative evidence on this point, almost all observers seem to agree that in almost all nations the woman has been given greater authority, respect and freedom within the family, and this relaxing of a patriarchal tradition has also improved the position of children. As will be noted later, the ideology of familial egalitarianism has its source in a broader stream of radical thought, and its impact can be observed in most countries. One of the most striking consequences of this change has been that women have come to be permitted to occupy responsible positions outside the family. Again it is difficult to quantify such matters, but it seems likely that egalitarianism in the occupational sphere has spread most rapidly in the socialist countries. It must be emphasized that I am not referring to 'women in the labour force.' After all, women have borne heavy burdens in all epochs and countries. Rather, I am pointing to a radically different phenomenon, the right of a woman to obtain a job (and the training necessary for it) and to be promoted within it, on the basis of her own merits without the permission of her husband or father. Needless to say, this factor supports egalitarianism within the family, since it reduces the dependence of women on the males, but it also creates a new respect for the woman as an individual.

Of course, with reference to all of these, the new civil codes are more advanced than the actual behaviour and attitudes of the populations concerned. The codes and new administrative rules are written by a new élite, who intend to lead these populations toward new types of family relations, but the process is relatively slow.

Moreover, it is not clear just how far such changes can go, whatever the ideological campaigns or the economic pressures. All such moves are purchased at some costs, and these may rise too high to be tolerated. It seems unlikely, for example, that any society can completely eliminate the parent-child bond as a way of creating the new civic man without particularistic ties to hamper the political programme. I doubt, too, that any society will in our lifetime be able to create genuine egalitarian relations between men and women.

In addition, we must keep in mind that each of these freedoms is a loss to someone, and most of them reduce the individual's emotional and even financial security. For the former, there may be no structural substitute. For the latter, various types of social welfare and pension programmes may suffice.

Even after taking note of these qualifications, we must concede, nevertheless, that the trends noted are steps toward the securing of human rights. Granted, they do not at first glance seem to be so dramatic or spectacular as the freeing of slaves or the abolition of a feudal system. On the other hand, those liberations may in fact have consequences similar to those of such grander political acts. If one could construct a numerical index, I would predict that the extensions of human rights to women and children in their domestic and occupational roles would loom as large as any other single step in the contemporary fight for human rights—certainly, far more real progress than has occurred in the areas of freedom of speech, religion, and publication, or the right of free elections or assembly. That step added as much or more to the economic production of the nations in which it has taken place and, very likely, at levels which we cannot easily explore here, helped to lay a firmer foundation for human rights in still other areas.

One of these levels does deserve brief attention here, which is that most of these extensions of human rights in the family area have not occurred only passively, but have been impelled by a positive and radical ideology of the family, which grows from but feeds back into a radical ideology of human relations in society.

The ideology of the conjugal family, as it is expressed in debates about family trends over much of the world, asserts the worth of the individual against the claims of caste, clan, or social stratum. It proclaims egalitarianism and the right to take part in important decisions. It urges new rights for women and children, and for adult males against the traditional claims of their elder kin. It demands the right to change exploitative relations among people.

. . .

However, we cannot evade the more problematic questions which I raised at the beginning of this paper. Even if most family systems of the world are moving toward granting more human rights to their members, can we assert that any particular kinds of family patterns or relations will produce a higher percentage of adults who will support the claims of their fellow citizens to the full enjoyment of human rights in the broader civic realm? Or, in a less cautious formulation, is it likely that the early experiences of the child in the family have *no* relationship with the willingness of the later adult to grant tolerance, freedom, and protection to others? Or, in a more utopian query, what type of family pattern would be most likely to produce adults who could live up to the really difficult role obligations that are demanded by the full extension of human rights to all?

The difficult task of socialization is not the inculcation of a love for one's personal freedom, which may be an easy goal: after all, any animal prefers at the outset to be free. But training children to support others' freedom and rights requires a more complex psychological and social pattern. Does any type of family pattern do that? Perhaps we might begin by taking note of a speculation often made by social philosophers and sociologists, essentially that extreme familism denies human rights to others. That is, when individuals are reared largely within the family and derive almost all of their satisfactions there, they are likely to overvalue the ingroup—the ethnic group, the tribe, the region. Consequently, they feel free to treat outsiders as of little value, not deserving of any protection. An extreme form of this unwillingness to grant human rights to others may be found in many peasant regions.

This suggestion, which we may explore at a later point, that immersion in the family unit fosters intense ethnocentric attitudes that run counter to the role obligations of human rights, also receives some slight support from the finding that children are more likely to be democratic in their social behavior if they spend more of their time with peers (who have roughly equal power) than with parents, who have superior power (we shall, however, consider this point).

This general hypothesis seems to be roughly correct, if not precisely stated, and of course many essays in the Western world have called on this and prior generations to abjure their loyalties to family and clan, in order to embrace a loyalty to all humanity.

However, the renunciation of extreme familism is hardly sufficient as a directive for rearing children who will support human rights. Speculatively, one would suppose that a high degree of permissiveness and egalitarianism within the family would be more likely to produce individuals who could not adjust easily to a repressive political system, or who would not create such a system.

Without attempting to summarize a considerable mass of data and critiques,[2] well known to the student of human rights, let me simply remind you of the central suggestions in those studies. By and large, they have asked the question, what kinds of socialization experiences create the type of personality that is most prone to deny human rights to Jews, Negroes and other ethnic groups? However, the answers suggest parallel hypotheses about the denial of human rights generally.

Authoritarian control of the family by the father is correlated with such traits as these: deification of the parent, high evaluation of the father role, the child's passive adjustment to the present situation, the suppression of the child's aggression, suppression of sexual impulses in the child, and the fostering of dependency in the child. 'Democratic' attitudes of fathers correlate with egalitarian treatment of children, encouragement of their independence, and affection as a means of control.[3]

Adults who exhibit intolerance of others' rights are more likely than other adults to have grown up under authoritarian parental control and, of course, to continue that tradition with their own children. The stereotyping that is so characteristic of those who consider people who differ from themselves as having few redeeming traits is emphasized by parental efforts to ascribe fixed, clearly distinct, traits to the two sexes; indeed, the more authoritarian the mother's attitudes, the greater the children's imitation of the like-sex parent.[4]

Additional suggestions as to the kinds of family relations that might maximize the support of human rights can be derived from Allport's description of the 'tolerant' personality,[5] which summarizes the findings of many studies. Perhaps central is the necessity of family interaction based on security and love, rather than threat, and that concedes the right of individuals to have pleasure without guilt. Under a régime of threat, the child—and later, the adult—feels the need to have precise instructions, for fear of making errors and being punished for it. There is, then, an intolerance of ambiguity, whereas in a society that guarantees human rights the individual must be able to interact with others without at all knowing exactly what they will do in turn; more important and more specific, the individual does not have to interact with them as members of neat categories, such as 'Communist,' 'deviationist,' 'bourgeois formalist,' 'decadent imperialist,' 'Jew,' 'Moslem,' and so on. Similarly, in such families, individuals are conceded to have their own unique traits, and not to be forced rigidly into the categories of 'male' and 'female'—for example, chores might be shared on the basis of need and capacity, rather than sex.

Given greater security in affection, and the right to have pleasure without guilt, the individual's tolerance of frustration is greater, and his need to attack others when things go wrong will be less. Thus, he is less likely to approve any denial of human rights to those who differ in political or other beliefs. In more technical terms he will have less repressed aggression, and less need to displace it against people who have not directly harmed him.

Certain family experiences do seem to correlate with some of the attitudes necessary for democratic participation in civic life.[6] Generally, a higher percentage of the people in countries granting more secure human rights feel that they were free as children to participate in family decisions. This finding parallels Allport's suggestion that in the family which fosters tolerance in a child the junior members are permitted to be critical. They need not dread the superior power of the parent.[7]

In addition, Almond and Verba report that a higher percentage also felt that they actually had some influence on these decisions, and were free to complain about matters if they did not like them. Correspondingly, a higher percentage actually did complain.

These findings also parallel the findings of several studies in the United States of America, showing that there is higher tolerance of deviance and a greater willingness to give civic rights to people with radical opinions, toward the upper social strata, whether this is defined by education or by holding positions of leadership. For it is also in such strata that the ideology and practice of sharing family decisions is more widely found.[8] Toward the upper strata, a higher percentage of adults felt that as children they were able to complain, and did so.

Those who participated in family decisions also feel more competent as adults to influence their own governments.[9] It is worth noting that this correlation is weaker within the higher educational levels, where other types of experiences may supplement any lack of participation within the family itself.

Bearing in mind that we are not searching for the most effective ways of developing the superego in the child, but a particular superego content, let us further suggest (on the basis of research outside the family, but supported by investigations carried out by Kurt Lewin, Ronald Lippitt and many others over the past ten years in a wide range of organizational settings) that a collaborative style of rearing is more likely to create adults who respect the wishes and contributions of others. By contrast, the autocracy that a Luther rejects in his father and his church simply re-emerges in his own pattern of repression as well as in his notion of fixed statuses and duties imposed by fiat.

One of the likely consequences of the collaborative style, in which parents and children cooperate to solve problems, is the development of faith or trust in other people. This, in turn, as most readers know, is negatively correlated with authoritarianism. Faith in people, it is interesting to note here, appears to be highest in countries in which human rights are more secure.[10]

A complex relationship exists between these factors and love. The manipulation of love is one of the most effective techniques for developing a strong superego, but there is some evidence that the threat of love withdrawal creates many psychological problems. Among these is a distrust of others. If love is dependent, for example, on performance, performance may be high but regression is also a possible outcome. It seems likely that the security of parental love must be great enough to permit the child to face aggression by parent or outsider without great anxiety. The ability to face hostility without any inner compulsion to aggress against those who oppose; or without any inner compulsion to bow to that opposition when it is powerful (seeking love by compliance) can be most effectively based on security in parental love.

This security would appear to be based, in turn, on conveying to the child that he is loved as a unique person, not because of his status as elder or younger, male or female. The recognition that each member of the family is unique, with his or her own needs and demands, rather than merely a set of ascribed statuses, should contribute to the generalized feeling that other individuals are also unique: they need not be manipulated to serve one's own needs, or rejected as outcasts.

Such a security has an added by-product of some consequence in the broader area of human rights. When adults or children fail to live up to the norms they themselves claim to accept, it is unlikely that they can face that fact, or improve their behaviour, if they can develop some kind of legitimation or rationalization for the discrepancy. As has been widely demonstrated, those who discriminate against others often assert nondiscriminatory norms, and avoid confronting the divergence between their behaviour and their norms. Thus they protect themselves against the strain of actually living up to those standards in the civic realm. It is unlikely that many individuals can achieve such a confrontation unless they have been given a considerable internal security, specifically a feeling that they are loved in spite of moral lapses.

This last point is linked, in turn, with a widely held psychodynamic notion, that self-acceptance is the strongest foundation for the acceptance of others. The child whose parents hammer into him a sense of his pervasive and continual moral failure is much less likely to accept himself as well as others. Reciprocally, those who as adults are authoritarian are more likely than others to express low evaluations of their own parents.[11] With reference to an hypothesis stated earlier, that intense familism is likely to be associated with an unwillingness to grant human rights to strangers, it should be noted that the personal autonomy arising from security permits the individual to be able to leave the family, to feel secure outside it, to trust even the stranger.

Finally, a collaborative style of family relations requires that youngsters take into account the needs and feelings of others. They become, therefore, more skilled at empathy. The authoritarian is less able to intuit correctly the attitudes and emotions of others. Correspondingly, it is not surprising that children from more democratic homes tend to be more popular among their peers than are children from authoritarian homes.[12]

But though such suggestions may be correct, and certainly deserve to be tested and made more precise by cross-cultural research, to persuade parents in many countries to change their ways is a difficult task. It is easier to push a highway through a jungle, or to purify a water supply, than to alter the details of family relations, as we know already from the repeated failures of birth control campaigns. Traditional parents are not more willing to share their authority with their children than are husbands to yield control over their wives. It is likely that the contemporary transformations in the political, economic, and social macrostructures of most nations will ultimately have more impact on the microstructure of the family than will any particular programme aimed at changing those internal relations of the family.

Equally ambiguous are the relations between personality variables and those of the larger social structure. No one has as yet succeeded in showing that personalities of particular types will create particular kinds of societies. Although adults who were reared under the ideal conditions sketched above would probably be more inclined to support human rights, it is not clear that traditional patriarchal, even authoritarian, family relations necessarily create authoritarian political and social structures. Perhaps the German family system contributed, as so many analysts claimed, to Nazism, but the Swiss, Dutch, French, Swedish and Belgian families were hardly less patriarchal or authoritarian.[13]

Nor can we cite as evidence the efforts of totalitarian régimes to control their family systems in order to gain support for their political system. Specifically, systems of high political control often do try to subordinate the individual directly to the state, by-passing the family where possible; and they also try to enlist the family members in campaigns to bring the apathetic or dissident members in line.

Such events prove, however, no more than that revolutionary leaders will use whatever instrumentalities they can command. Whether their hypotheses were correct is a separate matter for study. At present we do not know that these particular family experiences helped to produce adults who would wish to impose a repressive political control over others.

I think that these qualifications and doubts need not arouse pessimism as to the future of human rights in the world. For though the revolutions in many countries have merely substituted a tight political control in place of the old-fashioned, looser despotism, almost all of these new programmes have promised freedom, and derive much of their support from an ideology of human rights. Ultimately, they will have to fulfil the terms of that implicit contract.

Perhaps, at a still more fundamental level, the family patterns that are being preached in these countries and the trends that are now visible are precisely those most likely to produce a next generation which would rebel still more strongly against political repression, and would support more firmly a programme of human rights. Thus, the revolutionary ideologies of egalitarianism do more than accentuate those trends toward human rights in the limited area of family relations, but reciprocally, the new patterns of family relations will also produce individuals who are more likely to put into effect and uphold a broad programme of human rights. It is possible, then, that the changes in family patterns over the past half century are not only important in themselves;

they may also act as a catalyst that will eventually transform the massive flux of modern revolution into a clear movement toward greater human freedom.

In order to achieve the kind of social goals Goode discusses, it is obvious that the individual must be able to grow and become self-actualizing within the family. If the family can foster and encourage the growth of creative, self-actualizing individuals, such individuals can, in turn, foster a viable and creative society.

In the next selection, Olim examines the concept of self-actualization and extends it to a conception of "the fully functioning family."

18 The Self-Actualizing Person in the Fully Functioning Family: A Humanistic Viewpoint

Ellis G. Olim

Dr. Olim is Associate Professor and head of the Department of Human Development at the University of Massachusetts.

Any discussion of the American family today must take place within the context of what many observers regard as a crisis or, at best, a troublesome time of questioning and transition. We are beset by social unrest, the repolarization of racial attitudes, the disarray and underfinancing of our public school system and public health services, student revolts, dissent and civil disobedience, the pollution of our air and water supplies, crime in the cities and towns, experimentation with drugs, experimentation with new forms of social structure,[1] and alarm over both birth and abortion rates. This litany of troubles, it seems, adds up to a crisis. The crisis is occurring in the decade we call an "age of affluence." There is a connection between the affluence and the crisis, but not all would agree on what the salient features of that connection are, and even fewer perhaps would agree on the conclusions to be drawn from the connection.

.   .   .

From "The Self-Actualizing Person in the Fully Functioning Family: A Humanistic Viewpoint," by Ellis G. Olim, Associate Professor of Human Development and Head of the Department of Human Development, University of Massachusetts, article appearing in *The Family Coordinator,* Volume 13, No. 3 (July, 1968), reprinted by permission of author and publisher.

Man as Becoming

The view to which we subscribe is that man has a rendezvous only with the future. What we need today is a conception of man that is suitable for the world of tomorrow. We cannot accept the conception that parents know what is right and what is wrong, that they know what limits to impose on their children. Parents do not necessarily and automatically know what is good for the child, nor what is the good and what is the bad. And we certainly cannot accept today, in the face of research and clinical observation to the contrary, the idea that punishment and deprivation are good for children. True, if particular types of behavior intrinsically lead to unfortunate consequences for the individual, such punishment probably has some values. However, if punishment or deprivation is perpetrated by an agent, such as a parent or a teacher, there are unfortunate side effects, one of which is resentment and rebelliousness against the punisher. Of course the punishment may work in the short run but the undesirable behavior is merely driven underground, usually ready to reappear when the punisher is absent. If the internalization by the child of his conception of the parents' moral code is *too* effective, so that the child is a life-long victim of a harsh superego (Freud's conscience), the underground, undesirable behavior may never reappear, but in such instances, substitute forms will appear. In such cases, the victim is doomed to live in purgatory all his life, cheating himself of the opportunity to live fully and spontaneously.

We do have a new conception of man. It is a conception that enables us to go forward into the future instead of trying to hold back the course of human development. This new conception is that man is constantly becoming. Man need not be a fixed outcome of environmental influences except in the case of the abnormal man who suffers from being fixated at a level of personality development from which he cannot rise, or in the case of men in those preliterate societies which were static, which remained the same over thousands of years. But it is a truism that our society is an evolving one, constantly changing, an open society. Our society challenges its members to develop a flexible stance, a stance that enables them to adapt to changing conditions. What we want, then, is not to encourage a static type of personality based on traditional notions of right and wrong, but the kind of person who is able to go forward into the uncertain future. The man of the future should be self-actualizing. This means that he should ever be moving toward a greater realization of his human potential and, equally important, that he be constantly transcending himself. The idea of self-transcendence has two meanings. In one sense, it means that man should overcome his egocentricity and enlarge his self to include concern with humankind. Its other, more modern, sense is that man is in a constant process of evolving into higher and higher forms of humanness, that his self is constantly going beyond previous selves. Man's human potential is not finite; it is infinite. There are no limits to the process of becoming.

Thus, Maslow[2] talks of the "self-actualized" person; Rogers[3] of the "fully functioning" individual; Allport of man as having a "passion for integrity and for a meaningful relation to the whole of Being in his most distinctive capacity,"[4] Sullivan[5] of the basic direction of the organism as forward; Horney of the powerful incentive "to realize given potentialities," "an incentive to grow."[6]

.   .   .

The Humanist's Conception of the Ideal Personality

The conception of man as becoming, as self-actualizing, as moving toward the fully functioning individual, uses the conception of the "ideal" personality. It, too, however, is a value judgment. It has no support in traditional scientific methods of verification. Its support comes, in the main, from persons who have become self-actualizing or who have observed others become self-actualizing. Though this is not considered good scientific evidence by those who are addicted to a nineteenth century conception of science, it has been sufficient evidence to motivate some to give up the quest for man as a successful achiever, and to think of him as a process of becoming human. Though the humanistically oriented psychologists and psychiatrists believe that this is the road to self-fulfillment, they can not prove it. But they are willing to take a chance, to encourage people to move from static, fixed, stereotyped personalities to dynamic, ever-changing, variegated personalities.

Self-Actualization and the Family

How can we relate this conception of the self-actualizing person to the family? At the strictly sociological level of analysis it is customary nowadays to talk about the functions of the family not in terms of the older kinds of functions, such as that the family provides sustenance for its members, provides clothing and shelter, provides religious or other education and the like, but in terms of the family as an interaction system. The family is the primary socializing agent in early childhood. Personality development, from a sociological point of view, is a function of this socialization process. In the nuclear family of America, there are two other important functions[7]—the instrumental function, which is related to the external aspects of the family, to providing for the maintenance and physical well-being of the family; and the expressive function, which is related to the internal aspects of the family, to providing integrative and socio-emotional support for the family members. But this conception of the functions of the family as system does not demand that the children be socialized to any particular kind of behavior, that they develop any particular kind of personality. Nor does it require that the integrity of the family be maintained and sustained in any particular way.

. . .

What, then, might be some of the implications of the humanist view when applied to the family? What kind of family life would we have if every member of it were on the road to self-actualization? What kind of people would we produce in a fully functioning family?

The Fully Functioning Person

What is the difference between the fully functioning person (at this stage in history, such a person is more an ideal than a fact) and the kind of person here referred to as a conformist, as defensive, as operating at less than his potential, as not being on the road to self-actualization? One critical difference is that the fully functioning person has an acute sense of his own personal identity. As a consequence, he has also an awareness of his own powers to relate effectively to the world. He changes the world. He exercises mastery over it and over himself. The locus of evaluation of himself rests within himself. On the other hand, the normal personality, according to the classical Freudian description, or according to the view of a stimulus-response psychologist, places man in a reactive role. He reacts to environmental influences. He has little or no subjective awareness of his identity as a unique human being, but tends to see himself only as others see him, to see himself as a commodity.[8] He is molded by others; he is programmed as though he were a machine. For him technological progress becomes the automation of dehumanization, to use Kenneth Clark's apt phrase.

Let us now turn to how the fully functioning person might develop. He is not born fully functioning. The development does come about through environmental influences and, in early childhood, this means notably the parent-child relationship. Later it means also the relationship between the child and significant other persons in his environment. Still later his development will be affected by others through what he reads. The most essential ingredient for starting a child on the road to self-actualization is, according to Rogers, the presence of unconditional positive regard. This means that the growing child is appreciated as a human being. He is not punished for being human. He is not taught to become ashamed and guilty about his humanness. Valuing the child for his humanness means that he must be valued for the development of imagination, symbolization, aesthetic awareness, empathy, and reason. When the child is so valued, the initiative for learning and development comes from within the child, not from external rewards or punishments. Obviously the child must be taught some things. Each child cannot discover the whole history of man and man's thought all by himself. Nevertheless, wide latitude must be given to the child to discover and construct reality for himself, to find his own values, his own beliefs, his own moral code, what he wants to do with his life, his own identity. The roles he takes must be selected by him, not foisted upon him. If, as a parent, you wish to cripple your child, value him only when he does the things you want him to, disvalue him when he differs. Emphasize to him that he must assume certain social roles, and that he may not assume others. Concentrate on his roles; neglect his psychology.

To become a self-actualizing individual requires the courage to face the unknown. Therefore, the fully functioning individual is frightening to a conformist, who seeks the security of the known. It can be demonstrated that this is so because we have today in our midst young people who are on the road to self-actualization: the student activists. During the 1950's university students were called the "quiet" generation. They had "buttoned down" minds.[9] Polls, such as the Purdue poll, showed that students were unconcerned with deep values. They were complacent, status-oriented, committed only to exurbanite conformity. They wanted to wear gray flannel suits, become organization men, live in suburbia, and drive station wagons. Then suddenly in the 1960's, there burst upon us a new generation of young people. These people question. They protest. They are indifferent to the opportunity for status and income. These are not youths who were attracted to activism because they were economically deprived, or because their opportunities for upward mobility were blocked.[10] These are highly advantaged youths, whom some call the "victims" of an affluent society. Nor can these young people be explained as a generation in revolt. The youth of the early thirties were, by and large, a generation in revolt. These youths are not. Nor is it entirely a matter of generation gap. The good baby doctor stands shoulder to shoulder with the babies whose rearing he helped to shape. Studies have shown that the parents of student protestors often share their offsprings' views, that the parents are not conventional conformists.[11] Most activists come from a very special kind of middle or upper-middle class family. Both parents tend to be college educated, the father is a professional, the mother often has a career as well, both parents and children tend to be political liberals. The student activists state that their parents have been permissive and democratic. The parents describe themselves in these terms also. These youths do not want to find meaning in their lives in terms of status and role. Neither are the student activists, by and large, interested in copping out. They are willing to assume some of the dominant values of our culture. They are willing to contribute, but they are not willing to work for things that only have a price tag. They are not willing to make the compromises with their own sense of integrity that the upwardly mobile child from a deprived or non-affluent environment is all too willing to make. To the person willing to compromise and to the conformist, growing up means developing a cynical attitude toward the virtues. Thus, becoming conservative does not often mean desiring to conserve the best in man, but becoming a conformist, a compromiser, a "realist." The student activist rejects this. He has a basic concern with individual development and self-expression, with a spontaneous response to the world. The free expression of emotions and feelings is viewed as essential to the development and integrity of the individual. He is also concerned with self-development and expression in aesthetic and intellectual areas. Moreover, he is concerned with the social condition of others. He has a strong humanitarian outlook. This is what accounts for the popularity of VISTA and the Peace Corps, for students joining in civil rights struggles, and for student dissent.

The self-actualizing individual is above all a doubter. Descartes' famous affirmation of his existence, "I think, therefore I am" is well known. What is often overlooked is the context of the statement. It occurs in *Discourse on the Method* and expounded in his *Meditations on First Philosophy,* in which he describes how he arrived at his insight by starting with a profound doubt about the truth of anything.[12] The self-actualizing person doubts. He questions the meaning of life, of existence. This is a completely different kind of anxiety from the debilitating feeling with which Freud was concerned. Existential anxiety is the anxiety that one feels as one plunges into an ever-changing, unknown world. Doubt is the mark of man.

There is a serious clash in our society today between a "successful" and "affluent" society, which demands that behavior follow relatively fixed rules of conduct as defined by tradition, and the emerging values and doubts of the new humanists. One of the stated purposes of insisting upon rules is to protect the individual against unpredictable, and possibly destructive, impulses. Some fear that we will create monsters if we permit children to actualize themselves. This is an unfounded fear, a myth. There is nothing in our study of evolution or in our study of man that warrants the conclusion that if allowed to become human, man will be other than humane. Man, humane, is not interested in destroying himself. The humanist therefore rejects fixed rules. He is more flexible. He sees the spontaneous flow of feelings and ideas as intrinsically good, indeed essential, for optimal personal growth. To the child who has grown up in a humanistic environment, pursuit of the status goals encouraged in him by society, by the public school, by college means hypocrisy, and the sacrifice of personal integrity.

The Fully Functioning Family

Implicit in the foregoing is the notion that the fully functioning family is one in which all the individuals in it are open to one another, and are open to experience. They do not take stereotypical roles. They do not confuse conservatism with conformity. The fully functioning individual will find his way to traditional values that should be conserved. A person will not find his way to them if they are foisted upon him by moral exhortation, by citation of tradition and authority. The climate in the fully functioning family is thus flexible, highly fluid, in a continuous state of process, of becoming. The members in the family are defenseless before one another. They value one another in toto, not merely for certain aspects of their behavior. Do we not want to create people who are able to work not under coercion, not without any sense of self-fulfillment, but able to work joyously, to work with the thrill and excitement of the artist, the creator? And do we not want to create people who are able to love fully and deeply, to love not only those close to them but to love all mankind?

Humanistic parents raise their children in an environment relatively free of constraints, an environment that is favorable to experimentation, expressiveness, and spontaneity. Humanistic parents stress the significance of autonomous and authentic behavior, freely initiated by the individual and expressing his own true feelings and ideas.

Parents who are afraid of children like this, then, may not have understood the meaning of self-actualization. They have not understood what it means to have a mature mind. If doubt, questioning, and nonconformity seems too high a price to pay for growth, the alternative is likely to be the payment of a much higher price in tribulation, bitterness, and despair.

A family system that encourages the individual family members to strive for self-actualization is exciting. Certainly the traditional family has not always done this in the past. One of the areas in which the American society and family system has been somewhat repressive is that of sex roles. Masculinity and femininity, the social roles that go with male and female, have been rigidly defined in our culture as indeed they have been in almost all cultures. However, many in America are calling for a freeing of individuals from stereotyped sex roles. Although this movement is spearheaded by the feminists, it has great potential for men as well. The following reading examines our concepts of femininity and masculinity and ends by outlining a possible future society built on the strengths of both the male and the female rather than on stereotyped roles that ignore individual differences.

Dr. Lindemann is currently in Women's Studies at Santa Barbara City College in California. This article was especially written for this book and is used here by express permission of the author.

19 The Sex Role Revolution: Reexamination of Femininity and Masculinity

Barbara S. Lindemann

Women's liberation means many things to many people. To some it means liberating women from their enslavement to men, an enslavement which most people doubt exists. To some women, liberation means equal pay for equal work. To some who fear it, it means that men and women will reverse places, and women will come to dominate and/or tyrannize over men. To some who desire it, women's liberation means that women will no longer need men, but learn to live freely and happily separate from them.

Through all the debate, the misunderstandings, the extreme positions, there has emerged from the women's liberation movement a central vision which is less frightening and more profound than any of the above. This is a society that has transcended or gone beyond narrow stereotyped sex roles, "a vision of what it would mean to be a society not of feminine and masculine creatures, but comprised of humans."[1] We now define masculine roles as different from feminine roles. These role definitions limit individual choice and stand in the way of fully satisfying relationships between the sexes. Neither biological necessity nor social utility demands that the sexes live and act differently from each other. On the contrary, the needs of advanced industrial society will be best met by self-actualized people, individuals who do not fit into the stereotyped notions of masculine and feminine.

Presently, the first thing one notes upon meeting another person is whether he/she is male or female, because this one fact dictates the details of how we relate to others. The choice of words we use, the inflection in our voices, the content of our conversation, and the amount and kinds of physical contact we establish—all differ according to the sex of the other.[2] Furthermore, our assumptions about what the other is like and how he/she will behave differ according to the sex of the other. Thus male/female is the single most important description of an individual. The first question everyone asks when a baby is born is whether it is a boy or a girl. Even in the first hours this fact must be established so that people will know how to talk about and relate to the infant. The importance is reflected in our speech: it is impossible to use personal pronouns without indicating sexual identity.

Sex identity is so built into the fabric of our social relations that we are most uncomfortable when we do not know the sex of a person we are talking to, even when such knowledge is totally irrelevant to the particular social situation.

Such discomfort was reflected in a letter from a middle-aged man to his local newspaper:

> I've been having trouble lately with my eyesight. I see things that ain't so. After several harrowing experiences, perhaps it's time to ask your advice.
>
> It all started when a womanlike creature came to the door and inquired if we wished to list our property for sale. When I answered, "no Madame, we are not thinking of selling out at this time," the hairy person gave me a mean look and said, "I am not a madam." Which goes to show that maybe I need new glasses.
>
> Another time I saw a poor woman trying to cross a downtown street. When I rushed forward to assist the tottering creature, I discovered a mustache hidden under the fungus that I had mistaken for a feminine coiffure. When I said, "Excuse me, Miss," the creature glared at me.
>
> Today, some youngsters came to the door to collect the papers. Among them was a little girl who kept brushing her hair back and tossing her head, flinging her crop of ladylike hair first to one side, then to the other. Very gracefully done, too.
>
> When I told the neighbor boys that they showed rare taste in having such a pretty girl as a companion, the girl told me, "I ain't no girl. I'm a boy."[3]

The writer is not only complaining that he could not make the appropriate responses when he did not know the sex of these young people. He is also expressing his distaste that boys are looking like girls, a long-held taboo which, significantly, is not so strong in reverse. That is, it is socially acceptable for girls to dress and look like boys, but only so long as one can still clearly perceive them to be girls. If her sex is not clearly identifiable, then again interaction is difficult because important behavioral cues are missing. The dismay of the writer above would be more reasonable if he had been "girl-watching" at the time, or looking for a possible mate. But the striking thing about his examples is that in none of the situations he describes did gender need to make a bit of difference. He could have related to the others courteously without ever knowing their sex.

As women gradually come to be seen as the equals of men, gender designations will become less important. It will make no more sense to line up girls on one side of the room and boys on the other, than it does now to line up all redheads or black people or short people together. In a society where gender is not so important people will be free to relate to each other more fairly and honestly and with more true courtesy. Gender is stressed far beyond mating necessities because male and female now are expected to behave and live differently. Before we criticize these sex-role stereotypes, let us first examine how sex roles are defined and learned in our society.

Learning Sex Roles

Male and female grow up in the same families, attend the same schools, and work in the same offices; yet they live quite differently from each other and are expected to develop distinctive (many would say complementary) personality traits. Through play and imitation children learn the sex roles which they must perform as adults.

Girls can expect to do jobs, inside or outside the home, that are service oriented, supportive, and most likely to be performed indoors. Most jobs available to an adult woman—whether as wife, secretary, nurse, or teacher—require her to serve the needs and follow the directions of another person. A girl's upbringing prepares her to fit gracefully into these positions. Mothers tend to talk to girl babies more frequently than to boy babies, and to give girls much physical contact for more years.[4] The average girl is rewarded for neatness, consideration for others, docility, conformity, and display of affection. Through their upbringing girls become sensitive to the moods and expectations of those around them in order to conform properly. Thus as adults women tend to be far more sensitive to nuances of mood and meaning than are men.

Boys can expect to do jobs that are task oriented, self-initiated, and likely to be performed outdoors or to involve outside contacts. As young children they receive ambiguous signals. They are told that cleanliness and calmness are desirable traits which they should learn. And yet their parents smile with fond approval when they are assertive and engrossed in active games and construction that leave them dirty, torn, and scratched. "Boys will be boys," they are told with approval that implies that they cannot help their behavior. Society's love for the mischievous, clever, and independent little boy is seen in the continuing popularity of the Dennis the Menace comic strip. Through an upbringing which encourages a bit of rebelliousness, boys learn not to give too much regard to the expectations and demands of others. They learn to initiate activity and to concentrate not so much on other people as on the task at hand. In a society that defines adult work according to sex, such childhood preparation is realistic.

Society defines not only behavior, but also personality traits according to sex. As a child learns the expected male and female behavior it is also likely to develop the character traits considered appropriate to its sex. Boys learn early that society esteems men who are aggressive, independent, dominant, competitive, active, logical, direct, and outwardly unemotional. Girls learn early that it is socially desirable to be tactful, gentle, aware of others' feelings, interested in appearance, and expressive of tender feelings. These descriptions may seem overdrawn. But they are taken from a recent study which shows that "despite the apparent fluidity of sex-role definition in contemporary society as contrasted with the previous decades, our own findings to date confirm the existence of pervasive and persistent sex-role stereotypes." The respondents in the study held similar sex role stereotypes even though they came from a variety of socio-economic and religious backgrounds. The authors summed up that "sex role differences are considered desirable by college students, healthy by mental health professionals, and are even seen as ideal by both men and women."[5]

That sex role stereotypes are widely held in our society obviously does not mean that all men and women fit into these stereotypes. Few studies have been done to test how many men in our society are in fact aggressive, independent, competitive, etc., and how many women are tactful, gentle, aware of others' feelings, etc.[6] Since social expectations are known to profoundly affect individual behavior,[7] probably most men do share the competency/assertiveness, or masculine, cluster of traits while most women would measure high on the warmth-expressiveness cluster.

Criticism of Narrow Sex Roles

"Vive la différence," many people say. "Sure, men and women are different, different and complementary. What's wrong with that?" Granted, there will always be sexual attraction between male and female based on real and enjoyable physical differences. No one would want to change that. However, our narrow sex role definitions limit individual growth in women and, to a lesser extent, in men. Further, evidence strongly suggests that the male sex role puts pressure on men which takes its toll on their health and lives. And of equal importance, narrowly circumscribed sex roles make relations between the sexes difficult, especially in contemporary society.

Women who conform to feminine stereotypes are likely to suffer from low self esteem, since feminine characteristics are generally valued less than male characteristics. Although many people pay lip service to the idea that women, "while different," are "just as good as" men, the sentiment is not really believed. "The literature [of sociological studies] indicates that men and masculine characteristics are more highly valued than are women and feminine characteristics."[8] The traits that are considered desirable for men are the same traits believed to be normal for a healthy adult. Yet in one study, mental health workers perceived a "mature, healthy, socially competent adult woman" as "more submissive, less independent, less adventurous, less objective, more easily influenced, less aggressive, less competitive, more excitable in minor crises, more emotional, more conceited about their appearance, and having their feelings more easily hurt" than a healthy adult man.[9] Thus men establish the norm of adult behavior, and healthy women are expected to conform to an ideal that is deficient in terms of the adult/male norm. If she is truly feminine, then she is less than a mature and competent adult; if she has the traits of a mature and competent adult, she is criticized and perhaps shunned for not being a "real woman."

Women experience this "double-bind" in many areas of their lives. Female professions and jobs do not carry the prestige or money of male jobs. Elementary school teaching, nursing, clerical and secretarial work, and homemaking are all perceived as less prestigious than university teaching, being a physician, or electrical and carpentry work. Jobs which men do that are comparable to homemaking or lower in prestige—such as gardening, garbage collection, and dishwashing—are at least paid, while homemaking is not. Of course the assumption is that homemaking has important rewards unrelated to monetary compensation; yet that does not change the fact that when a woman takes on jobs that are appropriate to her sex, she accepts a status and income which is inferior to that of the men of her class.

Women in 1970 made up only 6.5% of all physicians, 2.1% of all dentists, 1.2% of all engineers, and 7% of all scientists. Full-time year round women workers in 1972 earned on the average 60% as much as male full time year round workers. Unemployment among women who were looking for work was 6.6% while the male unemployment rate was 4.9%. White women workers earn less than non-white male workers and non-white women have more difficulty finding jobs and earn less than any other group of workers. Women college graduates can expect to earn the same amount of money as men who drop out of school after the eighth grade.[10]

When women enter "masculine" professions, when they become physicians or lawyers, carpenters or police officers, they are likely to suffer internal conflict. They worry that they will lose their femininity and their attractiveness to men if they pursue this line of work.[11] This conflict may in some cases be intense enough that a young woman will give up her plans and instead follow a more traditionally feminine line of work. More commonly, women have been brought up so that they do not even consider anything except traditional jobs and marriage. They are thereby far more restricted than are men in the range of choices available to them. Regardless of their interest and skill, the majority of women go into limited kinds of jobs. Those who genuinely enjoy teaching or clerical work or nursing are among the fortunate ones. Although they will never earn much money in comparison to men of their class and educational level, they will be able to support themselves by doing work that they like.

Even these fortunate ones, if they have too fully internalized the social norms of femininity, may never develop into mature, healthy adults, in the sense that they may never develop the capacity for independent judgment or enjoy feelings of self-worth and competence. A talented and intelligent divorcee with one child, for example, married at seventeen and divorced at twenty-five, has an opportunity to pursue the college education she never got. Finding life alone too painful, she prefers to move in with a man who expects her to do the housework as well as aid him in his professional work. Only a woman with high self-esteem and an independent spirit would be able to risk the loss of his love by putting her own preparation for a future career before his work.

Men also pay a price if they internalize the masculine role stereotypes. While women may be stunted in their personal growth because *too little* is expected of them, men suffer physical and mental breakdowns because *too much* is expected of them. They feel pressure to support their family, to advance steadily in their work by doing better than other men, and to be decisive and competent leaders within the family and on the job. "Real men" are not supposed to admit defeat or even the fear of defeat; emotions such as grief or anxiety are to be sternly controlled in public, although a display of anger and indignation is generally acceptable. Crying, even in front of family members, is not socially acceptable, and tenderness must never reveal personal vulnerability. The pressures on men to be daring and successful may explain the high rate of accidental deaths among men between the ages of 18 and 65, and the higher incidence among men than among women of heart attacks, high blood pressure, and abuse of drugs, especially alcohol.

Traditional sex role definitions likewise make relations between the sexes often difficult. Marriage as traditionally defined provides a practical institution for the rearing and support of children. But today much more is commonly expected from marriage. The spouse is also to be one's best friend, to provide understanding, support, and companionship. A couple that has internalized the traditional definitions of sex roles will find it difficult if not impossible to establish this kind of close personal relationship with each other.

To begin with, the relationship is an unequal one in which the male has most of the power and the advantages. Since he is able to earn more money his job is seen as essential to the family, and he often claims prerogatives on the grounds of the importance of his work. He will argue that he should not have to wash dishes or bathe the children, as he is so tired from his work. His wife, although she too has often worked an eight to ten hour day by 6:00 P.M., finds this argument difficult to combat. If the couple is opposed to hiring outside help in the care of their children, then the greater earning power of the husband means automatically, for most couples, that he will take a job and his wife stay home. From that basic decision emerges the argument that since he earns the money, he should decide how it is spent. Of course he will "give" her as much as she wants/needs, but gradually a wife begins to feel trapped and resentful. She may want to raise her own children and enjoy being a homemaker, but she does not like the sense of utter dependence, of being treated like a servant to her husband. The longer she is absent from the paid work force the fewer options she has and her dependency may become ever greater and ever more galling to her.

For his part the husband may come to feel contempt for his wife, especially since all of their upbringing has prepared him and his wife to view him as the more talented and important partner. Her job seems easy to him, until, that is, he tries it. Then he wonders how she can tolerate the constant noise and demands of young children day in and day out. He may find her conversation about domestic occurrences and incidents at the supermarket tedious. Tired from a day of constant business with others, he may resent her craving for adult companionship, conversation, and news. As she becomes more trapped in the family situation he becomes ever more irritated that she expects so much from him; the temptation is strong to turn from a demanding and resentful wife to interests outside the home—sports, volunteer clubs, girlfriends. His wife will tolerate a distant and unsatisfactory relationship because her earning power and job opportunities are so limited, and most of her status and identity are wrapped up in the marriage. She may risk "potshots" at him, but not outright confrontation. Such vulnerability and indecisiveness may only increase his contempt for her.[12] Love based on sexual attraction, protectiveness, and dependency is possible between an inferior and a superior, but this kind of love provides a shaky foundation for years of companionship.[13]

The inequality built into the relationship is not the greatest obstacle to a close and mutually satisfactory marriage. Good communication between the sexes is limited by the very definition of masculine and feminine.

It is difficult to imagine a genuine loving relationship involving the stoical, unemotional, instrumentally oriented, dominating, aggressive, and competitive creature of the masculine stereotype. Moreover, both males and females view a husband's primary function as that of provider; there is no socially defined and sanctioned expectation that he confide, comfort, or share, and without these there is scarcely "love." It is, of course, equally difficult to imagine a male developing deep respect for the scatterbrained, passive, dependent, vain creature who would be 'feminine.'[14]

Biological Argument for Stereotyped Sex Roles

Traditional sex roles are said to be based on biological differences between the sexes. There is no doubt that profound physical differences with plausible psychological implications exist between male and female. A cataloguing of these differences could fill up many pages; they range from the obvious (genitalia, musculature, skeletal structure) to the more subtle (hormonal make-up, external appearance of the brain, chromosome structure). Yet among the myriad differences which exist, researchers until recently (when women have become more active in the field) have paid most attention to those differences which seem to explain and justify the superior position of men in our society.[15]

It is claimed, for example, that patriarchy developed and persists because men are physically stronger than women. Since women are more agile manually and men are stronger, it is proper that women type and assemble electronic components while men put in plumbing and operate heavy equipment. A variation of the same theme points to hormonal differences between male and female. The male hormone androgen makes men aggressive and the female hormones estrogen and progesterone make women passive and receptive, it is said. Therefore, it is "natural" that men assume leadership positions while women fill supportive and nurturing functions.

Such arguments have been used so long that they seem to us "just common sense." People note the physical differences between male and female and describe the different functions assigned to men and women in our society, and then assume that there is a direct correlation between the two. However, the evidence that suggests any necessary connection between these biological differences and the specific jobs/characteristics which our society ascribes to male and female is weak and contradictory. It could with as much reason and as little evidence be argued that women would make better political leaders because they are naturally less "assertive" than men and more sensitive to the needs and feelings of others. Similarly, women would make better brain surgeons because they are "naturally" so good at detailed and close work.

Recent research does indeed suggest that high androgen levels predispose an individual to high levels of activity and assertive (not aggressive) behavior. Girls with unusually high levels of androgen were found to be more active and to assume a leadership role among their playmates more frequently than a control group of girls with normal androgen levels.[16] Yet socialization has a far greater importance in sexual identity than does hormonal level.

Some babies are born each year who are not clearly male or female, but have a hormonal, genetic, and gonadal structure at variance with their external genitalia. The sex ascribed to them at birth may differ from their biological sex. A group of researchers at Johns Hopkins University has studied some of these babies over a twenty-year period.

> Of most interest to us here are those who were assigned one sex at birth and were later found to belong biologically (genetically, gonadally, and hormonally) to the opposite sex. In virtually all cases, the sex of assignment (and thus of rearing) proved dominant. Thus, babies assigned as males at birth and brought up as boys by their parents (who were unaware of their child's female genetic and hormonal makeup) thereafter thought of themselves as boys, played with boys' toys, enjoyed boys' sports, preferred boy's clothing, developed male sex fantasies, and in due course fell in love with girls. And the reverse was true for babies who were biologically male but reared as girls: they followed the typical feminine pattern of development—they preferred marriage over a career, enjoyed domestic and homemaking duties, and saw their future fulfillment in the traditional woman's role.[17]

Functional Argument for Sex Role Stereotypes

In discussing biological differences between the sexes we have thus far ignored the most basic differences: women bear and nurse infants. In most societies childrearing is done by women, no doubt because the women must nurse the infants for several years and thus as a matter of course they care for the older children as well. Girls must accordingly be taught to be responsible, obedient, altruistic, and nurturant. Acts of daring and risk-taking, while appropriate for warfare or for hunting and fishing, are not appropriate for childrearing or for the growing and preparation of food. Therefore women in most societies learn a different set of traits from men because their function requires it.[18]

This argument that women are different from men because of their function in society would seem to be as powerful as the argument based on biological (hormonal/structural) differences. Both seem to reinforce the contention that women must continue to fill their traditional roles. Yet from one culture to another women show an enormous range of difference. In one culture they are highly assertive and daring, while in another they may be docile and obedient. Some cultures value for all the members what we consider masculine behavior. In these cultures, the females on an absolute scale would rank as highly achievement oriented and self-reliant, whereas in comparison to the males of their own culture they are more nurturant and compliant. Similarly, in other cultures where feminine behavior is valued for both sexes, females still rank as more compliant and nurturant than males.[19] Some cultures raise male and female to be extremely different from each other, other cultures enforce few differences in behavior and character. The cultural stress on overall feminine or masculine behavior, and the degree of sexual difference demanded, seem to vary according to the economic requirements of the society. Hunting and fishing societies differ from agricultural societies, and advanced industrial societies differ from more simple societies.[20] Two facts of importance to us here clearly emerge from cross-cultural studies. First, male and female behavior is everywhere defined according to the needs of society. Secondly, babies regardless of sex have the potential to become either highly egoistic and aggressive, or firmly altruistic and obedient. Or they can learn to avoid both these extremes.

Sex roles are now under reevaluation in the United States, and are likely to change considerably. The reasons can be found in the profound economic and demographic changes which have occurred in the past fifty years. Before modern medical knowledge developed in the nineteenth century a high birth rate was essential for the survival of the human race. Infant and childhood mortality were so high that even without birth control the European population grew only slightly more than replacement level. Consequently childbearing was considered to be women's most important function and other female roles were defined accordingly. Today survival depends on a low birth rate.

World population now doubles every generation, that is, every thirty years. In the past few years dire warnings have been issued about the dangers of this "population explosion," and women in the United States are discouraged from having many babies. The population growth in the United States is now at replacement level, but even if it remains at that level indefinitely the population will not be stabilized for another eighty years, since people of child-bearing ages still make up a disproportionate part of the population. As childbearing becomes less important the society is gradually reassessing female capabilities and redefining feminine roles.

Masculine roles are similarly under attack. In our post-industrial society there is less and less place for the assertive individualist. Business enterprise is conducted not by a single energetic entrepreneur, but by massive conglomerates. Most people work in huge factories or offices where they carry out one limited and defined task; a tiny contribution to the final product. Within government and business alike planning and cooperation are assuming greater importance than competition and aggression as qualities essential not only to the realization of overall goals, but to the very survival of the nation. Eventually our childrearing practices will reflect these changed needs.

The Androgynous Person

Since post-industrial society requires less exaggerated differences in the definition of sex roles, we can assume that the society of the future will be androgynous. It will combine the best of male (andro) and of female (gyno) characteristics and will discourage individuals from acquiring the more extreme characteristics now associated with one or the other sex. We already have an idealized model of an androgynous person in Abraham Maslow's concept of a self-actualized person: an individual with a healthy ego who is able to relate fully to others. Self-actualized people, as described by a psychologist who worked with Maslow, are "relatively spontaneous in behavior. . . . simple, natural. . . . They are honest with themselves and with others. They are not self-satisfied, but they have come to accept themselves with equanimity, without self-consciousness."[21]

Self-actualized people form deep and close relationships with a small, select group. "They are capable of more fusion, greater love, more perfect identification, more obliteration of ego boundaries than other people would consider possible." At the same time they are kind and friendly and patient with almost everyone they meet. They enjoy periods of solitude and have a greater need for privacy than the average person.

Self-actualized people spend little time thinking about themselves. Rather they dwell on problems outside themselves. They are able to concentrate to the point that they become unconscious of their physical comfort and surroundings. They are comfortable with their own bodies and are not usually perturbed by minor discomforts. "They are self-starters, active, self-disciplined, responsible. . . . They can make decisions, plan without fluster, direct themselves smoothly."[22]

This description of a self-actualized person sets up an ideal attractive to both sexes. Conventional sex roles appear foolish and insignificant when placed before this model of developed maturity. The self-actualized person has no need to assert dominance nor to play the coquette. The self-actualized person would not hide his tears nor mask her competence. Not surprisingly, Maslow found the qualities of self-actualization to be the same for men and women. Yet only a small fraction (in one study group one twelfth) of his subjects were women. Why, asks Esther M. Lloyd Jones, were there so few women among his subjects?

> Because in our society they [women] tend to be less conspicuous, are they, therefore, harder to find and identify? Or does our culture not encourage or even permit our girls to individuate, to develop their uniqueness? Do we not hold, perhaps unconsciously, as our model for femininity something of the Eastern idea of the beauty and wonder of the person who has suppressed the development of her ego? Have we been "protecting" women from developing their full strengths, protecting them from the hard realities of our world, from making hard conscious moral decisions and thus stunted their growth?"[23]

The female sex role as defined by our society encourages traits quite different from those of a self-actualized person. Women who internalize the female sex role learn to be dependent, fear being left alone, are concerned about their appearance, and suffer doubts about their own competence and self worth. The male sex role diverges from the self-actualized ideal to a much lesser extent than does the female sex role. For at least a hundred years our society has held up two ideals before women: the "feminine" ideal, and the ideal of a mature or self-actualized person. The stereotyped concepts of femininity are losing whatever social benefit they may once have had. It is now time to replace traditional images of masculine and feminine with the single ideal of a self-actualized person. When we raise children with this end in view we will be well on the way to achieving an androgynous society.

In an androgynous society children strive for competence in many areas without regard to sex. They develop motor skills through running and jumping, and hand-eye coordination through needle work, art work, and handling of tools. They learn the skills necessary to take care of themselves, such as cooking, sewing, and household repairs. They play with friends of both sexes, in school as well as out. They engage freely in games of competition as well as games of cooperation with friends of the other sex and friends of the same sex. They learn to respect (or to dislike!) each other on the basis of individual differences, not according to sexual category.

Children learn not only self-confidence and a sense of mastery but also attitudes of caring and concern for others. Both sexes are held and touched often as infants and after. They learn to understand and express their own feelings and to recognize the needs and feelings of those around them. Verbal and physical displays of emotion are encouraged as long as they are not harmful to other people.

This kind of early childhood training prepares the way for adolescent relationships very different from those we know today. In an androgynous society dating is no longer a battle between a boy seeking "conquest" and a girl looking for status, each lonely and insecure. Instead an adolescent is likely to form a friendship with a member of the opposite sex which realistically meets his/her needs of support and understanding in the search for meaning and identity. The practice of "going steady" and the incidence of promiscuous sexuality are both less likely in a society where both sexes enjoy self-esteem and recognize their common needs and interest. At an appropriate age, possibly in the late teens, couples are encouraged to form stable sexual relationships, living either together or in separate households. Pregnancy, if not banned outright by public sterilization measures, is discouraged at this stage.

During their teens both sexes prepare for work by which they can support themselves as adults. And yet they cannot anticipate what most of the years ahead will hold. Their future is less predictable than that of any previous generation. They will no doubt change careers once or twice in their lifetime; they may or may not have children; they will probably change long-term partners at least once in their adult lives. And they will have many years of leisure when they will not have to work. Thus these years of adolescence are not used (as they were in the past) to set a person on the specific path he/she will take during much of life. Rather these years continue the education begun at birth, an education designed to create a self-confident, flexible, and loving person with a wide variety of skills.

Many different living arrangements will be available to adults, although for the sake of social stability the laws and society should encourage long-term relationships. In our future androgynous society, individuals can choose to marry, to live with a partner without marriage, or to join one of various kinds of communal living groups. In each of these living arrangements work and income are shared. That is, household tasks are done by all in the household and outside income is pooled to provide for the members of the couple or the group. People live with others in order to enjoy love, companionship, and emotional support of all kinds. The childrearing practices described above are designed to prepare people for close personal relationships which encourage individual growth, not stifle it as is the case in so many marriages and living arrangements today.

The decision to have a child would carry with it specific responsibilities. Parenthood would no longer be seen as a privileged right of every man and woman. Given population pressures, it may even be that in the future the state will take measures (such as adding something to the drinking water) to sterilize the population; consequently, a couple wanting children would have to get permission from the state. Let us hope that such drastic measures will never be taken. In any event, parenthood requires a firm commitment for a number of years, a commitment to the other parent and to the child. In an androgynous society laws will require parents to support their child jointly, although each couple will divide up financial support and actual physical care of the child according to individual interests and talents. Parenthood will replace marriage as a firm legal commitment, and society will make it extremely difficult to break that contract—as it was once difficult to break the marriage contract.

To make possible these innovations in living arrangements and in parenthood, a great many social and economic changes are necessary. True choices of living and working arrangements are possible only when women have available to them jobs at the same level of pay as men. Otherwise, in any living group, the males have greater incentive to work outside the home than do the females, and traditional patterns repeat themselves. Similarly, all jobs must be open to both sexes and jobs now seen as "women's" jobs must be paid on a level comparable to those of "male" jobs.

In this new society the nine-to-five job gradually becomes less the norm, as employers establish more flexible working hours and make available interesting part-time jobs with full fringe benefits. Lifetime career patterns also change, as more and more people change careers in mid-life. Employers and employees alike come to consider a job or career in terms of a ten to twenty year commitment rather than a thirty to fifty year commitment. A forty-year-old person who changes fields is not discriminated against, but rather is considered to have as much promise as an inexperienced twenty-year-old applying for the same job. A man or woman who chooses to devote much of her/his first "career period" (ages 20–35) to child rearing thus does not find his or her options limited at the end of that time, but joins others of the same age who are in the process of changing careers.

In our androgynous society child care takes on new importance as the number of children born decreases. Parents receive a great deal of social support and help which was not proffered in the past. The changes in career patterns discussed above furnish an indirect means of support for parents, in that half-time jobs enable the parents to spend more time with the child. Those who commit themselves to child rearing are not penalized professionally for their choice. But direct aid is also available. If the parents are part of an extended living group, the other adults in the group may share child care. Since not all adults have children, this enables more people to share the important experience of watching and helping a child grow.

Parent controlled child care centers also are available in an androgynous society. They are well funded and staffed with highly trained personnel aided by young and second career people who are considering this as a possible field of work. Child care centers serve as consulting centers as well as care centers; that is, they help parents and children with childrearing problems.

A society that has gone beyond narrow ideas of femininity and masculinity to the ideal of the self-actualized person offers the widest possible range of choices to its members. It is a society that has reached a level of material comfort that allows it to put resources into human rather than material development. Many of the reforms suggested here are ideas made familiar by the women's liberation movement. Yet the real issue is not the liberation of women so much as the liberation of humanity, the establishment of a society where men and women have a real opportunity to fulfil their hopes and dreams unhampered by oppressive and irrelevant sexual stereotypes.

Dr. Lindemann calls for a revamping of society and family so as to do away with sex role stereotypes.

Other more strident voices are being heard criticizing the family in the United States. The "hang-loose" ethic espoused by a small portion of our youth calls for a drastic freeing of man from his traditional sexual mores, yet youth spends little time thinking about the kind of family system that might evolve in the ensuing climate of sexual freedom. It is difficult to reconcile the "flower child's" idea that sex is meaningful communication and love, with the classified advertisements requesting sexual partners that appear in the underground newspapers. Such behavior seems little different from their loudly expressed criticism of the establishment's creation of a love object to be manipulated, as exemplified by the bunny or playboy made famous by Hugh Hefner in *Playboy* magazine. At times the "hang-loose" ethic sounds exactly like the superficial establishment prescriptions for the detachment of sex from love and emotional involvement that Harvey Cox criticizes in *The Secular City*. Each ethic rests pompously secure in its own self-righteousness and prescribes the proper behavior for the turned-on sexual person. For example, *Playboy* fulfills a special need.

> For the insecure young man with newly acquired free time and money who still feels uncertain about his consumer skills (sex consumption included), *Playboy* supplies a comprehensive authoritative guidebook to this forbidding new world to which he now has access. It tells him not only who to be; it tells him how to be it, and even provides consolation outlets for those who secretly feel that they have not quite made it.
>
> The happy issue is always a casual but satisfying sexual experience with no entangling alliances whatever. Unlike the women he knows in real life, the *Playboy* reader's fictional girlfriends know their place and ask for nothing new. They present no danger of permanent involvement. Like any good accessory, they are detachable and disposable.[24]

It is difficult to differentiate between an advertisement in an underground newspaper for a sexual partner and the girl offered by *Playboy* to the young man's imagination. Yet among the sincere and thoughtful youth, there are some validities to the "hang-loose" ethic.

Just what are some of the alternatives to the nuclear family being proposed today? The following article delineates many of the possible alternatives currently being discussed.

20 The Alternatives: Changing Sexual and Family Mores

Frank D. Cox

In the meantime, if marriage and paternity are to survive as social institutions, some compromise is necessary between complete promiscuity and lifelong monogamy. Although it is difficult to decide the best compromise at a given time certain points seem clear:

— Young unmarried people should have considerable freedom as long as children are avoided so that they may better distinguish between mere physical attraction and the sort of congeniality that is necessary to make marriage a success.
— Divorce should be possible without blame to either party and should not be regarded as in anyway disgraceful.
— Everything possible should be done to free sexual relations from economic taint. At present, wives, just as much as prostitutes, live by the sale of their sexual charms; and even in temporary free relations the man is usually expected to bear all the joint expenses. The result is that there is a sordid entanglement of money with sex, and that woman's motives not infrequently have a mercenary element. A woman, like a man, should have to work for her living, and an idle wife is no more intrinsically worthy of respect than a gigolo.[1]

Bertrand Russell

Attending to the contemporary mass media, one finds that the institution of marriage is everywhere under attack. After years of man and woman enduring a misguided relationship with each other, it is at last possible to have newer (?), far more ideal (?) relationships. Traditional marriage will die and in its place will arise the new, more perfect union.

The naiveté of such a view emerges clearly when one assumes an historical vantage point. What is traditional marriage? History has no ready answer, especially if the institution is observed cross-culturally. Is the new really new? Consensual marriage, living together without legal sanctions, is certainly not unique to this time or to current college students. Many states have for years recognized common-law marriages, i.e., if you live together long enough the state accords you marital status without the formalities. It may be of interest to note that the opening quotation was written in 1936.

What then can be gained by examining some of the highly touted new (?) forms of male-female intimacy? Your author holds that: *a free and creative society will offer many structural forms of the family by which its functions such as child-rearing and meeting sexual needs may be fulfilled.* What is perhaps different about modern America is its permissiveness toward and acceptance of multiple forms of intimate relationships. Other cultures have had different marital systems but have usually disallowed deviance from the system chosen at a given historical time.

The reasons for America's permissiveness are partially philosophic and partly economic. Although it is not our purpose to trace exhaustively the roots of this permissiveness, it is worthwhile to discuss briefly the economic influence.

Although we can find every conceivable family type by examining other cultures, many forms have little relevance to a modern industrialized society such as ours. Marriages in an affluent society may assume many more forms than in a poor society. Even during the industrial revolution, marriage forms were limited mainly because the woman was unable to earn a decent enough wage to maintain her children without a man. She was economically tied to the man (the breadwinner) regardless of the success of their personal relationship.

With affluence it becomes more possible to consider alternate life-styles and marital forms. Affluence allows greater education which, if successful, plants new ideas and knowledge. One is made aware of other life-styles than the one in which he is raised. Affluence brings mobility. Population transiency affords contact with new people, new life-styles without the constraint of immediate supervision by parents. If one finds greater personal satisfaction in some alternate life-style, affluence allows one to seek out others with like interests. Affluence postpones the assumption of adult responsibility, thereby allowing wider experimentation and lessening the consequences of failure. Affluence with full employment has allowed the woman greater freedom since she can maintain herself and her children economically without a man. Although she is not yet economically equal to the male in America, she is gaining more and more economic independence.

In part then, because of America's affluence, it seems that the young have a broader choice of acceptable relationships available than did their grandparents. Perhaps it will be true that a given couple, by choosing wisely the roles that best fit them as individuals, will be able to create a growing intimate relationship that is more fulfilling than was found in the past. Only time will tell.

Many alternate relationships (not necessarily accepted by the society at large) are briefly presented along with statements of possible advantages and disadvantages. Since there is little empirical evidence on the outcome of such alternate unions, the evaluations of them are often based on opinion rather than fact. It is hoped that these opinions will stimulate the reader to make his own evaluations.

1. Changing Thoughts on Parenthood

Children have long been the central function of the family. Historically, in most cultures, many children were produced through the childbearing years since infant mortality was high and had to be offset. A woman might have ten children but see only three grow into adulthood. With modern medicine, the infant mortality rate has declined drastically, especially in western countries. This and the recognition of the population problem have brought about a reduction in the reproduction rate in the United States. Increasing awareness of ecological problems, especially in the United States, has influenced some young couples to avoid having children. Only ten years ago, the newly wed couple was pressured to have children. Family and friends began to ask what was wrong if a child didn't appear within a year or two of the marriage. The couple was chastised as being selfish if they hinted that they did not want children. Today, however, increasing numbers of young people are saying that they choose to remain childless. Of all women who ever marry, about one in twenty never become mothers and one-half of these are childless by choice.[2,3] This ratio is currently shifting, with more favoring childlessness than in the past. Recently, couples opting for a childless life are finding some support. For example, *The Case Against Having Children,*[4] *The Baby Trap,*[5] and *Those Missing Babies*[6]—all are supportive of childlessness. Only time will tell whether the young will continue to feel this way throughout their childbearing years. The birthrate in America has recently dropped to its lowest level, so it appears that some portion of our married population is drastically reducing the number of children they have.

In 1800, American women averaged seven children each (five survived). During the depression year of 1936, this had fallen to 2.1. There was a baby boom after World War II when the rate climbed to 3.8, but by 1957 that had begun to decline until at the end of 1973 the rate was only 1.9 children per fertile woman, an insufficient number to replace the population. To replace the population, 2.11 children would have to be produced by each woman. At the current reproduction rate it will take about 50 years for the population to stabilize, at which time America's population will be 260 million.[7] Unfortunately, such trends are limited to only a few of the industrial countries, with the so-called underdeveloped areas such as Asia, Africa, and South America reproducing at 2.3 percent a year, far faster than food supplies are increasing.

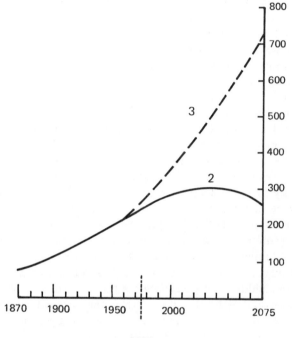

Fig. 1   U.S. Population and Projections for Two- and Three-Children Families

Childlessness offers numerous advantages to the couple. The major advantage is increased freedom. The couple does not have to contend with the responsibilities of children. They are monetarily unencumbered. Current estimates range to $25,000 to raise a child to eighteen years of age. The couple's time is their own to devote to careers, each other, hobbies, travels, and adult life in general. Often the childless couple is a *two-career family* where each is free to invest his energies in his work while meeting with the spouse during leisure times.

The interest in *child-care agencies,* early schooling, and communal child-rearing on the part of some parents may reflect their desire to live as the childless couple lives while at the same time having children. As in the kibbutz settlements of Israel, the parents can be freed of the negative aspects of childrearing while enjoying the positive aspects. The wealthy have long used nurses and servants to relieve themselves of the day-to-day burdens of parenthood. "Why can't state agencies be used in the same way?" ask some of the less fortunate parents.

Parenthood as a career is still the majority choice. Parenthood is a central focus for the spouses. Joy is taken in helping children to grow. Satisfaction is derived from the children's successes. Caring relationships between all family members including grandparents and grandchildren offer the spouses many additional relationships that buffer them against loneliness and feelings of unproductiveness and lack of worth.

With decreasing emphasis on children, remaining *single* is regaining a modicum of respectability. Although the society still discriminates against the single person, remaining unmarried to devote oneself to a career or to avoid the perceived difficulties of marriage is becoming more acceptable. It really was not many years ago when careers such as teaching and nursing actually discouraged marriage for their members. Although such discouragement to marry will probably never reappear, one may at least again contemplate remaining single to devote oneself to a career, a cause, or simply because one enjoys the single life-style. In 1960, 28 percent of twenty- to twenty-four-year-old women were single. This increased to 36 percent in 1970.[7] Freedom to do your own thing is the major advantage of remaining single. Possible loneliness, failure to relate intimately, and a sense of meaninglessness are potential disadvantages. In addition, rigidity and failure to develop interpersonal relating skills are possible disadvantages, as is a higher incidence of mental illness. (See figure 2.) It is difficult to say just why the incidence of mental illness is higher for single persons compared to married. Perhaps those with a proclivity toward mental illness are bypassed by those seeking mates and are thereby forced to remain single. Living closely with another person does serve a corrective function since the other person validates or invalidates many of one's thoughts and actions, thus serving to keep one closer to reality than might otherwise be the case without this interaction. In addition, the social onus placed on the single person may act to increase mental stress.

A life-style recently more acceptable is *single parenthood*. Until very recently, adoption of children was strictly limited to carefully investigated married couples. In some states, such as California, a few placements are now being made with single responsible adults. Single parenthood is also created by the illegitimate child. In the past, illegitimacy was a stigma and remains so through much of the American society. However, among some subgroups the unwed mother carries her baby about as a badge of her daring to be different. In 1971, 20 percent of the black and 9 percent of the white female heads of family were single, never married.[8] Such a statistic must be treated cautiously, since data on socially unacceptable behavior are always suspect. There are advantages to single parenthood. Having complete control of the child vested in only one authority avoids the possible conflicts engendered by split authority. One can enjoy parenthood without having to be married. Naturally the single parent is burdened with the entire responsibility of the child. Also, the growing child is less likely to learn the marital role of the missing spouse. Financially, for most single parents, survival is far more difficult than for the couple pulling together to support the children. The problem of child care while the single parent works is still far from solved and presently takes a good deal of the single person's budget.

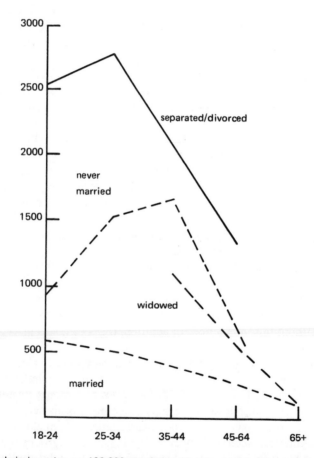

Fig. 2   Admission rates per 100,000 population 18 years and over by marital status, Outpatient Psychiatric Services, United States, Publishing Co., 1972), p. 169

(From Statistical Note 79, April, 1973. HEW. Public Health Service. National Institute of Mental Health)

2. Inclusivity versus Exclusivity

Ideally, traditional marriage in the United States has usually meant exclusivity of mates. The spouses devote themselves, both physically and emotionally, to one another. Emotional or physical involvement with another is avoided. If it is not, the marriage would be wrecked and divorce the logical result.

In practice, the exclusive nature of marriage is often transgressed by both wives and husbands. Such transgressions have been kept secret in the past. Today, however, among a small but increasing minority, such transgressions have become a part of the marriage. Indeed multirelationships by spouses are being institutionalized in group and swinging marriages. Hard data are difficult to gather on these marital forms because of the general social taboos surrounding such behavior, thus most of the following evaluations are essentially mere opinion.

Group or multilateral marriage is marriage among three or more persons. The advantages of such an arrangement are said to be (1) a broader base of companionship, therefore less loneliness, (2) the benefits of multiple parenting received by the child, (3) a more enriched sexual life, (4) a stabler economic foundation, (5) increasing personal growth opportunities, and (6) a more fulfilled life.

To date most group marriages have been quite unstable. They have collapsed quickly, in part, because of negative social pressures. The major reason for collapse, more probably, is the drastic increase in complexity. Instead of the normal two-way interaction, one must now cope with multiple interactions. If one considers the many roles in marriage such as woman, wife, and mother and then adds multiple interactions in each role, it is apparent that complexity of relationships can be overwhelming. Pleasing one wife or husband is difficult, but pleasing two or three is impossible for many.

Far more common than group marriage is *swinging.* This usually refers to sexual openness while maintaining emotional exclusivity. Again, what research evidence there is on swinging is highly suspect. Some say that sexual openness keeps interest and freshness alive from which one gains a more confident self-image. The secretiveness and ensuing tensions are removed from adultery. The simplest rationale offered is, sex is fun so why not enjoy it.

It is interesting that most swingers return to the traditional marital format after two or three years, apparently because the life-style is so strenuous. Research suggests that many people cannot make the transition to swinging because of inhibitions and guilt. Swinging is disruptive of marriage when it is tried but can't be accepted. Divorce rates among swingers are higher than average. Venereal disease becomes a real possibility.

A study[9] of 1,175 couples who dropped out of swinging indicated the following kinds of problems. About 10 percent of the couples cited jealousy as their reason for dropping out of swinging. Husbands reported more jealousy than wives. Some became quite concerned about their wives' popularity or endurance capabilities. Wives were more apt to become jealous if the marriage was threatened. Other reasons cited for dropping out were guilt, threat to marriage, development of outside attachment, boredom, separation or divorce, fear of discovery.

Not all couples that dropped out of swinging reported only negative results. About one-third reported at least temporary improvement in their marital relationship. The reasons given by these couples were excitement, sexual freedom, greater appreciation of mate, learning new sex techniques, sexual variety, and better communication or openness between partners.

It is usually the husband who initiates interest and makes the first contacts, but it is the wife who often is the first to seek an end to the swinging arrangement.[9] Swingers allow individuals freedom of choice and do not coerce people into doing things against their wishes. There is a high rate of female homosexual behavior, but male homosexuality appears to be rare. There seems to be no evidence that swingers have any more personal problems than nonswingers of similar background. Most swingers feel that it has helped their marriage but stress that swinging would probably harm a marriage already in trouble. Most swingers believe that they are honest and open about sex and that this is a desirable quality.[10,11]

Communes represent another possible alternative to the traditional nuclear family pattern. They will be investigated more thoroughly in Reading 24.

3. Permanent Commitment versus Permanent Availability

Consensual marriage simply means a man and woman choosing to live together without the formalities of a socially sanctioned marriage. This is not a new phenomenon. Throughout America's early frontier lands, common-law marriage was recognized in part because of the lack of legal officials to perform a proper marriage. Today living together merely for convenience or to avoid the negative restraints of formal marriage or to test the relationship (*trial marriage*) in preparation for legal marriage is becoming more acceptable. A few studies of living-together couples have appeared. A recent one compared living-together couples with going-together couples. There were no significant differences between the groups in level of trust and reported happiness, both of which were high. A difference was found in the reported degree of commitment to marriage. The going-together males and females were most committed to future marriage. The living-together males were the least committed, far less even than the girls with whom they were living. The researchers' tentative conclusions were, in part:

> To a striking degree, living-together couples did *not* reciprocate the kinds of feelings (of need, respect, happiness, involvement, or commitment to marriage) that one would expect to be the basis of a

good heterosexual relationship. The question of whether such a lack of reciprocity is typical of such relationships and thus reflects the difficulties of bringing off a successful nonnormative relationship or whether it is merely typical of those who volunteered for our research cannot be answered.[12]

Many who live together state their desire to avoid what they perceive to be the constraining, love-draining formalities associated with legal marriage. They say, "If I stay with my mate out of my own free desire rather than because I legally must remain, our relationship will be more honest and caring." "The stability of our relationship is its very instability."

It appears that "living together" has numerous connotations which may not be true for every cohabiting couple. First, it is clear that many of these experiences are no more than short-lived sexual flings. Among male students in the largest research to date on cohabiting students, 82 percent of those 20 years of age or younger reported their longest cohabitation as three months or less. Of males aged 21 and 22, 63 percent reported the same. Among females in the 20-and-under age group, 67 percent reported three months or briefer cohabitations, while 48 percent of the 21-and 22-year-olds reported the same.[13] These couples do not stay together long, and there are no firm future plans.

There are those couples who see cohabiting as a true trial marriage. As one young woman explained, "We are thinking of marriage in the future, and we want to find out if we really are what each other wants. If everything works out, we will get married."[14] Some of these couples go so far as to set a specific time period.

In addition, there are those couples that view cohabiting as a permanent alternative to marriage. They often express philosophical rejection of the marital institution as being unfavorable to healthy and growing relationships.

There are also the casual couples that live together out of convenience. Their relationship is not inclusive, although it may be sexually intimate or not. Such couples often live together after a very short acquaintance.

"Living together" does not necessarily portend some great new experiment leading to improved marriage despite the medias' popular presentation of the great new way to happier life.[15]

Children complicate the living-together idea. Margaret Mead has proposed a *two-step marriage* to provide for children. The first step would be a looser relationship legally than our current marriage in which parenthood would have to be avoided. This first step would be similar to living together in that it could be broken upon request of either partner. If successful, this first-step relationship may then evolve into the second step, a parenthood marriage which would have stronger legal commitments.[16]

To date, living together seldom survives long as a permanent form of relationship. Most couples either break up or legally marry after living together.

Contractual marriage is another approach. In essence, the couple must

TABLE 1 A Comparison of Cohabiting and Noncohabiting College Students[15]

Most formal studies of cohabitation to date have had fairly small samples. The study to be reported here is the first with a relatively large sample size. Eleven hundred undergraduates completed a questionnaire requesting details of their heterosexual relationship experiences while in college. One-third of the sample reported some period of living with a member of the opposite sex.

Are you now, or have you ever 'lived' with someone of the opposite sex?

Yes:	Men	33.4%
	Women	32.3%
	Total	32.8%

When class standing is considered it becomes obvious that the chances of cohabitation experience increase greatly as age and college standing progress.

Percent having cohabitation experience by class standing

Males		*Females*	
Freshmen	19%	Freshmen	25%
Sophomores	25%	Sophomores	26%
Juniors	34%	Juniors	32%
Seniors	47%	Seniors	45%

Exactly half of the cohabitors reported engaging in more than one such arrangement. Sixty-two percent of the males and forty-one percent of the females had cohabited more than once.

Sixty percent of the cohabiting experiences involved a living situation that included third parties, other roommates, etc.

The cohabiting experiences were rather short for the majority.

	Length of Cohabitation	
	Less Than 6 Months	More Than 6 Months
Males	85	15
Females	75	25

Fifty percent of the males and 31 percent of the females reported that their longest cohabiting experience lasted less than a month.

The authors ran many other analyses of the data. In general, the overall conclusions from the study appear to be:

1. The opportunity to cohabit has increased in recent years, especially as college housing arrangements have become less restrictive and the fear of pregnancy reduced by improved contraception.
2. There is limited commitment although commitment increases with age and class standing.
3. Most cohabitation experience is probably not in the nature of a "trial marriage" because of its short duration and the living situation in which there are often other persons.
4. A minority of parents are told of the cohabiting experience.
5. Marriage is still the popular choice for cohabitors although cohabitation on a more permanent basis ranks higher than for noncohabitors.

periodically renew their marriage contract. Such a contract might be tied to a given time period, say, five years, or to critical life junctures, such as the coming of children as in Mead's two-step marriage. The new contract could be made with the same person or a new person. In a way, such a system now operates informally in the United States. *Serial monogamy* is the system of marriage whereby one has several partners but only one at a time. As divorce becomes easier, as for example with California's new no-fault, no-contest system, more and more people will marry several spouses over their lifetime.

Summary

"Perhaps, in conclusion, I should note some of the risks involved in the new life-styles. The major risk in opening up choice is error in choice. When choices open up, one must carefully consider priorities. The older restricted system exacted a price: it placed a person in a mold which did not enable him to choose a life-style that would allow maximum self-growth and social contribution. The current, more open system runs the risk of one's acting impulsively. Such precipitate action might destroy aspects of life of higher priority. For example, one may impulsively get involved in a sexual encounter, and thereby cause a break in a meaningful relationship; or one may hastily get involved in divorce proceedings, and thereby avoid facing up to faults in oneself. Thus, the price of a more open system is the greater need for a rational examination of the alternatives.

"The old system had many people trapped in a rut; the new one may have many people constantly running from one style of life to another, unable to choose wisely."[17]

Regardless of the specific kind of union between a man and a woman, to be successful it is still basically the quality of the relationship between two human beings. I may live in a nuclear family, be a single swinger or a commune member, but in each case I must relate successfully on a one-to-one basis with another person if my life is to be totally fulfilled. If I cannot make such relationships, the form of the union makes no real difference. In the following article, William Masters and Virginia Johnson examine the meaning of commitment and the emotional elements that can make or break any relationship. In reality, the success of a relationship depends upon two personalities and their interaction rather than on the form of the institution.

21 The Pleasure Bond: A New Look at Sexuality and Commitment

William H. Masters
Virginia E. Johnson

The Circle of Commitment

Today, when almost all the old assumptions about love and marriage are being questioned, the trend is to deny the importance of commitment. And so, tantalized by talk of open marriages and sexual freedom, afraid to seem over-possessive, many couples feel confused. What does it mean, then, to be "committed" to another person, either in a marriage or in a long-term relationship?

Put in its simplest terms, a commitment is a pledge to do something. One person tells another, "I promise," and the promise is kept, the obligation fulfilled. Trust has been asked for; trust has been given; trust has been repaid.

This is the basic meaning of commitment. It is the cement that binds individuals and groups together. Even a legal contract depends on the keeping of a pledge. For if a contract is broken, the commitment not kept, the law can penalize the person who failed to perform as he had promised; but penalizing him leaves the obligation unfulfilled, the job undone, the need unmet.

That is all there is to commitment insofar as it relates to associations that exist for practical purposes. When the association is for emotional reasons, however, the meaning of commitment changes. It still can be defined as a pledge to do something, but the pledge possesses a radically different dimension. "I promise," one person tells another, "because I care about you."

Caring flows from two related but different kinds of feelings. One is a feeling of being *responsive* to someone, of *caring for* that person; the other is a feeling of being *responsible for* someone, of wanting to *take care* of him or her. These feelings are generated in entirely different ways. Responsiveness occurs sponta-neously, before the mind is consciously aware of what is happening—a sudden surge of interest and attraction triggered by another person's physical pres-ence. Responsibility is consciously, though often unwillingly, invoked by the mind—an acknowledgement of obligation.

Most parents experience these elemental feelings when holding their infant. This combination of emotions—a wish to take care of someone for whom one cares—creates an overpowering sense of involvement and identification, of oneness. Some people call it love, and it is the original source of commitment.

As such, however, it is still a one-sided commitment. The parents are committed; the baby is dependent. There is nothing mutual about the bond. Before too long, however, emotionally mature parents stop identifying with their child in such a total way. Gradually they accept him or her as a separate human being whose needs are not only different from their own but also in conflict often with their immediate desires. Thus, long before parent and child are equals in any sense of the word, each needs something of the other: acceptance, appreciation, affection. And the smallest child soon learns that his parents hope to receive from him precisely what he expects from them— pleasure. *Mutual pleasure sets a seal on emotional commitment.*

This is the foundation on which all future affectionate relationships will be constructed. The search for pleasure—and pleasure is an infinitely deeper and more complex emotional matter than simple sensual gratification—continues throughout life. The quality of marriage is determined by whether the pleasure derived exceeds the inevitable portion of displeasure that human beings must experience in all their associations. When there is more displeasure than pleasure in a marriage, a husband and wife are more aware of the obligations of marriage than they are of its rewards, and their bond can be characterized as a commitment of obligation.

In contrast there is the commitment of concern, a bond in which a man and a woman mutually meet their obligations not because they feel *compelled* to do so but because they feel *impelled* to, by impulses, desires and convictions that are deeply rooted within themselves. When they act in each other's best interests, even though this may at the time be in conflict with their own immediate wishes, they are saying to each other, in effect: "I care very much about your feelings—because your feelings affect mine. Your happiness adds to mine, your unhappiness takes away from mine, and I want to be happy."

So obvious does all this seem to most young couples that they believe they know all there is to know—or certainly all they need to know—about how and why being committed to each other is linked to sexual pleasure. They met as two strangers and eventually became lovers, and because this is how life is expected to move, they accept it as a natural sequence of events, a matter of elementary logic: Love leads to sex, which leads to greater love, which in turn leads to better sex, and so it goes. This, at least, is how they expect it to be, and if it turns out otherwise, they have convenient explanations: insufficient love, inadequate sex. It is as simple as A B C. Like the alphabet, however, it does not mean much by itself.

In a more reflective mood they might say: "Since we enjoy being together, the greater our enjoyment, the more reason we have to stay together." They are describing the circle of commitment. Being together gives them satisfactions, including sex, that reinforce their decision to live together as a couple; these satisfactions, which are highly valued, must be safeguarded. Each partner, to protect his or her own happiness, tries to sustain the other partner's happiness so that their relationship will flourish; and these reciprocal efforts intensify the satisfactions they find in living together—which further strengthens their wish to remain a couple. They live according to the commitment of mutual concern, and pleasure is the bond between them.

They expect to be faithful because they want to be. Furthermore they realize that if either or both of them seek sexual satisfaction with other partners, the circle of commitment will have been broken. The more satisfactions they find with other people, the fewer satisfactions they need from each other; and the less they need from each other, the easier it is for them to go their separate ways. Beyond all rationalization, extra-marital affairs would demonstrate two things: first, that husband and wife were incapable of meeting each other's most basic physical and emotional needs and, second, that they did not consider each other a unique source of satisfaction and pleasure.

Just as no one stops to think about what is required for him to breathe until he has trouble breathing, so couples give little thought to what is needed for their happiness to continue until the day they discover that theirs is no longer a happy marriage. Then, to the extent that they never really understood what united them as lovers, they find it difficult to understand what has made them strangers once again. It seems as though the movie of their life has been put in reverse.

If their life together had actually been filmed and could now be reviewed, they might better appreciate some things that in the beginning of their relationship greatly contributed to their satisfaction in being in each other's company. There was, for example, the simple fact of acceptance.

The importance of being accepted as the person one happens to be is incalculable. Its contribution to self-esteem is well established, and it plays a significant part in sexual responsiveness. This can be discerned in the remark of a man who said that he first truly believed that his wife-to-be loved him the evening she drank from his glass of water. To him the gesture communicated total acceptance, and this acceptance of oneself as a physical being heralds the acceptance of oneself as a sexual being.

This is particularly important in the beginning of a sexual relationship. What is needed is not simply to be admired or desired, vitally important though that is, but to be confirmed as a sexual person. It is comparatively simple, after all, for anyone to establish the extent to which his personality seems to appeal to other people. But a person's sexuality, which is just one dimension of personality, is more difficult to assay. It finds its fullest expression in mutually appreciative physical relationships. Even emancipated men and women don't have too many of these.

In one lifetime, therefore, most men and women will have few reflections of themselves as sexual beings. Consequently, each relationship has the potential to exert a powerful emotional effect, for better or for worse. In every sexual encounter, no matter how absorbed the partners may be in their individual physical and emotional responses, each remains distinctly conscious of the other's reactions. In part this reflects concern for the partner: Was it good? And in part it reflects uncertainty about oneself: Was I good?

This is one of the satisfactions that all couples seek in their relationships—a validation of their sexual selves. On one level a man wants to be reassured that he is like other men; the woman, that she is like other women.

Beyond that, however, lies a need to be appreciated in an entirely specific way as a unique individual. In the intimacy of a sexual relationship, few things matter more to each partner than to be perceived as the individual he or she is. Indeed, it is this perception that makes mutual, sustained pleasure possible.

To make an emotional commitment to someone is to be a steadfast ally; it is essentially an expression of loyalty. But there is another dimension to commitment. Becoming committed to someone is, by definition, to entrust one's physical and emotional well-being to that person; it is an act of faith and an acceptance of vulnerability.

This vital distinction between *making a commitment* and *becoming committed* is obscured by the English language, which fails to provide words that differentiate one emotional dimension from the other. To say that a man and a woman are committed to each other, for instance, in no way indicates the nature of their bond. A woman may be committed to her husband in the sense of being his loyal wife, his co-operative partner in maintaining a family—and yet *not* be committed to him in the sense of trusting him with her deepest feelings, of being emotionally vulnerable to him.

Because this distinction between making a commitment and becoming committed has not been widely appreciated and generally goes unremarked, considerable confusion results. Not infrequently, men and women discover to their astonishment that they have become committed in spite of themselves, and without ever having openly made a commitment.

A case in point involves a woman in her early 30s who had been married for six years to a professional man who was sexually inactive. After having tried unsuccessfully to encourage him to be more responsive, she decided to have an affair. Since her marriage offered her many material and social advantages that she valued, she did not want a divorce.

Consequently, the wife chose to have an affair with a man who appeared to have little in common with her. He was younger than she was; he worked as a baker; and having recently come to the United States, he spoke little English. But sex between them was very good, and in the warmth and security of the physical relationship each began to unfold. Without being aware of what was happening, they started to become committed to each other. All they knew was that they chose to be with each other as often as possible and they permitted themselves to reveal more and more of their deepest feelings.

Perhaps because language was an obstacle, they learned to watch each other's face, and to listen with extraordinary intensity to whatever was said.

The experience was shattering for the young woman because her role at home seemed one of catering to her husband's wishes, while he often appeared totally oblivious to her presence. Finding herself truly perceived and appreciated as an individual by her foreign-born friend, she flowered; friends who did not know what was going on commented on her obvious happiness, which was a reflection of the fact that she was discovering aspects of her own personality —a level of sensual awareness—that she had never known existed. This was especially true in sex; as she expressed it, she was discovering in parts of her body feelings that she hadn't dreamed were there. She was finding her own sexual identity.

Ultimately this led her to leave her husband and go to live with her friend. In doing so she believed that she was making a new commitment. What she did not realize was that this commitment had been in the making for more than a year.

When a man and a woman marry, what sometimes happens, through no fault of their own, is that they begin to think of themselves, not as two individuals who have the capacity to enhance each other's joy in being alive, but as a couple mutually committed to tasks they must complete. They want to make money, to advance in their careers, to set up a home or become socially established and, sooner or later, to have children. These all are reasonable and praiseworthy goals, but secondary in importance to their original commitment: the mutual need to flourish as individuals in the climate of pleasure that each afforded the other.

Rarely do they understand what has happened. They have forgotten that before their marriage they were two people who tried to be together as much as they could because they found comfort and security in each other's acceptance, appreciation and understanding. This was the commitment of mutual concern. With marriage, however, they have become husband and wife, individuals who expect to take care of specialized responsibilities and who increasingly follow separate paths if their day's work is to be done. They slowly become emotionally uncommitted—and are left with the commitment of obligation.

Commitment to goals of achievement pre-empt the mutual commitment. All the forces that brought them together are now losing intensity. Instead of being joined as a male and a female who can give each other support and pleasure, they now play the roles of husband and wife, or mother and father, who must separately struggle with onerous obligations. And because they are less directly involved in each other's lives, each partner experiences this "disinvolvement" as being less cared for, less valued.

This is one of the main reasons why sex between them grows unsatisfactory. In the early years of their relationship, both before marriage and probably for some time afterward, their love-making would occur at the end of a day during which, for a few hours, at least, they had been closely involved. Intercourse then expressed the feelings that had been accumulating all the while they were enjoying other aspects of their life.

But after years of marriage, sex becomes a postscript tacked on at the end of the day. Having had little opportunity to spend time together and little to say beyond discussing their separate obligations, they meet in bed and expect to turn on passion as though it were an electric switch. It is hardly surprising, under these circumstances, that sex, which earlier in marriage was one of the strongest forces drawing them together, later may be experienced as an obligation close to being an imposition. Instead of uniting them, sex separates them.

Such changes are not always attributable to the fact that a husband and wife have devoted their energies to other goals they consider more important than their intimate relationship. Frequently the deterioration of the sexual bond stems from the husband's and wife's lack of a secure sense of themselves as sexual beings. The insecurity may come from negative sexual attitudes and early repressions, from unfortunate sexual experiences or simply from a lack of sexual information.

In the beginning of their relationship, this inadequacy may go unremarked because the earliest sexual encounters generally—although certainly not always—prove stimulating enough to propel them into a sexual union. One naked body touching another is, after all, sufficient to generate a powerful drive that can carry both individuals past inhibitions.

Even if this were not the case, however, some lack of satisfaction in their early encounters would be what any two inexperienced individuals might anticipate, since either one or both may have had little chance to learn what sex is all about.

There is no particular reason for a couple to doubt that in time, and with a commitment secure enough to allow them to be vulnerable without fear, they will become fully functional sexual beings. Each usually will become responsive *if* he or she has some concept of what it means to be a sexual person. It means more than just the acceptance of male or female identity.

Being a sexual person means being responsive to one's sexual feelings—that is, being conscious of spontaneous sexual impulses generated within the body, accepting them as natural, healthy and "good," enjoying them without shame or guilt and permitting them to build up into the tensions that then require some sort of release. It means being responsible for the satisfaction of one's sexual feelings—that is, actively reaching out for ways to achieve that release, whether through masturbation, intercourse or any mutually acceptable caress. And finally, it means deriving pleasure not only from released tension and from sensual gratification but from the total experience as an affirmation of one's sexual nature. Only with security in these feelings about oneself is it possible to pursue sexual pleasure as an active goal with one's partner, to be committed to sex as a couple.

One reason couples become trapped in sexually distressed situations is that they are afraid. This is usually the basis for their lack of commitment to their own sexuality, to their right as human beings to sexual pleasure. For the chief obstacle to sexual pleasure is fear—fear in all its forms: the fear of being hurt, physically or emotionally; the fear of being wrong or making a mistake and being punished or ridiculed; the fear of being considered ugly, clumsy, foolish, incompetent, unresponsive, undesirable . . . an almost endless list.

In sex, fear frequently masquerades as acute embarrassment, and its effects are so insidious that it can undermine any sense of security a man or woman may have. One recently married young woman, for example, had just finished showering and on impulse decided to walk out of the bathroom naked. She approached her husband with a smile, anticipating approval at the very least, if not admiration and even desire. He looked at her and he too smiled, but his smile was one of embarrassment. Then he reached out and flicked her nipple with his finger in what was intended to be a teasing gesture. It was, in fact, the only way he could think of to meet a situation for which he was totally unprepared. He felt dismayed at the possibility that something was being requested of him that he was too inexperienced to deliver. His crude gesture was enough to humiliate his wife, to make her feel not only rejected but foolish. It was a moment she never forgot, and in telling of it years later, long after her divorce, she still found the incident emotionally disturbing.

What her husband had done was to put commitment in reverse. His wife had approached him in total vulnerability, expecting that this would unite them, and he had taught her never to make that mistake again. She had approached him in nakedness, but from then on she was always certain to be covered when his eyes were on her. It is concealment personified, one human being protecting herself from another, remaining separate—and separating herself—from the one person with whom she should have been able to reveal herself without fear, in total physical and emotional nakedness.

Just as the willingness of a man and a woman to reveal themselves to each other and to become vulnerable brings them closer together, so their unwillingness to be vulnerable leads them *not* to reveal themselves and to become uncommitted. A natural sense of self-protection takes over. In learning not to be vulnerable to each other, a married couple are usually re-enacting a childhood scenario. With the marriage partner, as probably with parents in the past, one of them hides behind defensive barriers. In time the partner too becomes guarded, if not equally defensive. Neither is willing to be emotionally vulnerable. They may depend on each other but they do not entrust themselves to each other.

In successful marriages of this kind, the husband and wife are, in effect, business partners in a venture in which both are willing to invest time and effort and from which both hope to profit, an arrangement that allows them to get the major jobs done without too much emotional stress. Because their commitment is governed by reason and practical considerations rather than by emotion, their feelings are generally low-keyed. The bond between them may be primarily one of toleration, each respecting what the other contributes. Or they may even appreciate each other's individuality and share the kind of affection that reflects a sense of comfort with familiar things.

Either way, they relate to each other much as they do to the telephone company. They pay whatever price is required for service to continue—for the house to be cleaned, meals prepared, children cared for, bills paid, possessions purchased, entertainment provided and, when either partner chooses, for sexual relations. They attend to each other's needs to the best of their ability, but passion is something they must go to the movies to see.

To the extent that each fulfills his or her obligations, the marriage survives. Sex becomes perfunctory at best; more often it is either dull, dormant or dead. In many such cases the husband and wife live essentially celibate lives—at least, celibate within the marriage.

Viewed from the outside, such unions seem to fulfill the marriage commitment, and in a sense they do: They fulfill the commitment of obligation. The husband and wife remain faithful to each other, but they do so because they are committed to their marriage, not to each other as sexual beings. Their fidelity is not the expression of their sexual commitment; it is the passive acceptance of a way of life they either do not want to change or do not know how to change.

There is a profound difference, however, between being unwilling to change and being unable to change—although not infrequently couples do not discover until they have sought professional help that one or the other partner does not want to change the nature of their sexual relationship. This can be illustrated by a comparison of two cases that at the outset seemed to have much in common.

Both husbands were troubled by impotence. Both couples had been married almost 30 years and had children who were young adults. As usual, the difference between success and failure in treatment was related directly to the level of interpersonal commitment. Failure (in the classical sense) is perhaps the wrong word to use, because one couple abruptly terminated treatment. It was the wife who refused to continue. Her decision was made the day after she and her husband, following instructions that they had been given by their therapists, had taken turns stroking each other's bodies, trying only to give and get the sensual satisfaction that comes from such caresses, to experience the kind of sensual gratification that even a child is familiar with.

The next day the wife reported that she had felt nothing at all when her husband touched her—but that was not why she insisted on terminating treatment. What bothered her unendurably was that when she touched her husband, his pleasure was evident and his physiological response was immediate and unmistakable. To him, to be freely touched by his wife was like a miracle, and he could hardly contain his joy. This was precisely what the wife could not bear. It was only when she was confronted by her husband's happiness that she realized how unwilling she was to be the source of such satisfaction. From her point of view, he had treated her so wretchedly over the years that she had no reservoir of good will to draw from, no incentive to do anything more for him than she absolutely had to do—and no hope that there could be any reward in sex for her. It would not be an exaggeration to say that the only pleasure left for her in her marriage was to deprive her husband of his pleasure.

The other couple offered a striking contrast. Although for almost 30 years intercourse had taken place infrequently and generally unsatisfactorily, the husband and wife had remained affectionate and close, more sad than angry about their sexual frustration. Most important, the wife never mocked or attacked her husband for his inadequacy in bed—she said that she always knew that he felt miserable enough without her saying a word.

Thirty years of deprivation had not embittered them, nor had it extinguished for either partner a genuine desire to find sexual happiness together.

In treatment they followed their therapists' directions, and almost immediately discovered the pleasure to be derived from the opportunity to touch each other in ways they had never before permitted themselves. The husband was one of myriad men who have grown up believing that there must be something wrong with him if he needed any "help" from a woman in order to become physically aroused. Once released from the bondage of ignorance, both he and his wife eagerly took turns pleasuring each other.

The ability of a man and a woman to become sexually committed stands or falls primarily on their willingness to give and receive pleasure in all its forms. But this is not the willingness that reflects an application of will power, which says more of mental deliberation, discipline and obligation than of desire. It is the willingness that flows from wishing or wanting something, from caring for someone, when the mind serves only as a catalyst and the body asserts itself in ways that the mind might not have anticipated.

Giving and getting pleasure does not mean bartering favors. It involves a mutuality, a flow of excitement and gratification that shuttles back and forth between the partners, who frequently find it impossible to draw a line between the pleasure they are receiving and the pleasure they are giving. It is the same as it is with a kiss—only if a man and a woman are *not* caught up in the kiss will either of them be aware of the physical separateness of their lips.

If a man and a woman are committed to the enjoyment of their own sexual natures and to each other as sexual persons, intercourse allows them to express their emotions in whatever ways seem desirable and appropriate at the moment, revealing themselves not only to each other but to themselves. Liberated from the domination of reason and discipline, they are able to communicate spontaneous wishes that need no justification.

This does not mean that every sexual embrace is a transcendent experience. On the contrary, precisely because both partners are under no pressure to perform or pretend, any sexual embrace can be as casual as a good-night kiss, if that is what both partners want or if that is what one of them needs and the other is pleased and privileged to provide. Moreover, in such a relaxed atmosphere each has earned emotional credit in the other's bank. If, as it occasionally must, sex proves unsatisfactory or disappointing or even frustrating to either husband or wife, their security as a committed couple lies in knowing that there is always a tomorrow.

Total commitment, in which all sense of obligation is linked to mutual feelings of loving concern, sustains a couple sexually over the years. In the beginning it frees them to explore the hidden dimensions of their sexual natures, playing with sex as pastime and passion, seeking the erotic pleasures that give life much of its meaning. Then when carrying the inescapable burdens that come with a family and maturity, they can turn to each other for the physical comforting and emotional sustenance they need. Finally, in their later years, it is in the enduring satisfactions of their sexual and emotional bonds that committed husbands and wives find reason enough to be glad that they still have another day together.

Masters and Johnson speak of commitment and sexuality. Their discussion focuses mainly on the former while little is said directly about human sexuality. The family is above all a sexual union in almost all cultures. Nowhere does one find man's sexuality unregulated by his culture. True, the regulations can and do vary drastically from one society to another, yet it is always regulated.

Man is biologically a sexual animal, but is an understanding of his biology sufficient to understand his sexual behavior? Emphatically, no, it is not. The following reading discusses the biological, psychological, and sociological determinants of human sexual behavior. From there, the authors attempt to define some fundamental standards for human sexual behavior.

22 Fundamental Questions About Human Sexuality

Herant A. Katchadourian
Donald T. Lunde

. . .

We can hardly deny that the origins of human sexual behavior are rooted in biological makeup. But we must also consider other factors because, although important, biology is not all there is to sex. How we behave is a result of three types of forces—biological, psychological, and social. In discussing these determinants of sexual behavior, we do not intend to imply that a choice among these factors is necessary; it is understood that they are complementary rather than mutually exclusive.

Biological Origins of Sexuality

Biological explanations of sexual behavior have generally been based on the concept of instinct. This notion of an innate force has proved quite useful, but scientists have so far failed to define specifically enough what terms like "instinct" and "drive" mean.

As sex and reproduction are so intimately linked in most living beings, we tend to forget that there are also asexual modes of reproduction and organisms that duplicate themselves merely by dividing into two identical "daughter cells." Sexual reproduction, in which two dissimilar cells (sperm and egg) combine to form a new being, is nevertheless the reproductive mode of most animals, including man.

It is thus understandable that one explanation of sexual behavior is simply the need to reproduce. Sex, in this sense, is part of a larger reproductive "instinct," a deep-rooted biological incentive for animals to mate and perpetuate their species. But lower animals cannot possibly know that mating results in reproduction. For that matter, we do not know who made the momentous discovery, at some point in prehistory, that coitus leads to pregnancy. As lower animals are ignorant of this association, what mysterious force propels them to mate?

Although the reproductive consequences of copulation are obvious to us, sexual behavior cannot be scientifically explained in teleological terms, as behavior in which animals engage in order to reproduce. Besides, a great deal of animal and human sexual activity serves no reproductive function.

A simpler and more likely explanation is that man and other animals engage in sex because it is pleasurable. The incentive is in the act itself, rather than in its possible consequences. Sexual behavior in this sense arises from a psychological "drive," associated with sensory pleasure, and its reproductive consequences are a by-product (though a vital one). We are only beginning to understand the neurophysiological basis of pleasure. It has been demonstrated, for example, that there are "pleasure centers" in the brain (in the thalamus, hypothalamus, and mesencephalon) that, when electrically stimulated, cause animals to experience intense pleasure. (Stimulation of certain adjacent areas causes extreme discomfort or pain.) When an animal has the opportunity to stimulate these pleasure centers, it will persist in doing so to the exclusion of all other activity: It will not take time to eat even when starving.

What about sex hormones? They are a fascinating but currently problematic subject of study. We know, for instance, that they begin to exert their influence before birth and are vital in sexual development. Yet, in the mature animal they seem relatively dispensable to the maintenance of sexual functioning. Although these hormones are intimately linked to sexual functioning, the link is clearly not a simple one, and we have yet to discover a substance that might represent a true "sex fuel."

Thus, the biological basis of our sexual behavior involves certain physical "givens," including sex organs, hormones, intricate networks of nerves, and brain centers.

Psychological Determinants of Sexual Behavior

If biological explanations of sexuality were totally satisfactory, it would not be necessary for us to go farther. But, as they do not at this time suffice, we must look for additional factors to explain sexual behavior.

In discussing psychological determinants of behavior, we often must deal with different levels of analysis of the human organism. In one sense, psychological or social forces are merely reflections and manifestations of underlying biological processes. For example, Freud argued that the libido, or sex drive, is the psychological representation of a biological sex instinct.

In another sense, psychological factors are more independent, even though they must be mediated through the neurophysiological mechanisms of the brain, for neither thought nor emotion can occur in an empty skull. But these mechanisms are considered only as the intermediaries through which thought and emotion operate, rather than as their primary determinants. Let us again use hunger as an example. When the brain motivates a person to eat, in response to a feeling of hunger (due to certain sensations in the gastrointestinal system or to a decrease in blood sugar), the response of the individual is relatively independent of psychological and social considerations. Although such factors have some influence on the individual's behavior, they are not the main determinants. On the other hand, when a person dislikes pork or is expected to abstain from eating it, he acts from personal preference or religious conviction. His motivation is still mediated through the brain, but it originates in learned patterns of behavior, rather than in biological factors. We have used the example of hunger, rather than of sex itself, because in the latter the biological imperative is less clear.

Theories of the psychological motivation for sexual behavior are thus fundamentally of two types. In the first, which includes psychoanalytic theory, psychological factors are considered to be representations or extensions of biological forces. In contrast, many learning theories assume that patterns of sexual behavior are largely acquired through a variety of psychological and social mechanisms.

While the causes or determinants of a given type of behavior must not be confused with the purposes that it serves, and though such distinctions are not always easy to recognize, it is, nevertheless, also useful to examine the various aims of sexual behavior. For instance, when a person engages in sex expressly to satisfy physical desire or to relieve "sexual tension," we may say that sex occurs "for its own sake." But for most people sex has an emotional component as well; it takes on added significance as an expression of affection or love for the partner. We can argue, of course, whether this affective component ought to be a basic part of sex or a desirable addition to it, but this question comes under the third main section of this chapter.

Certain secondary (though not necessarily unimportant) goals of sex are clearly "non-sexual" in origin. The contribution of sex to self-esteem is, for instance, most important. Each of us needs a deep and firmly rooted conviction of personal worth. Although no one can hope to be universally loved and admired, we must receive some appreciation from "significant others" and from ourselves. An important component of a person's self-esteem is his sexual standing in his own eyes, as well as in those of others. The role of sex in self-esteem varies among individuals and groups, and some sexual attributes have more widespread significance than do others. For example, confidence of virility is vital to most males, and impotence before old age is humiliating. A man who is often impotent is likely to lose confidence in himself and to feel uncertain and incompetent even in areas in which sexual virility has no direct bearing. Others may be driven to compensate for their sexual weaknesses by acquiring political power, wealth, or knowledge or through antisocial behavior.

In contrast, women have traditionally been much less concerned about their ability to experience orgasm, though this attitude is changing, at least in the West. In some conservative groups in the Middle East, for instance, a women who fails to reach coital orgasm may be aware of a lack, but her self-esteem is not affected by it. The disaster for her is not frigidity but sterility.

The more striking changes in female awareness of orgasm have been occurring in the West, particularly in countries long influenced by the "Victorian ethic." Respectable Victorian women, for instance, risked actual loss of self-esteem if they experienced sexual pleasure (at least, so the predominantly male chroniclers of the age tell us). In contrast, the sophisticated modern Western woman is rapidly becoming as preoccupied with orgasm as males are and as vulnerable to loss of self-esteem at failure. For most women, however, the association between sex and self-esteem has always seemed less direct than for men. Women are more concerned with being attractive, desirable, and lovable, and deficiencies in these attributes are more apt to damage their self-esteem than sexual responsiveness as such. Also, these attributes and sexual responsiveness are often mutually enhancing: A woman who feels admired and desired is more likely to respond sexually and a responsive woman in turn is more ardently desired.

Sexuality is clearly an important component of an individual's self-concept, or sense of identity. Awareness of sexual differentiation precedes that of all other social attributes in the child: He knows himself as a boy or girl long before he learns to associate himself with national, ethnic, religious, and other cultural groupings.

Although developing an awareness of one's biological sex is a relatively simple matter, the acquisition of a sense of sexual identity is a more complex culturally relative process. Traditionally we have assumed that biological sex (maleness and femaleness) and its psychological attributes (masculinity and feminity) are two sides of the same coin. In traditional and stable societies this assumption may have been (and may still be) valid. But in the technologically advanced and structurally more fluid societies such direct correspondence between biological sex and psychological attributes is being challenged more and more vigorously as occupational and social roles for men and women become progressively blurred.

Finally, sex figures prominently in an individual's moral or spiritual identity. At least in Western cultures, it is used as a moral yardstick more consistently than any other form of behavior, at both the personal and public levels: Many of us feel greater guilt and are often punished more severely for sexual transgressions than for other offenses. Common as sexual themes are in our mass media, the level of tolerance is nowhere near that for aggression and violence.

Although both personal and public attitudes are changing in this regard, a common first reaction as to whether or not a person (particularly a woman) is moral or "honorable" is to think in sexual terms. We are not implying that this should or should not be so, but are merely pointing out the enormous influence that sex has on our standing as individuals and members of society.

Social Factors in Sexual Behavior

Just as psychological functions are intimately linked with biological forces, they are equally tied to social factors. In fact, distinctions between what is primarily psychological and what is social often tend to be arbitrary. As a rule, in referring to social or cultural factors the emphasis is on the interpersonal over the intrapsychic and on group processes over internal ones.

Sexuality is often considered a cohesive force that binds the family unit together. In this sense it is subservient to a social goal, and social organizations reciprocally facilitate sexual aims by providing sexual partners and contacts. Sexuality can, of course, also have a divisive influence, and this potential may be one reason for the ambivalence with which sex is viewed in many societies.

Sex also functions as a form of communication. Through it we express affection and love—as well as anger and hatred. When, after coming home from a party, a wife who is herself sexually aroused refuses to sleep with her husband because he has been flirting with other women, she is using sex to communicate a message ("I am angry") and a lesson ("Next time behave yourself"). On the other hand, a woman who is sexually unstimulated may engage in coitus to reward her husband for good behavior. Similarly, promiscuous sexual activity may communicate messages like "I am lonely," "I am not impotent," "I dare to misbehave," and so on.

Sex also symbolizes status. The dominant male animals in a troop and the men with power in society usually have first choice of the more desirable females, as well as the juicier cuts of meat. Beauty is naturally pleasing to the eye, but beyond this attraction the company of a beautiful woman is a testimony and a tribute to a man's social standing, even though she may be tedious in bed. A woman's status is more often enhanced by the importance than by the looks of her man. The value of sex as an indicator of status prompts men in some cultures to keep mistresses; similarly, in prison a dominant inmate may have a "girl" (a sexually submissive male). In both instances, the actual sexual interest may be quite desultory.

The association of sex and aggression is very broad and encompasses biological, psychological, and social considerations. We need only point out here that aggressive impulses may be expressed through sexual behavior and vice versa and that there is a fluid and intimate relation between these two powerful "drives" in all kinds of sexual liaisons.

For some people sexual activity is a form of self-expression in a creative, or aesthetic, sense. What matters most is not simple physical pleasure as such but the broadening of sensual horizons with each experience and the opportunity to express and share these experiences in a very special and intimate way with another person. Such feelings, though very real, are difficult to describe.

In various places and at various times, sex has been used for the loftiest, as well as for the basest, ends. Although sexuality is foreign to the major modern Western traditions of religious worship, other religions have had distinctly sexual components, as the erotic statuary adorning Indian temples and phallic monuments from Classical times attest. Some Muslim men still offer brief prayers before coitus.

On balance, sex has been more crassly and mercilessly exploited than has any other human need. The female body in particular has been a commodity since remotest antiquity. Although women have benefited financially from prostitution, men have had more than their share of profits from this commerce. Prostitution is the most flagrant example of the use of sex for practical gain, but it is by no means the only one. Sexual favors are exchanged for other services between spouses and friends. Sex is used to maintain social standing, to gain popularity, to ensnare and hold spouses, and so on. The overt and covert use of sex in advertising hardly needs to be pointed out.

Other uses of sex are legion. The ancient Romans wore amulets in the form of male sex organs. Some people use sex to cure headaches, to calm their nerves, or to end insomnia. Sex can thus be used for "nonsexual" as well as "sexual" ends. Conversely, sexual gratification can be achieved through orgasm as well as by the displacement and sublimation of the sexual drive with countless ordinary and extraordinary "nonsexual" activities.

.   .   .

How We Should Behave Sexually

According to an old saying, a stiff penis has no conscience. The world, however, is not populated by penises and vaginas but by men and women, and they do have consciences. In fact, the moral questions related to sex, as well as to any other area of life, may well be the most critical ones. They certainly are the most difficult.

There are several well-known approaches to the discussion of sexual ethics. First is the straitlaced attitude, which at its worst stands for dullness, hypocritical double standards, tedious lists of "don'ts" with a few "dos" (that are hardly worth doing), and an outlook that generally inhibits all that is spontaneous, imaginative, and exciting in sex.

The opposite alternative is the callously libertine approach advocated by assorted sexual "liberators." Their central message is a cavalier insistence on discarding sexual shackles, casting off "Victorian" (and often long dead and buried) inhibitions, and "letting oneself go." The proponents and practitioners of this ethic are not always concerned with the consequences of their acts and even less bothered by offending the sensibilities of others.

Then there is the intermediary stance that is becoming increasingly prevalent, whereby permissiveness is tempered with consideration. There is little concern here with abstract principles; the attitude is rather one of "as long as it gives pleasure to all concerned and hurts no one, it is moral."

In the search for a sexual ethic, it is tempting to bypass basic moral issues by dismissing them as "philosophical" abstractions of no practical immediacy and instead to try to go directly to specifics of sexual behavior. This shortcut usually fails, for before we can sensibly discuss whether premarital sex, for example, is right or wrong, we must agree on what "right" and "wrong" mean. Nor can we be satisfied with the mere enunciation of moral generalities, for the specifics of sexual acts must also be recognized: Agreeing that sexual exploitation is wrong is insufficient to determine whether or not certain episodes of premarital sex are wrong. Premarital sex may or may not be exploitative, and, besides, exploitation is not the only kind of immorality.

The answer to a given moral question is dependent upon the content and application of specific principles. For example, the following considerations could enter into judgments about heterosexual intercourse: Children are best raised by their parents; sex is most satisfying in the context of stable relationships; and secrecy is inimical to honest relationships. In a particular sexual act these components *(content)* of moral judgment are then *applied* to the specific act. In the case of extramarital intercourse, it is likely that children resulting from the union will not be raised by both parents or that children in an existing marriage will lose a parent; that the relationship will be unstable; and that the relationship will have to be kept secret. Therefore adultery could be judged morally wrong on any or all counts.

In contemporary Western society, however, neither the content of moral judgments nor their applications are agreed upon. In the above example, some people would argue that it is preferable to raise children in communes, that casual sexual encounters can be satisfying and need not result in pregnancy, that it is possible to have stable relationships without the benefit of marriage, and that what you do not know will not hurt you. There are marked differences of opinion in these matters between groups divided along generational, educational, and socioeconomic lines. Even within clergy of the same denomination opinions are likely to be conflicting.

.   .   .

Fundamental Standards for Sexual Behavior

Given the uncertainties about why and how people behave sexually and the confusion between judgments of private and public behavior, the dilemma of absolute versus relative moral standards, and changing moral values, how do we decide how we should behave sexually here and now?

New Year's resolutions notwithstanding, most of us do not regulate our sex lives formally. At best we have general feelings about how we should behave sexually. Most of us conform out of inertia or fear and break rules mainly on impulse. We reject some activities totally because of the enormity of their social consequences or the threats that they pose to our self-esteem. We find others unappealing or difficult of access. When we change our moral views, we usually do so with guilt and primarily to justify acts already committed. Hopefully, some of us also just grow wiser with time.

Our behavior and attitudes are determined by complex and often unconscious processes that explain the apparent irrationality with which we conduct
our lives. That is "human nature," and little can be done to change it. We are
not, however, totally helpless in this respect, even though it may be convenient
to assume that we are. At some point every thoughtful and responsible person
must exercise his "free will" and make choices. The first, and basic, choice is
whether he wants to be a "moral" person, by whatever standard, or to take
what he can for himself and the rest of the world be damned. The ambiguities
and difficulties in making ethical judgments can be used as an excuse for
avoiding them altogether: As no one really "knows" what constitutes right and
wrong, why pay attention to them at all? Why not do as we please and let other
people fend for themselves?

. . .

To live in society in reasonable peace we have to know its rules and to be
able to differentiate between those that can be broken with relative impunity
and those that cannot. But what if the rules are irrational or unfair? Is adjustment to society the ultimate goal? The answers again involve personal choices.
Most people follow the main trends of sexual behavior, and this majority
provides stability. Many people, however, refuse to conform themselves, and
some attempt to change others' behavior as well. Those who do should remember that deviation from the norm and forging ahead of one's time are the
prerogatives of prophets and fools: One must be sure of his calling. Despite
these imponderables, can we isolate some components of a fundamental standard of sexual behavior? There are at least five that seem worth major consideration.

Acceptance of Sexual Realities. Knowledge and acceptance of sexual realities
are indispensable to sexual fulfillment and honesty. First comes the willingness
to recognize biological facts, including practical knowledge (not necessarily
from formal study) of the sexual organs and their functions. More important
is acceptance of sexual feelings as legitimate biological and psychological
manifestations, rather than as afflictions that must be exorcised or only grudg-
ingly tolerated.

Next is a willingness to accept behavioral facts, to recognize how people
behave, regardless of how we think that they ought to behave. People have
remarkable capacities for self-deception. When an investigator reports statistics on the prevalence of some socially unacceptable behavior, there is always
a public outcry. People object not because they have more reliable data but
because the findings "don't make sense." "There cannot be so many homosexuals," they may say, but what they mean is that there should not be so many
homosexuals. The tendency to think in stereotypes is often as strong as the
tendency to deny. According to some people, for example, any artist or intel-

lectual, any man who is refined or gentle, is a homosexual. The behavioral realities are there, whether we recognize them or not. By ignoring, distorting, or denying them we merely fool ourselves. On the other hand, recognizing reality does not necessarily require condoning it.

Of all the various phases of our sex lives perhaps the most crucial is how well we face up to our own sexual thoughts and feelings. It is not possible to come to terms with ourselves as long as we refuse to confront our own sexuality. Some extraordinary individuals willingly recognize their sexual needs, yet delay or inhibit satisfying those needs for what they consider to be higher causes. That is one thing; simply to look away is another. We must be honest with ourselves and others in all things but especially in sex, for in this area pretense wears thin, bravado sounds hollow, and in bluffing others we bluff ourselves.

Enhancing Sexuality. Sexuality is not a wild horse that must be tamed and then exercised periodically. It is a potential with which we are born and which must be developed and nourished. It is every bit as important to be concerned about fulfilling our sexual capabilities as about fulfilling our intellectual or artistic capabilities.

The biological origins of sexual functioning do not ensure its automatic operation. Monkeys reared in isolation, for instance, do not know how to interact sexually. They are physically healthy and the sex drive is present, but the behavior that would lead to gratification is disorganized. Sexuality thus requires a certain milieu in which to develop. It needs warm contacts with other people, and it needs nurture.

To start with, there must be acceptance of the fundamental value of sex, in addition to acceptance of its reality. Such acceptance must come early and be incorporated into the personality structure of the child. His intimate relationships must enhance this feeling and permit the growth of his sexuality while instilling the restraints required for successful social living.

A fundamental standard must therefore include incentives as well as prohibitions. There is at times the assumption that one can do no wrong sexually as long as one does nothing at all. This approach is too negative and makes sexuality appear a necessary evil at best.

When a person enters a relationship that has a legitimate sexual component, is he not obligated to act effectively in a sexual way? When a parent does not provide for his family to the best of his ability or fails to care for his children we rightfully condemn him. But what about the spouse who makes no effort to maintain and improve his or her sexual attractiveness, who is lazy and inept in bed, and who tries to pass off sexual incompetence as innocence or decency?

Integrating Sex into Life as a Whole. Ultimately sex must make sense in the context of one's overall life. At certain periods sexual pressure is overwhelming, and sometimes we go to great lengths for its sake. But these instances are unusual and transitory and generally give way to more prosaic but steady sexual needs.

The place that sex occupies in our overall lives varies from one person to another. It is possible that we are born with different genetic predispositions in drive strength. Physical characteristics certainly have great influence on personality development and sexual behavior. For example, a pretty girl discovers very early the impact of her appearance upon others. The families that raise us and the community values that we learn to share or reject combine to shape our sexual behavior.

For some people sex becomes the pivot of their lives. Others hardly seem to care. The important point is not how many orgasms we achieve during a week or in a lifetime but whether or not our sexual needs are satisfied in a manner consistent with the strength of our desires, the requirements of our consciences, and the basic goals and purposes of our lives.

Some sexual dissatisfactions are caused by false or excessive expectations. Gratifying as sex may be, we can derive only so much from it. It cannot be substituted for all other needs, just as substitution of other satisfactions for those of sex can also be stretched only so far.

A fundamental standard that does not facilitate the integration of sexuality into life as a whole has limited usefulness. There are those who feel or act morally in all respects but sexually; sex is thus their secret vice. To a degree such schisms are unavoidable, but beyond certain limits they constitute points of weakness that are vulnerable to stress.

The Relation of Sex to Marriage. The aspect of heterosexual intercourse that raises the most frequent moral concern is whether it occurs within or outside of marriage. Marriage in its various forms is a universal institution. Sex almost always plays a part in it, but, of course, marriage involves much more than sex. At least in principle, however, there are important cultural differences in whether or not sex is restricted to marital partners.

In the West the traditional expectation has been that sex will be restricted in this way. In practice there have been many departures from this expectation, particularly among men. Currently the trend is toward less rigidity on this point for both sexes, particularly in relation to premarital sex. Statistical estimates of the incidence of virginity have been one of the more popular forms of sex research on university campuses. Current assessments vary, but half the student population in some colleges may well be engaging in coitus with some frequency. Extramarital coitus poses different kinds of problems, for it involves consideration of the spouse's feelings as well as of one's own conscience. The incidence of extramarital sex is apparently also on the rise, but again there are wide variations among social groups.

Because of the long-term mutual commitments of married couples, marital sex has particular significance. The marital relationship entails much more than sex. Nevertheless, sexual incompatibility is a frequent cause of marital discord. Of course, marital discord arising from other sources also leads to sexual problems. The issue is not how much sex is necessary or "good" for the couple but whether or not sex plays a mutually satisfactory role in the relationship.

These areas are those to which a fundamental standard must apply. The matter has been discussed time and again and continues to be a major topic.

Sex and Love. Each era and culture has had its views on love, and many of man's most eloquent expressions have been those of love. It is a tribute to the enduring strength of the sentiment to which it refers that the word "love"—hackneyed, abused, and exploited as it has been—still retains so much meaning.

A common, and justified, criticism of "sex manuals" is that they neglect appropriate consideration of love: Either they omit mention of it altogether, or they include only insipid platitudes. By the same token, however, essays on love tend to neglect or etherealize sex to a point at which it seems more suited to angels than to human beings.

The relation of sex to love, like that of sex to marriage, is a frequent source of controversy. The well-known Western ideal attempts to combine all three: sex, love, and marriage. But relatively few people seem able to attain this ideal or to sustain it over periods of years. Currently some people are willing to settle for love and sex alone, and love too may be on its way out as a necessary condition for sex. This change is viewed as moral degeneration by some people and as sexual regeneration by others.

Should sex, which is equally complex, not be viewed as an entity in its own right? If we can have love with or without sex, why can we not legitimately have sex with or without love? Everyone must ultimately face this question, and a well-thought-out fundamental standard may be preferable to the usual compromises reached under the pressures of the moment.

The last paragraph is particularly important to the single adult. A newly divorced man or woman, for example, must decide what to do with their sexuality. Do I simply sleep with every person that offers sex? Do I wait until I remarry? Can I sleep with another man in my own house if the children are home? Do I give up sex altogether? In addition, there are many other problems for the single person, especially the recently divorced or widowed. For example, the economics of running a household with only one parent are considerably different than when there are two parents present.

The feminists' plea for monetary equality for the woman becomes especially crucial when the single-parent family is considered. The vast majority of single-parent families are headed by a woman. About one of every ten families is a one-parent family. It is estimated that 10 percent of the children in the United States are living in single-parent families. In the cases where the absent husband cannot or will not continue monetary help to the family, the woman is hard put to support herself and her children even when she has marketable skills. For example, in 1972 the median salary for full-time, year-round workers was $8,966 for white males, $5,323 for white women.[1] The median wage for full-time women workers was 60 percent of that for men. Such earnings figures directly affect 8.9 percent of all white families and 24.9 percent of Negro families since these are the percentages of families headed by women in the United States.[2] This represents about 2¼ million families. Although this figure represents only about one-twelfth of all families with children, they make up more than one-fourth of all that are classified as poor. Thus, compared with the intact family, the single-parent family often lives at a marginal economic level.

The following selection by E. E. LeMasters, a professor in the School of Social Work at the University of Wisconsin, discusses the characteristics, advantages and disadvantages of the single-parent family.

23 Parents without Partners

E. E. LeMasters

In thinking about parents, it is easy to assume a model of what might be termed "the biological parent team" of mother and father. In this model two parents act as partners in carrying out the parental functions. Furthermore, both of the parents are biological as well as social parents. It is this parent-team model that is analyzed in most of the chapters in this book.

What is not realized by many observers, especially by parent critics, is the fact that a considerable proportion of contemporary American parents do not operate under these ideal conditions. These parents include "parents without partners" (mostly divorced or separated women, but including some men also); widows and widowers with children; unmarried mothers; adoptive parents; stepparents; and, finally, foster parents.

Some of the groups in the list above are amazingly large—Simon, for example, reports that in the 1960s in the United States there were about *seven*

Reprinted from LeMasters, *Parents Without Partners*. By permission of The Dorsey Press, Homewood, Ill., 1974 ©.

million children living with a stepparent.[1] This means that approximately one out of every nine children in modern America is a stepchild.

In this chapter we wish to do two things: (1) summarize the statistics on these parental subgroups, and (2) analyze the role complications these parents are confronted with. Some of these parents may actually have certain advantages over so-called normal parents, and where this seems to be the case we will analyze this also.

Mothers Without Fathers

One of the by now familiar parental types in our society is the mother rearing her children alone. As of 1960 about one household out of ten in the United States was headed by a woman.[2] In an earlier, more innocent America, this mother without father was seen as a heroic figure—a brave woman whose husband had died who was struggling to rear her brood by scrubbing floors, taking in family laundry, and so on. This was the brave little widow of an earlier day.

After the end of World War I, as the divorce rate began to climb, this picture —and this woman—underwent a radical change. With the rapid improvement of American medicine, marriages in the early and middle decades of life were no longer broken primarily by death; now the great destroyers of marriages came to be social and psychological, not biological.

With this shift, the public's attitude toward the mother with no father by her side changed drastically—it became ambivalent. In some cases she might be viewed with sympathy and understanding, if she happened to be your sister or a close friend, but more often she was perceived as a woman of questionable character—either the gay divorcee of the upper social class levels or the AFDC [Aid for Dependent Children] mother living off the taxpayers at the lower social class levels.[3] In either case the image was a far cry from that of the heroic little widow of the Victorian era.

Statistically, and otherwise, these mothers without fathers fall into five different categories: divorced, separated, deserted, widowed, and never married. All of these categories overlap, so that some mothers might at some point in their lives occupy all five positions in the list.

Generic Features of Mothers Without Partners

1. *Poverty.* It has been estimated that while households headed by a woman comprise only about 10 percent of all U.S. households, they constitute about 25 percent of the families in the so-called poverty group in American society.[4]

In the best study yet published on divorced women, Goode found financial stress to be a major complaint.[5] At any given time, approximately 40 percent of the divorced husbands in this study were delinquent in their support payments, a pattern that seems to be nationwide.[6]

Poverty is extremely relative, as is deprivation. A divorced woman receiving even $1,000 a month in support payments may have to reduce her standard of living from what it was before her divorce.

The reasons for the financial difficulties of these mothers are not mysterious or difficult to identify. Most American men cannot afford to support two living establishments on a high level. This is one reason why some support payments are delinquent. The man usually gets involved with at least one other woman, and this costs money.[7] Often his new woman is not well off financially, and the man may find himself contributing to her support also.

Since a considerable proportion of divorced women are apparently employed at the time of their divorce,[8] they had what is commonly called a two-income family. The mother may continue to work after the father has left the home, but with two living establishments to maintain, two cars, and so on, the financial situation tends to be tight.

In a study of AFDC mothers in Boston, it was discovered that these women faced financial crises almost monthly.[9] They coped with these difficult situations by accepting aid from members of their family; by pooling their resources with neighbors and women friends in the same plight, and by occasional aid from a boy friend.

In several counseling cases with divorced women, the writer was impressed with the annoying feature of the relative poverty experienced by these women —one woman did not have the money to get her television set repaired and this created tension between herself and her children. Another woman, who lived in an area with inadequate bus service, could not afford an automobile. Any person in our society can understand how frustrating problems of this nature can be.

2. *Role conflicts.* Since these women have added the father role to their parental responsibilities, they tend to be either overloaded or in conflict over their various role commitments. The presence of a husband-father provides more role flexibility than these women now have—if the mother is ill, or has to work late, the husband may be able to be home with the children.

When these mothers are employed outside of the home, as a sizable proportion are,[10] the work hours usually conflict with those of the school system. Children leave for school too late, get home too early, and have far too many vacations for the employed mother. There are also childhood illnesses that must be coped with.

It is true that the termination of the marriage has reduced or eliminated the mother's role as wife, but she is still a woman in the early decades of life and men will be in the picture sooner or later. Thus, she may not be a wife at the moment but she will soon be a girl friend, and the courtship role may be even more demanding than that of wife.

It is the writer's belief, based on numerous interviews with divorced women, that being the head of a household is, for most women, an 18-hour day, seven days a week, and 365 days a year job. It would seem that only the most capable, and the most fortunate, can perform all of the roles involved effectively.

3. *Role shifts.* Since the vast majority of the mothers being discussed here —80–90 percent—will eventually remarry, they face the difficult process of taking over the father role and then relinquishing it.[11] This is not easy for most of us; once we have appropriated a role in a family system, it is often difficult to turn it over to somebody else.

Furthermore, these mothers operate in an unusual family system in that, for an indefinite period, they do not have to worry about what the other parent thinks. They are both mother and father for the time being.

This is not entirely true, of course, in the case of the divorced woman, but it seems to be largely true, even for this group.[12] The departed father starts out with the best intentions of "not forgetting my kids," but a variety of factors tend to reduce his parental influence as time goes on.[13]

One divorced woman talked to the writer about the problem of "shifting gears" in her parental roles: "I found it very difficult," she said. "When my husband and I were first divorced he continued to see the children and participated in some of the decisions about them. Then he moved to another state and we seldom saw him after that—but he did continue to send the support checks.

"At this point," she continued, "I assumed almost all of the parental responsibilities, except for the money sent by my former husband and some advice (of questionable value) that my mother chipped in from time to time.

"And then I met the man I am now married to. At first he stayed out of the children's lives, not being sure how long he and I would be going together. But as we moved toward marriage the children became attached to him and gradually he became a foster father to them. Now he has taken over a considerable amount of parental responsibility and I am back almost to where I was before my divorce—I am just a mother again."[14]

Once these women have remarried, there is a sort of built-in strain in that one of the parents (the mother) is a natural parent while the other (the father) is only a stepparent.

4. *Public attitudes.* These mothers are operating in deviant family situations, and for the most part the community tends to regard them and their children as deviants.[15] Except for the widow, all of these mothers are viewed with some ambivalence in our society. They receive some sympathy, some respect, and some help, but they are also viewed as women who are not "quite right"—they did not sustain their marriage "until death do us part."[16]

The unmarried mother, of course, never had a marriage to sustain, and the public has no ambivalence about her; they simply condemn her and that is that.[17]

If these mothers require support from public welfare, they will find the community's mixed feelings reflected in their monthly check—the community will not permit them and their children to starve, but it will also not allow them to live at a decent level.[18]

5. *The well of loneliness.* Any parent rearing children alone will suffer some degree of emotional deprivation. This syndrome appears repeatedly in interviews with divorced and widowed parents. The love partner has been taken away, and whether this was the result of death or divorce, the psychological impact is similar—one half of the parental team has been lost. Sooner or later all (or most) of these parents will reach out for a new life partner, but in the interim it is a very lonely world.

Specific Features of the Subsystems in the One-Parent Family

1. *The divorced mother.* The divorced mother has several advantages over the deserted mother: she at least has had the help of a domestic relations court in spelling out the financial responsibility of the father, also the legal arrangements for custody. In this sense divorce is a lot less messy than desertion in our society.

The divorced mother is also legally free to associate with other men and to remarry if she finds the right person—advantages the deserted woman does not have.

The divorced father, it seems to us, is not in an enviable position in his role as father. He may be happy not to be married to his children's mother any more, but he often hates to be separated from his children.[19] In a sense he still has the responsibility of a father for his minor children but few of the enjoyments of parenthood. To be with his children he has to interact to some degree with his former wife—a process so painful that he was willing to have the marriage terminated.

In the unpublished study of 80 divorced men one of the most frequent regrets expressed by the men was their frustration and concern about their relationships to their children.[20]

The divorced mother has one parental advantage that she shares with all other parents without partners; she does not have to share the daily parental decisions with a partner who might not agree with her strategy. In the Goode study of divorced women, the mothers seemed to think this was an advantage.[21] The parental partner can be of great help if he can agree with his mate on how their children should be reared, but when this is not the case one parent can probably do a better job going it alone.

2. *The deserted mother.* It has already been indicated that desertions in our society are more messy than divorces.[22] There are two reasons: (1) desertion is more apt to be unilateral, with the decision to pull out being made by one party alone; and (2) there is no court supervision of the desertion process—it is unplanned from society's point of view.

The deserted mother is likely to have more severe financial problems than the divorced mother because support payments have not been agreed upon.

Psychologically, desertion is probably more traumatic than divorce, partly because it is more unilateral but also because it is less planned.[23] To the extent that this is true—and we recognize that the evidence on this point is not conclusive—then the deserted mother is handicapped in her parental role by her emotional upheaval or trauma.

This woman also has other problems; she is not legally free to remarry and in a sense not even free to go out with other men since she is technically still a married woman. These feelings, of course, will tend to reflect the social class and the moral subculture of the particular woman.

3. *The separated mother.* If we assume that most marital separations in modern America have been arrived at by mutual agreement, then this mother has certain advantages over the deserted mother. One disadvantage is that her courtship status is ambiguous; another is that she is not free to remarry.[24] Psychologically, the separated mother should reflect patterns similar to those of the divorced mother: her marriage has failed but she has done something about it and now has to plan for her future life.

4. *The widowed mother.* The one big advantage of this parent is the favorable attitude of her family, her friends, and the community toward her. This tends to be reflected in her self-image, thus giving her emotional support. Once she emerges from the period of bereavement, however, she has to face about the same problems as the women discussed previously—she probably will have financial problems; she will have to be father as well as mother; she may need to get a job; and eventually she will have to consider whether to remarry.

It is difficult to say whether the widowed woman suffers more or less emotional trauma than the women whose husbands are still alive but whose marriages are dead. Both have experienced "death" in one form or another—either psychological or physical.

It is undoubtedly true that some of the marriages of widowed women had also failed before the husband died, but there is no way to discover how large this group is.

5. *The unmarried mother.* This is not the place to review the status and problems of the unmarried mother in our society—the literature on this woman is quite voluminous.[25] It only needs to be said here that this mother has all of the problems of the women discussed before plus a few of her own. She is more likely to be a member of a racial minority—one of the extra burdens she has to shoulder. She is also more likely to be on public welfare[26] —a major burden in itself in our society. Her chances for marriage are not as gloomy as some people once thought,[27] but her chances for a successful marriage may be more dubious.

The unmarried mother has one dubious advantage over the divorced, the deserted, and the separated mothers. She does not have to juggle the ambivalent feelings of the general public toward her; she knows that they disapprove of her almost unanimously.

We are talking here, of course, of the unmarried mothers who keep their children. Those who give up their children for adoption, and those who terminate their pregnancies via the abortionist, have their own problems.

It is interesting to note that some women in our society have occupied *all* of the positions discussed so far. They have been unmarried mothers, divorced, deserted, separated, and widowed, although not necessarily in that order. We have interviewed two such women and they both were remarkable persons.

One of these women was an unmarried mother at 16, deserted at 18, divorced at 20, widowed at 23, and remarried at 25. Along the way she had accumulated six children and had been separated any number of times.

What impressed us about this woman was not only her lonely journey through the wars of matrimony but her intense concern for the welfare of her children. The general public would undoubtedly have viewed her as a "bad" mother, but our own judgment was that she did quite well with children—her problems were largely with husbands and boy friends. It is too bad that women like this do not write books, for they could tell all of us much that we need to know.

Father-Only Families

As of 1972 the U.S. Bureau of the Census estimated that there were 796,000 families in which fathers were rearing one or more children under 18 years of age with no mother present.[28] Of this number, 249,000 of the fathers were reported to be widowers, while the rest had either never been married or had experienced marital failure. The writer has been unable to discover any published studies of these father-only families.

It seems likely that these fathers do not continue indefinitely to rear their children alone, that the majority of them remarry, in which case they would experience the same problems of role shifts discussed earlier for mothers on their own.

It also seems likely that these men experience role conflicts between their jobs, their social life, and their parental responsibility.

It is doubtful that these solo fathers would suffer from poverty to the extent found among solo mothers—but the writer has no data to cite in support of this statement.

The rat race experienced by mothers rearing families without the help of a father would likely be found among these men also; it simply reflects what might be termed "role overload."

Psychologically, judging from case studies to be presented shortly, these men probably suffer from the same syndrome found among mothers who have lost their husbands—loneliness, sorrow, perhaps bitterness, often a sense of failure, plus a feeling of being overwhelmed by their almost complete responsibility for their children. About the only effective treatment for feelings of this nature is to find a new partner and get married—the solution most adult Americans rely on for whatever ails them. These fathers are no exception to this statement.

It would appear that these men have a few problems that would be less likely to bother mothers: the physical care of preschool children and the tasks of home management, such as shopping for food and clothes, preparing meals, doing the family laundry, and cleaning the house. Some men become quite adept at this work after awhile, but for others a stove or an iron remains a mystery forever.

Case Studies of Fathers Without Mothers

1. *Case of desertion.* A man of 45 talked to us at length about his struggle to complete the rearing of his three children after his wife had deserted him.

"I came home one night from work and she was gone. A note said that she no longer wanted to live with me and that she thought the children would be better off with me."

"Later on I had a letter from her from California with no return address."

Fortunately, one of this father's children was of high school age and could help with the younger children.

This man says that he went "through hell" for several months—the blow of being deserted, plus the added responsibility for his children, were almost too much for him.

The final solution in this case was the willingness of a widowed sister, with no children of her own, to move in with this family and take over most of the responsibility for the children. After a one-year trial this arrangement seemed to be working out.

2. *Case of divorce.* A man interviewed by the writer had divorced his wife because of an affair she had with a friend of his. Since he felt quite strongly that his wife was not competent to rear their four children, he applied to the court for custody of the children and his petition was approved.

This man was quite definite that he and the children managed better without the mother than they had ever done when she had been present.

"She was always feuding with either me or one of the children. She was moody and negative about life. And she hated any kind of housework. After she left the kids and I got along fine. I did the cooking, they did the housecleaning, and we hired a woman to do the laundry. It worked out just fine."

This man—a remarkable person—even took his four children on a year's tour of Europe after his divorce. Using a combined passenger car and bus, they camped all over Europe, settling down in one country for several months so the children could attend school and study a foreign language.

This man has now remarried. He still has custody of the four children and reports that "everything is fine."

3. *Case involving the death of a mother.* This man talked freely of his life after the death of his wife. He said that since only one of his three children (a boy of ten) was still at home when his wife died, he had decided to "bach it"—in other words, he did not attempt to employ a housekeeper, nor did he invite any of his grown children to move back into the family home.

He said, "I felt that the boy and I could manage by ourselves and that we would be better off that way."

This was a small town and many relatives were nearby if help was needed.

This man had been very much in love with his wife and had no desire to remarry.

Eight years after his wife's death, when the boy was ready for college or a job, the father did remarry. He feels that the plan worked out well for both him and the boy—but when the son was about to leave home, the father felt the need for companionship and so he got married.

The writer does not present these cases as being typical. They simply illustrate some of the patterns to be found in the father-only family in our society.

Is the One-Parent Family Pathological?

Most of us probably assume that the one-parent family is inherently pathological—at least for the children involved. It seems only logical to assume that two parents are better than one—the old adage that two heads are better than one.

In his text on the American family, Bell summarizes several studies that question the assumption that two parents are better than one—judging by the adjustment of the children.[29] This, however, does not say anything about the impact of solo child rearing on the parent, which is the major concern of this book.

If one wishes to debate the number of adults required to socialize children properly, the question can be raised, Who decided that *two* parents was the proper number? Biologically this is natural enough, but this does not prove its social rightness.

As a matter of fact, a family sociologist, Farber, has asked the question, "Are two parents enough? . . . in almost every human society *more* than two adults are involved in the socialization of the child."[30]

Farber goes on to point out that in many societies a "third parent," outside of the nuclear family, acts as a sort of "social critic" of the child.[31]

In 1968 Kadushin reviewed a mass of studies in an attempt to determine whether the one-parent family system was inherently dysfunctional or pathological. The basic purpose of this study was to determine whether adoption agencies would be justified in considering single persons for adoptions. Kadushin concluded that "the association between single-parent familyhood and psychosocial pathology is neither strong nor invariable."[32] Kadushin also makes the statement: "The material suggests a greater appreciation of different kinds of contexts in which children can be reared without damage."[33]

It is obvious to any clinician that the two-parent system has its own pathology—the two parents may be in serious conflict as to how their parental roles should be performed; one parent may be competent but have his (or her) efforts undermined by the incompetent partner; the children may be caught in a "double bind" or crossfire between the two parents;[34] both parents may be competent but simply unable to work together as an effective team in rearing their children; one parent may be more competent than the other but be inhibited in using this competence by the team pattern inherent in the two-parent system.

It is quite clear that much of the so-called pathology of the one-parent family in American society results from inadequate institutional planning for such families—such as the lack of adequate day-care programs for preschool children.

Foster Parents

A relatively new type of parent in the United States is the "foster parent" utilized by social work agencies to care for children whose biological parents are unable or unwilling to assume parental responsibility. As of 1962 about 176,000 children were living with foster parents in our society. This represented about 70 percent of all American children being cared for by private and public welfare agencies.[35]

Kadushin points out that foster parents have largely replaced the "children's home" in our society: as of 1923 about 65 percent of the homeless children in the United States were living in institutions built for such children, whereas today over two-thirds are living in foster homes.[36]

This is not the place to review the whole foster-home movement, but, in view of the increase in foster parenthood in our society in recent decades, a few observations are in order.[37]

1. *Foster parents have no parental rights.* Although about 75 percent of all foster-home placements turn out to be permanent—the child never returns to his own parents—the foster parents usually have no right to permanent custody of the child.[38] As a rule they cannot adopt the child, nor can they prevent the agency from taking the child away at any time for any reason. The agency is not required to "show cause" when it decides to remove a child from a foster home; there is no appeal to the courts.

About the only clear-cut right the foster parent has is the right to be paid —about 95 percent of them receive compensation for taking care of the child.[39]

2. *The foster-parent role is ambiguous.* Foster parents are supposed to express instant love or affection for the foster child, but at the same time they

are not supposed to become so attached to a child that they cannot give the child up at any time.

Kadushin points out that the foster-parent role is quite complex: "Because foster parenthood is an ambiguously defined role," he writes, "its enactment is likely to occasion difficulty."[40]

The role is ambiguous in that it combines a commercial arrangement with an expectation of affection or a willingness to perform beyond the call of duty. When a child is sick, the workday is 24 hours, with no overtime from the agency.

The foster-parent role is ambiguous in that while the job pays, it does not pay very well—and yet the care of the child is supposed to be first class.

Every natural parent and every adoptive parent knows that nobody could pay enough to properly rear a child—even a million dollars would not cover the heartaches and the anguish experienced by most parents at one time or another.

The foster-parent role is also ambiguous in that what is planned as a temporary placement may turn out to be permanent, while a placement that was intended to be permanent may be terminated in a few days if things do not go well.

It is the writer's belief that the foster-parent role is one of the most complex roles attempted by any parent in our society, and the research seems to support this belief.[41]

Adoptive Parents

As of 1963 about 120,000 children were being adopted annually in the United States.[42] Of this number, almost half (47 percent) were adopted by relatives. About two out of every 100 children in our society are reared by adoptive parents.[43]

Unlike the foster parents discussed in the preceding section, adoptive parents have all of the rights that biological parents have once the final adoption papers are signed by the court having jurisdiction. Adoptive parents not only have the same rights as natural parents, but also the same responsibilities.

In a well-known study of adoptive parents, Kirk concluded that they have "very special" problems—intense worry as to how the adoption will "turn out," deep feelings of insecurity and/or inadequacy, apprehension, and so on.[44] Reading this book it seemed to us that the feelings Kirk found in adoptive parents are *universal* reactions to parenthood, not just those experienced by adoptive parents.[45]

Biological parents never really know how their children will turn out; most of them feel inadequate and insecure; and almost all of them are literally frightened when they take their first child home from the hospital and realize the awesome responsibility they have assumed—18–21 years of daily responsibility for another human being.

Actually, as we see it, adoptive parents have several advantages over biological parents.

1. *They get to choose their child.* This may not always be the case, but at least they can reject a child that they consider grossly unsuited for them. Biological parents have to accept and keep what "the Lord sends"—bright, dull, retarded, deformed, beautiful, or otherwise.

2. *Adoptive parents are voluntary parents.* These fathers and mothers do not become parents by accident. The adoption process is such that persons who do not know what they are doing are screened out—they never receive a child. Nobody knows how many children in our society were not actually wanted by their biological parents, but the number must be substantial.

3. *Adoptive parents have a probation period and can return the child if necessary.* In most states there is a probationary period of six months to a year in which the adoptive parents can decide whether they wish to assume permanent responsibility for the child. With biological parents the point of no return comes at the moment of conception—except for those willing to seek an abortion.

For the above reasons it seems to the writer that the role of adoptive parent is less complex and less fraught with difficulty than is generally thought. Kadushin estimates that 75–85 percent of all adoptions in our society are "reasonably successful."[46] Whether as much can be said for biological parents in American society may be debatable.

Summary and Conclusion

It would seem that a sizable proportion of American parents operate in situations that are far from ideal—they do not coincide with the dream that most of us have when we start a family.

If one fourth of all marriages in the United States end in divorce, this alone would produce a significant proportion of parents who are either rearing their children alone (those who do not remarry) or are involved in the stepparent role (those who do remarry). If we add to this the families in which a father or mother has died, we get an additional group.

And then, to all of these must be added the unmarried mothers, the separated, and the deserted who are not yet (or even) divorced.

It is not correct to just add all of these categories because almost all of them overlap at some point in time.

Actually, there are many additional deviant parent situations that we have not even mentioned: mothers whose husbands are away from home because of military service; fathers whose occupations keep them away from their children most of the time; parents who are temporarily in a mental hospital or other medical treatment facility—a tuberculosis sanitarium, for example.

It would seem, from the above, that the total number of American parents who face difficult situations in carrying out their parental responsibilities is larger than most of us realize.

24 Communes and Cluster Families as Viable Alternatives to the Nuclear Family

Frank D. Cox

Communes represent a viable alternate marital pattern that some find attractive. It is difficult to discuss communes as if they were a single entity. Some communes are agrarian, some urban, some limit sexual contact, drugs, and alcohol, others do not, some are based around Jesus and Christianity, others around utopian ideas such as B. F. Skinner's book *Walden II*. One helpful classification of communes is shown in Table 1.

TABLE 1   Characteristics of Three Classifications of Communes[1]

Utopian Commune	Evolutionary Commune	Religious Commune
Drop-out orientation	High achievers	Highly structured
Do your own thing	Highly mobile	Authoritarian leader
Loosely organized	Straight jobs	Work ethic
Usually subsidized	Upper middle class	Usually self-sustaining
Youth oriented	Opinion leaders	Withdrawn from society
Sometimes revolutionary	Most over 30	Family oriented
Usually short-lived	Many post-children	

In trying to capture the diversity found within communes, Rogers lists the following groups:

1. A rural commune of eleven adults and six children functioning pretty much as an extended family but with freer sex relationships outside of paired bonds.
2. An urban commune of a dozen professional men and women (and one child) who are paired off, engage in sexual experimentation, and employ encounter-group procedures to achieve harmony.
3. A semirural commune, open to anyone, and eventually closed as a public health menace.

4. A coed house near a college, inhabited mostly by students, with great turnover but an eight year record of stability; work is shared, relationships consist of brother-sister type, and sexual companionship is found outside the house.
5. An urban house containing three men and three women practicing group marriage; far from harmonious, the group finally developed a chart designating who was to sleep with whom on a given night.
6. A group of agricultural communes, unified by religion, going back over 400 years.
7. A highly organized commune of thirty men and women (only two children) stressing work, cleanliness, and sexual freedom.
8. A relationship of urban communes bound together by charismatic leadership, highly structured and emotional group sessions, and a history of drug addiction among members.
9. A rural commune, bound together by Eastern mystical beliefs, and limited to twenty-five members.

In general, communes are joined in order to escape increasing individual alienation and isolation and to gain a more whole life via a less fractionalized life-style. This second reason is especially true on the rural commune where work and living are done in the same place. Additionally the commune offers sanction for ideas or behavior that differ from the on-going society at large. This allows one to experience a different social philosophy, and perhaps organization, which in turn leads to personal growth and development.[2]

Table 2 compares the conventional family with the communal family in eight categories. The table gives some idea of the advantages claimed for communal living.

Actually, most communes live less than one year. Only those that are authoritarian seem to last, and as one contributor to the *Whole Earth Catalog* ironically noted, "If the intentional community hopes to survive, it must be authoritarian, and if it is authoritarian, it offers no more freedom than the conventional society."[4]

The major reasons communes fail appear to be (1) inability to handle inter-personal conflicts, (2) failure to survive economically, (3) jealousy, (4) failure to find a secure one-to-one relationship and the insecurity of relating to an amorphous group, (5) the greater difficulty of maintaining multiple relation-ships, (6) failure to grant a measure of privacy, and (7) the attempt to live anarchistically with individuals who are not mature and responsible.[2]

Research, especially on rural communes, finds that the actual living styles may not be as radically different from the traditional as mass media lead one to believe. Despite women's liberation, the traditional male and female roles, for example, remain essentially old-fashioned in many communes. The women do the daily cooking, cleaning, and child-rearing jobs while the men work the income-producing jobs. Ira L. Reiss concludes that the commune picture that

TABLE 2 Evaluation of Conventional and Counterculture Families[3]

Problem or issue	Conventional	Counterculture
Child-rearing	Inhibited, control-oriented, achievement, competition, conditional love, insecurity in isolation	Child as "treasure," relative freedom, cooperation, security in multiple adults
Labor, economics, leisure	Private economic struggle, materialism as an end, sex-role stereotypes, cash- and things-oriented leisure	Economic sharing, utility orientation toward things, attempt to break stereotypes, simple leisure and productive recreation
Conflicts	Inhibited, circumscribed conflict by "rules" and games, little growth and change, stable tensions unresolved	Growth- and change-oriented, open tension toward either resolution or breakup, more options for change
Family solidarity	Externally derived, often contrived and artificially supported, ingenuine at times but secure	Internally derived, at times primarily a response to external pressures, normative struggle to create rules, order
Privacy	At times may be too much, (children?) but in general implies isolation of the family unit	Mostly too little currently due to norms of sharing and economic privations, making housing a problem, need for better information
Sex	Inhibiting, but with "approved" adaptations, essentially nonproductive of growth—rather encourages duplicity and gaming (e.g. sexuality) cocktail party	Sensual hedonism, respect for variations, openness, but with problems of working in normative vacuum (or within old cultural framework hanging over)
The aged	Little place, little promise	Little place, some promise—based on idea of return to older forms utilizing aged
Religion	Social control oriented, externally supported, ritualized for control purposes, guilt-directed	Meditative, self-unity oriented, noninstitutionalized, at times community directed, personal-natural, integrative, positive, accepting

emerges from the research is not one of radical change in marital relations. "The radical change seems to be the attempt to achieve close relations in one household, among a relatively large number of people. This is a departure from the suburban nuclear family ranch house, but in many other ways, it is not a departure from the conventional marriage. Perhaps, in time, with a second generation on the commune scene, more radical changes will appear. But even so it looks as though some form of marital relationship is well established in the commune setting."[5]

Herbert A. Otto described some of the various kinds of communes in *Saturday Review*:*

Begun by the under-thirty generation and hippie tribal families, the 1960s have seen the growth of a new commune movement. This movement has started to attract significant segments of the older, established population. For example, I recently conducted a weekend marathon in Chicago—under the auspices of the Oasis Center—that was open to the public. Seven out of thirty-six participants were members of communes. Three of the seven were successful professional men in their mid-forties. Another participant, a college professor in his early thirties, mentioned that he had been a member of a commune composed of several psychiatrists, an engineer, a teacher, and a chemist. When I visited New York following the Chicago weekend, a senior editor of a large publishing house casually mentioned that he and some friends were in the process of organizing a commune. They were looking for a large brownstone close to their offices.

The commune movement even has its own journal, *Modern Utopian.* Issued by the Alternatives Foundation of Berkeley, California, it is in its fourth year of publication. In 1969, this journal published the first comprehensive directory of intentional or utopian communes in the United States and the world. The addresses of close to two hundred intentional communities in this country are given. (It has been estimated that there are four to six times this number of communes in the United States.) California leads the *Modern Utopian* directory with more than thirty listed. New York has twenty-eight and Pennsylvania thirteen, with communes listed from thirty-five other states. Half a dozen books that I know of are currently in preparation on the commune movement.

Communes of various types exist, varying from agricultural subsistence to religious. To provide a base for economic survival, many of the communes furnish services or construct marketable products such as hammocks or wooden toys for preschoolers. Others operate printing presses or schools. Most communes not located in cities raise some of their own food. Relatively rare is the commune that is self-supporting solely on the basis of its agricultural operation. Sizes vary with anywhere from twelve persons or fewer to a hundred persons or more as members of an intentional community. The educational and vocational backgrounds of members also vary widely. The young people and school dropouts are currently being joined by a growing number of "Establishment dropouts." Many of these are people who have made successful contributions in their chosen vocations or professions and have grown disillusioned, or who are seeking to explore new life-styles.

Communes often have their beginning when several persons who know each other well, like each other, and have similar values decide to live together. Sometimes a commune is formed around a common interest, craft, or unifying creative goal. Political views or convictions may also play a role in the formation of a commune. There are a number of peace-movement and radical communes; sometimes these are composed of political activists, and sometimes of people who see the commune movement as a "radical approach to revolution." Members of one such group, the Twin Oaks community in Virginia, think of themselves as a post-revolutionary society. As detailed in *Modern Utopian,* this "radical commune" was organized as the result of a university conference:

Twin Oaks was started by a group of people who met while attending an "academic" conference during 1966 at Ann Arbor, Michigan, on the formation of a Walden II community. One of the Twin Oakers related how this conference resulted in a very elaborate, academic type plan on how to get a Walden II community going. But when the conference was over, the professors all returned to their teaching posts, and nobody had any idea where they could get the several million dollars that the plan called for to start the thing. So eight people decided to start right away with whatever resources they could get together. . . .

For while Twin Oaks was designed to be a living experiment in community, it also aims to stimulate others to do the same. As one member said, "We generally hold to the opinion that people who *don't* start communities (or join them) are slightly immoral." It's all part of the revolution being over—they define revolution as a "radical restructuring" of society, both economic and, more important, cultural. (But maybe you can't really separate the two.) One member summed up a desirable post-revolutionary society as: "A society that creates people who are committed to non-aggression; a society of people concerned for one another; a society where one man's gain is not another man's loss; a society where disagreeable work is minimized and leisure is valued; a society in which people come first; an economic system of equality; a society which is constantly trying to improve in its ability to create happy, productive, creative people."

The personal property a member brings to a commune remains his, although he may be expected to share it when needed. Some purists object that, since members do not donate personal property for the benefit of the group, the current social experiments should not be referred to as "communes." Obviously, the term has acquired a new meaning and definition. The emphasis today is on the exploration of alternate models for togetherness, the shaping of growing dynamic environments, the exploration of new life-styles, and the enjoyment of living together.

A number of communes are deliberately organized for the purpose of group marriage. The concept of group marriage, however, differs widely. Some communes exclusively composed of couples have a living arrangement similar to the "big family" or group family that originated in Sweden in 1967. These married couples share the same home, expenses, household chores, and the upbringing of the children. Infidelity is not encouraged. Other group-marriage communes tolerate or encourage the sharing of husbands and wives. On the other end of the group-marriage continuum are communes such as The Family near Taos, New Mexico. This group of more than fifty members discourages pairing—"Everyone is married to everyone. The children are everyone's."

The life-span of many communes is relatively short due to four major disintegrative pressures that fragment intentional communities. Disagreement over household chores or work to be performed is a major source of disruption. When members fail to fulfill their obligations, disillusionment and demoralization often set in. Closely related are interpersonal conflicts, frequently fueled by the exchange of sex partners and resultant jealousy. Drugs do not seem to create a major problem in most communes, as there is either a permissive attitude or drug use is discouraged or forbidden. A small number of religious/mystical communes use drugs for sacramental purposes and as a means of communion.

The problems associated with economic survival generate considerable pressure. A final strong force that contributes to the collapse of communes stems from the hostility of surrounding communities. There are innumerable instances of harassment by neighbors, strangers, civil authorities, and police. The persistent and violent nature of this persecution is probably traceable to deep-seated feelings of threat and outrage when the neighboring communities discover a group in their midst suspected of having unorthodox living arrangements. These pervasive feelings of resistance and anger (which may be partially subconscious) are conceivably engendered in many persons by what they perceive to be a threat to the existing family structure.

Time magazine recently featured "The American Family" and discussed modern communes as follows:*

Most of the new communards are fleeing what they regard as the constriction, loneliness, materialism and the hypocrisy in straight society and the family life on which it is based. Yet some of the same old problems reappear—for example, the tug of war between individualism and submission to the group. One contributor to the *Whole Earth Catalog* summed up his own experience. "If the intentional community hopes to survive, it must be authoritarian, and if it is authoritarian, it offers no more freedom than conventional society. Those communes based on freedom inevitably fail, usually within a year."

But when they fail, their members often go on to join other tribes, now that there is a network of communes available to them. Benjamin Zablocki, a Berkeley sociologist who has visited more than 100 communes in the past six years, insists: "The children are incredibly fine. It's natural for children to be raised in extended families, where there are many adults." Yet in spite of the talk of extended families, the extension in the new communes does not reach to a third generation. Indeed, the "families" have a narrow age span, and it is possible that the children have never seen an adult over 30.

Deformed Monstrosity

Writes Brandeis' Sociologist Philip Slater, in *The Pursuit of Loneliness:* "It is ironic that young people who try to form communes almost always create the same narrow, age-graded, class-homogeneous society in which they were formed. A community that does not have old people and children, white-collar and blue-collar, eccentric and conventional, and so on, is not a community at all, but the same kind of truncated and deformed monstrosity that most people inhabit today."

Some communes actually form compromises with the nuclear family. Nowhere is this point better made than at Lama, a contemporary commune 18 miles north of Taos, N. Mex., which was re-revisited last week by Correspondent David DeVoss after an absence of 19 months.

"We work together—we collectively grow and distribute the crops, but we go back to our individual nests at night," explains Satya De La Manitov, 28, who has now moved from a tepee into a still unfinished A-frame house that took him $1,500 and twelve months to build. Most couples are in their upper 20s, are married, have children, own their own homes, have a deep respect for property rights and believe in the value of honest toil. Although the concept of complete sexual freedom retains its followers, it plays only a minor role in Lama society today. Indeed, reports DeVoss, "were it not for their long hair, predilection for grass and rejection of the American political system, Lama residents could pass for solid, middle-class citizens."

Most of today's communes are in the cities, and they indeed do have appeal for many middle-class citizens. To Ethel Herring, 30, married to a Los Angeles lawyer and active in Women's Lib, a city commune seemed the answer to growing frustrations, which culminated when she realized that she was spending $60 to $70 a week for baby sitters; the Herrings had no live-in grandparents or nearby relatives to care for their three children while Ethel was attending her frequent feminist meetings. In effect, she says, "we were suffering from the nuclear family setup."

With six other sympathetic couples in similar circumstances, the Herrings scouted around and finally found a U-shaped, six-unit apartment building in southern Los Angeles. They purchased it last September, and converted it into a successful, middle-class (most of the men are lawyers) city commune. Knocking out walls and doors, they built interjoining apartments and a communal nursery, TV room and library. "The apartments open up so that the kids' rooms can run into each other," Ethel explains, "and yet there is still plenty of privacy for adults."

The families share their services, following a schedule that calls for each couple to do all of the cooking and housework for one week. "That's KP once every six weeks per couple, which keeps everybody happy," says Ethel. Her husband, for instance, has curtailed his practice so that he can spend one day a week at home on child-care and cooking duty. Says Ethel, "The truth is that most men are deprived of a close relationship with their children, and our men are finding out what they've been missing. It's groovy."

The kibbutz of Israel represents yet another approach to family and child-rearing. Essential to most kibbutz systems is institutionalized child care. A major consideration in the establishment of a system of kibbutz collective child-rearing was the belief (certainly well supported in clinical literature) that "bad mothering" was to blame for most childhood problems. Properly controlled social rearing could and should reduce parent-child strains according to kibbutz theory. By giving over to the kibbutz all education and socialization of the child, time spent by the child with the parents could be only enjoyment and happiness time. If the parents need not concern themselves with control and teaching the child, parental-child conflict would be drastically reduced.

Allowing the kibbutz to assume child-rearing responsibility theoretically reduces the parent-child conflict for several other important reasons. The child does not place additional economic burdens on the parents, since he is supported by the kibbutz. The importance of the nurse allows the child to love someone in addition to his parents. Jealousy and anger that have to be repressed in the family can be expressed in the kibbutz because the child can find more legitimate objects of aggression among his peers. The collective framework shields the child from overprotective or domineering parents who might block his efforts to become independent. Ideally, abolishment of family-centeredness creates an atmosphere in which parents and children can maximize love and affection.[6]

Kibbutz Settlements

"Operationally a kibbutz is a relatively small agricultural settlement, though in recent years most of them have added small industries. Their size varies from less than one hundred to a maximum of two thousand inhabitants. What is unique about them is that each community forms a single unit: economic, political and social. All property belongs to the community except for some small personal belongings, and even the latter is a recent development. Originally, not even the clothes he wore belonged to the person, but came and went from a common supply, and this is still true for the children. Again: Only recently was it decided to give each member a very small yearly allowance (about thirty dollars) to spend as he wished.

"On becoming a member of the kibbutz, the person turns over to the community all his private possessions, though on leaving he is not entitled to receive them back, nor any share of the communal property.

"Everything is provided by the community. And the community, through its general assembly, decides what should thus be provided: for example, whether each member should be given a radio, or how many trips a year to a cultural event in a neighboring city may be paid for out of community funds.

"Not only is the community run as a single economic unit, but as a single big household. It provides food, clothing, shelter, and all necessities of life, plus small luxuries when feasible. Food, for example, is provided by a communal kitchen, and is eaten in a common dining hall, though here again an important relaxation has lately set in. Members are now given some food items and a hot plate so that they can fix tea and snacks in their rooms.

"All services, including all schooling and medical care, are provided by the community. Big decisions are made by a general assembly of all members. (There are always a number of nonmembers living in a kibbutz: parents of members who did not themselves become members; persons who want to become members but are in their trial year; visitors; and of course all the children of the kibbutz.) The assembly meets weekly and is headed by a secretariat elected by the assembly. The secretariat usually consists of a secretary and treasurer, plus the farm manager, the manager of the factory, etc.

"It is the secretariat that prepares the agenda for the weekly assembly and carries out its decisions through committees. One committee, for example, assigns to each member his daily work. Another committee is in charge of all education. Still another one decides who may take a trip that extends beyond the weekly day off, or the two-weeks' yearly vacation. In practice the chairman of these committees carries a great deal of weight in the committee's decision."*

Regardless of the structure of the volunteer commune family, it still lacks a legal identity and a long-term permanence. Recently fourteen young people living together as two volunteer families went to court to protect themselves

*Bruno Bettelheim, *The Children of The Dream.* (New York: The Macmillan Co., 1969), pp. 331–332.

from the application of local zoning laws that prohibited more than four persons from occupying the same dwelling unless members of one family. The group tried to establish themselves as a legal single family. The judge concluded that such volunteer cohabitation did not constitute a legal family.

"There is a long-recognized value in the traditional family relationship which does not attach to the 'voluntary family'! " Reinforced by biological and legal ties, the family "plays a role in educating and nourishing the young; it has been a means of satisfying the deepest emotional and physical needs of human beings." The judge was impressed with the sincerity of the families' members, but found that "communal living groups are voluntary, with fluctuating memberships who have no legal obligations of support and cohabitation." He concluded that communes "are legally indistinguishable from such traditional living groups as religious communities and residence clubs. The right to form such groups may be constitutionally protected, but the right to insist that these groups live under the same roof in any part of the city they choose is not."[7]

Because of the state's interests in property and "legitimacy of issue," volunteer communes will find it difficult to survive unless legal marriage is permitted within their structure. Nevertheless people are seeking new ways in which to make meaningful lives together and the idea of the extended family system seems to be enjoying at least a mild revival.

"Cluster" or *"extended" family* is another attempt to regain some of the lost sense of community felt by many Americans.

A Sense of Community and Modern America*

I grew up in an urban neighborhood in a large city in the East. Actually I don't suppose it was really necessary to specify urban, because in those days there were no suburbs to speak of. I lived for many years rather far out on the west side of the city on a quiet little street only a half block from the corner grocery store. There weren't any supermarkets in those days. All of us bought our groceries from rather small, one-man neighborhood stores.

I came to know the grocer and his family very well over a long period of time. His son was about my age and we became good friends, played together every day. I was often at his house and he at mine. I had dinner with his family on Sunday from time to time, and in summer went with them now and again to a little shore place that they owned on a river not far off.

When I was eleven or twelve, the grocer hired me to help his son deliver groceries on Saturdays, and to work at restocking the shelves in

*"The Meaning of Community: Being with people who know you." Dr. John Crane, Unitarian Church Sermon, January 6, 1974

the store. As I worked I would listen to him talking to each customer in an easy, congenial way, as he cut the meat or got canned goods down off the high shelves with long-handled pincers. He clearly enjoyed the work, and the customers plainly found pleasure in encountering him. They would report on happenings in their families, discuss illnesses, successes and failures. The arrival of each customer meant not only a business transaction, but a social encounter as well. The customers and the grocer knew each other, had known each other over a period of years.

We are so constructed as creatures that we need to have in ourselves a sense of community with others of our kind for our well-being. That's how we are made.

A sense of community is something we come to feel over a period of time, as we move among people we know well, are close to, people we trust, feel safe with, feel warm toward.

This sense of community used to arise in us naturally, without any conscious effort, in years past, when most of us lived out our lives in the area in which we were born. We met the same people day after day, week after week, some of whom we were quite close to, confided in, and were given confidences from in return. We knew all of the storekeepers and tradesmen, often had known them from the time they were children.

In this stable kind of community, with a low level of mobility, we gained both a sense of community and a sense of identity. It didn't require any effort or attention, it was just something we breathed in from our social environment. We came to know ourselves by moving among people who knew us and had known us for some time. We saw ourselves in their eyes each day, in the expression on their faces, in the tones of their voices as they responded to us.

It isn't like this today. It is not like this at all. To take a small example, now, as we come up to the checkout counter of the supermarket, the checkout girl puts on a warm smile for us. She doesn't know us and we don't know her. She does know, however, that a warm smile is far better for commerce than a frozen face, so she smiles and says hello. It's much the same with the stewardesses we encounter as we enter and leave the airplanes by which we propel ourselves swiftly around the country. As we leave the planes the stewardesses smile warmly at us, bid us good-by, as though we had shared a significant human experience in the hour or two on the plane. Actually, however, we leave knowing nothing of each other.

Characteristically, in this place, in this time, we move among people, who work efficiently, smile warmly, and do not know us. Hence the decay in our sense of community, our sense of personal identity.

A cluster family is an artificially contrived family group that meets together for companionship, recreation, and to share other meaningful experiences.

They may on occasion eat together, play together, work together, exist together. The point is that each person has a larger circle to which he may relate. The artificially constructed extended family was started by the Santa Barbara Unitarian Church, Santa Barbara, California, and since its inception in 1971, it has been copied across the United States as well as in some foreign countries.

Those interested in joining such a family are randomly grouped together after being sorted for age, sex, and marital status. Thus, there are married couples, children, and singles in the families. Ideally the family numbers from fifteen to twenty people. There is a nonprofessional facilitation leader although he/she need not remain in this role past the first three months. It is necessary, however, that there be steady, sensitive leadership for the extended family group to prosper.

Each family develops in directions of their own choosing. Whoever joins a family must commit to it for a minimum of three months. They are expected to make an effort to know and understand the family members as well as allow themselves to be known. Joining a family means "playing, laughing, loving, opening yourself, giving and receiving. It means growing close to people who, over time, with shared experience, come to matter to you."[8]

Morton Hunt, author of *The Natural History of Love,* recently tried to prognosticate the future of marriage for *Playboy* magazine. The following abridged article includes all of his major points. After reading the many articles included in this volume, it will be interesting for you to compare your conclusions about the future of marriage with Mr. Hunt's.

25 The Future of Marriage

Morton Hunt

. . .

Marriage as a social structure is exceedingly plastic, being shaped by the interplay of culture and of human needs into hundreds of different forms. In societies where women could do valuable productive work, it often made sense for a man to acquire more than one wife; where women were idle or relatively unproductive—and, hence, a burden—monogamy was more likely to be the pattern. When women had means of their own or could fall back upon relatives, divorce was apt to be easy; where they were wholly dependent on their husbands, it was generally difficult. Under marginal and primitive living conditions, men kept their women in useful subjugation; in wealthier and more leisured societies, women often managed to acquire a degree of independence and power.

For a long while, the only acceptable form of marriage in America was a lifelong one-to-one union, sexually faithful, all but indissoluble, productive of goods and children and strongly husband-dominated. It was a thoroughly functional mechanism during the 18th and much of the 19th centuries, when men were struggling to secure the land and needed women who would clothe and feed them, produce and rear children to help them, and obey their orders without question for an entire lifetime. It was functional, too, for the women of that time, who, uneducated, unfit for other kinds of work and endowed by law with almost no legal or property rights, needed men who would support them, give them social status and be their guides and protectors for life.

But time passed, the Indians were conquered, the sod was busted, towns and cities grew up, railroads laced the land, factories and offices took the place of the frontier. Less and less did men need women to produce goods and children; more and more, women were educated, had time to spare, made their way into the job market—and realized that they no longer had to cling to their men for life. As patriarchalism lost its usefulness, women began to want and demand orgasms, contraceptives, the vote and respect; men, finding the world growing ever more impersonal and cold, began to want wives who were warm, understanding, companionable and sexy.

Yet, strangely enough, as all these things were happening, marriage not only did not lose ground but grew more popular, and today, when it is under full-scale attack on most fronts, it is more widespread than ever before. A considerably larger percentage of our adult population was married in 1970 than was the case in 1890; the marriage rate, though still below the level of the 1940s, has been climbing steadily since 1963.

The explanation of this paradox is that as marriage was losing its former uses, it was gaining new ones. The changes that were robbing marriage of practical and life-affirming values were turning America into a mechanized urban society in which we felt like numbers, not individuals, in which we had many neighbors but few lifelong friends and in which our lives were controlled by remote governments, huge companies and insensate computers. Alone and impotent, how can we find intimacy and warmth, understanding and loyalty, enduring friendship and a feeling of personal importance? Why, obviously, through *loving* and *marrying.* Marriage is a microcosm, a world within which we seek to correct the shortcomings of the macrocosm around us.

The model of marriage that served the old purposes excellently serves the new ones poorly. But most of the contemporary assaults upon it are not efforts to destroy it; they are efforts to modify and remold it. Only traditional patriarchal marriage is dying, while all around us marriage is being reborn in new forms.

Divorce is a case in point. Far from being a wasting illness, it is a healthful adaptation, enabling monogamy to survive in a time when patriarchal powers, privileges and marital systems have become unworkable; far from being a radical change in the institution of marriage, divorce is a relatively minor modification of it and thoroughly supportive of most of its conventions.

Not that it seemed so at first. When divorce was introduced to Christian Europe, it appeared an extreme and rather sinful measure to most people; even among the wealthy—the only people who could afford it—it remained for centuries quite rare and thoroughly scandalous. In 1816, when president Timothy Dwight of Yale thundered against the "alarming and terrible" divorce rate in Connecticut, about one of every 100 marriages was being legally dissolved. But as women began achieving a certain degree of emancipation during the 19th Century, and as the purposes of marriage changed, divorce laws were liberalized and the rate began climbing. Between 1870 and 1905, both the U.S. population and the divorce rate more than doubled; and between then and today, the divorce rate increased over four times.

And not only for the reasons we have already noted but for yet another: the increase in longevity. When people married in their late 20s and marriage was likely to end in death by the time the last child was leaving home, divorce seemed not only wrong but hardly worth the trouble; this was especially true where the only defect in a marriage was boredom. Today, however, when people marry earlier and have finished raising their children with half their adult lives still ahead of them, boredom seems a very good reason for getting divorced.

Half of all divorces occur after eight years of marriage and a quarter of them after 15—most of these being not the results of bad initial choices but of disparity or dullness that has grown with time.

Divorcing people, however, are seeking not to escape from marriage for the rest of their lives but to exchange unhappy or boring marriages for satisfying ones. Whatever bitter things they say at the time of divorce, the vast majority do remarry, most of their second marriages lasting the rest of their lives; even those whose second marriages fail are very likely to divorce and remarry again and, that failing, yet again. Divorcing people are actually marrying people, and divorce is not a negation of marriage but a workable cross between traditional monogamy and multiple marriage; sociologists have even referred to it as "serial polygamy."

Despite its costs and its hardships, divorce is thus a compromise between the monogamous ideal and the realities of present-day life. To judge from the statistics, it is becoming more useful and more socially acceptable every year. Although the divorce rate leveled off for a dozen years or so after the postwar surge of 1946, it has been climbing steadily since 1962, continuing the long-range trend of 100 years, and the rate for the entire nation now stands at nearly one for every three marriages. In some areas, it is even higher. In California, where a new ultraliberal law went into effect in 1970, nearly two of every three marriages end in divorce—a fact that astonishes people in other areas of the country but that Californians themselves accept with equanimity. They still approve of, and very much enjoy, being married; they have simply gone further than the rest of us in using divorce to keep monogamy workable in today's world.

Seen in the same light, marital infidelity is also a frequently useful modification of the marriage contract rather than a repudiation of it. It violates the conventional moral code to a greater degree than does divorce but, as practiced in America, is only a limited departure from the monogamous pattern. Unfaithful Americans, by and large, neither have extramarital love affairs that last for many years nor do they engage in a continuous series of minor liaisons; rather, their infidelity consists of relatively brief and widely scattered episodes, so that in the course of a married lifetime, they spend many more years being faithful than being unfaithful. Furthermore, American infidelity, unlike its European counterparts, has no recognized status as part of the marital system; except in a few circles, it remains impermissible, hidden and isolated from the rest of one's life.

This is not true at all levels of our society, however: Upper-class men—and, to some extent, women—have long regarded the discreet love affair as an essential complement to marriage, and lower-class husbands have always considered an extracurricular roll in the hay important to a married man's peace of mind. Indeed, very few societies have ever tried to make both husband and wife sexually faithful over a lifetime; the totally monogamous ideal is statistically an abnormality. Professors Clellan Ford and Frank Beach state in *Patterns of Sexual Behavior* that less than 16 percent of 185 societies studied by anthropologists had formal restrictions to a single mate—and, of these, less than a third wholly disapproved of both premarital and extra-marital relationships.

Our middle-class, puritanical society, however, has long held that infidelity of any sort is impossible if one truly loves one's mate and is happily married, that any deviation from fidelity stems from an evil or neurotic character and that it inevitably damages both the sinner and the sinned against. This credo drew support from earlier generations of psychotherapists, for almost all the adulterers they treated were neurotic, unhappily married or out of sorts with life in general. But it is just such people who seek psychotherapy; they are hardly a fair sample. Recently, sex researchers have examined the unfaithful more representatively and have come up with quite different findings.

- Many of the unfaithful—perhaps even a majority—are not seriously dissatisfied with their marriages nor their mates and a fair number are more or less happily married.

- Only about a third—perhaps even fewer—appear to seek extramarital sex for neurotic motives; the rest do so for nonpathological reasons.
- Many of the unfaithful—perhaps even a majority—do not feel that they, their mates nor their marriages have been harmed; in my own sample, a tenth said that their marriages had been helped or made more tolerable by their infidelity.

It is still true that many a "deceived" husband or wife, learning about his or her mate's infidelity, feels humiliated, betrayed and unloved, and is filled with rage and the desire for revenge; it is still true, too, that infidelity is a cause in perhaps a third of all divorces. But more often than not, deceived spouses never know of their mates' infidelity nor are their marriages perceptibly harmed by it.

At this point Hunt discusses in some detail free sex and swinging among married couples. See Reading 20 for a discussion of this phenomenon.

. . .

There seems to be a far broader and more thorough rejection of marriage on the part of those men and women who choose to live together unwed. Informal, nonlegal unions have long been widespread among poor blacks, largely for economic reasons, but the present wave of such unions among middle-class whites has an ideological basis, for most of those who choose this arrangement consider themselves revolutionaries who have the guts to pioneer in a more honest and vital relationship than conventional marriage. A 44-year-old conference leader, Theodora Wells, and a 51-year-old psychologist, Lee Christie, who live together in Beverly Hills, expounded their philosophy in the April 1970 issue of *The Futurist:* " 'Personhood' is central to the living-together relationship; sex roles are central to the marriage relationship. Our experience strongly suggests that personhood excites growth, stimulates openness, increases joyful satisfactions in achieving, encompasses rich, full sexuality peaking in romance. Marriage may have the appearance of this in its romantic phase, but it settles down to prosaic routine. . . . The wife role is diametrically opposed to the personhood I want. I [Theodora] therefore choose to live with the man who joins me in the priority of personhood."

What this means is that she hates homemaking, is career oriented and fears that if she became a legal wife, she would automatically be committed to traditional female roles, to dependency. Hence, she and Christie have rejected marriage and chosen an arrangement without legal obligations, without a head of the household and without a primary money earner or primary homemaker —though Christie, as it happens, does 90 percent of the cooking. Both believe that their freedom from legal ties and their constant need to rechoose each other make for a more exciting, real and growing relationship.

A fair number of the avant-garde and many of the young have begun to find this not only a fashionably rebellious but a thoroughly congenial attitude toward marriage; couples are living together, often openly, on many a college campus, risking punishment by college authorities (but finding the risk smaller every day) and bucking their parents' strenuous disapproval (but getting their glum acceptance more and more often).

When one examines the situation closely, however, it becomes clear that most of these marital Maoists live together in close, warm, committed and monogamous fashion, very much like married people: they keep house together (although often dividing their roles in untraditional ways) and neither is free to have sex with anyone else, date anyone else nor even find anyone else intriguing. Anthropologists Margaret Mead and Ashley Montagu, sociologist John Gagnon and other close observers of the youth scene feel that living together, whatever its defects, is actually an apprentice marriage and not a true rebellion against marriage at all.

.   .   .

If these modifications of monogamy aren't quite as alarming or as revolutionary as they seem to be, one contemporary experiment in marriage *is* a genuine and total break with Western tradition. This is group marriage—a catchall term applied to a wide variety of polygamous experiments in which small groups of adult males and females, and their children, live together under one roof or in a close-knit settlement, calling themselves a family, tribe, commune or, more grandly, intentional community and considering themselves all married to one another. (See Reading 24.)

As the term intentional community indicates, these are experiments not merely in marriage but in the building of a new type of society. They are utopian minisocieties existing within, but almost wholly opposed to, the mores and values of present-day American society.

Not that they are all of a piece. A few are located in cities and have members who look and act square and hold regular jobs; some, both urban and rural, consist largely of dropouts, acidheads, panhandlers and petty thieves; but most are rural communities, have hippie-looking members and aim at a self-sufficient farming-and-handicraft way of life. A very few communes are politically conservative, some are in the middle and most are pacifist, anarchistic and/or New Leftist. Nearly all, whatever their national political bent, are islands of primitive communism in which everything is collectively owned and all members work for the common good.

In the next section, Hunt overestimates the number of communes that encourage sexual permissiveness. Indeed, the most stable communes are those with a religious orientation where sexual interaction is closely controlled. Hunt also uses the term "group marriage" interchangeably with the term "commune" which is misleading. A "group marriage" is the sharing of all aspects of life, including sex, with each member of the marriage. "Commune" is a much broader term denoting living in a large group of people. Many communes consist of monogamous couples living in separate quarters but sharing parental duties and/or economic responsibilities. It is also interesting to note that there is a great deal of communal living among the elderly. "Merrill Court is a small apartment building near the shore of San Francisco Bay, and the home of 43 people. As persons over the age of 62 they are called, by the public housing authorities who built the project, 'senior citizens.' Most of the residents are conservative, fundamentalist widows (37 of the 43 are women) from the Midwest and Southwest and as such they might not seem likely candidates for 'communal living' or 'alternatives to the nuclear family.' Nonetheless their social life together is, in many ways, communal and it suggests an alternative way of life for many other older people as well."[1]

Their communism extends to—or perhaps really begins with—sexual collectivism. Though some communes consist of married couples who are conventionally faithful, many are built around some kind of group sexual sharing. In some of these, couples are paired off but occasionally sleep with other members of the group; in others, pairing off is actively discouraged and the members drift around sexually from one partner to another—a night here, a night there, as they wish.

Group marriage has captured the imagination of many thousands of college students in the past few years through its idealistic and romantic portrayal in three novels widely read by the young—Robert Heinlein's *Stranger in a Strange Land* and Robert Rimmer's *The Harrad Experiment* and *Proposition 31*. The underground press, too, has paid a good deal of sympathetic attention —and the establishment press a good deal of hostile attention—to communes. There has even been, for several years, a West Coast publication titled *The Modern Utopian* that is devoted, in large part, to news and discussions of group marriage. The magazine, which publishes a directory of intentional communities, recently listed 125 communes and the editor said, "For every listing you find here, you can be certain there are 100 others." And an article in *The New York Times* last December stated that "nearly 2000 communes in 34 states have turned up" but gave this as a conservative figure, as "no accurate count exists."

All this sometimes gives one the feeling that group marriage is sweeping the country; but, based on the undoubtedly exaggerated figures of *The Modern Utopian* and counting a generous average of 20 people per commune, it would still mean that no more than 250,000 adults—approximately one tenth of one percent of the U.S. population—are presently involved in group marriages. These figures seem improbable.

Nevertheless, group marriage offers solutions to a number of the nagging problems and discontents of modern monogamy. Collective parenthood— every parent being partly responsible for every child in the group—not only privides a warm and enveloping atmosphere for children but removes some of the pressure from individual parents: moreover, it minimizes the disruptive effects of divorce on the child's world. Sexual sharing is an answer to boredom and solves the problem of infidelity, or seeks to, by declaring extramarital experiences acceptable and admirable. It avoids the success-status-possession syndrome of middle-class family life by turning toward simplicity, communal ownership and communal goals.

Finally, it avoids the loneliness and confinement of monogamy by creating something comparable to what anthropologists call the extended family, a larger grouping of related people living together. (There is a difference, of course: In group marriage, the extended family isn't composed of blood relatives.) Even when sexual switching isn't the focus, there is a warm feeling of being affectionally connected to everyone else. As one young woman in a Taos commune said ecstatically, "It's really groovy waking up and knowing that 48 people love you."

There is, however, a negative side: This drastic reformulation of marriage makes for new problems, some of them more severe than the ones it has solved. Albert Ellis, quoted in Herbert Otto's new book, *The Family in Search of a Future,* lists several categories of serious difficulties with group marriage, including the near impossibility of finding four or more adults who can live harmoniously and lovingly together, the stubborn intrusion of jealousy and love conflicts and the innumerable difficulties of coordinating and scheduling many lives.

Other writers, including those who have sampled communal life, also talk about the problems of leadership (most communes have few rules to start with; those that survive for any time do so by becoming almost conventional and traditional) and the difficulties in communal work sharing (there are always some members who are slovenly and lazy and others who are neat and hard-working, the latter either having to expel the former or give up and let the commune slowly die).

A more serious defect is that most group marriages, being based upon a simple, semiprimitive agrarian life, reintroduce old-style patriarchalism, because such a life puts a premium on masculine muscle power and endurance and leaves the classic domestic and subservient roles to women. Even a most sympathetic observer, psychiatrist Joseph Downing, writes, "In the tribal families, while both sexes work, women are generally in a service role. . . . Male dominance is held desirable by both sexes."

Most serious of all are the emotional limitations of group marriage. Its ideal is sexual freedom and universal love, but the group marriages that most nearly achieve this have the least cohesiveness and the shallowest interpersonal involvements: people come and go, and there is really no marriage at all but only a continuously changing and highly unstable encounter group. The longer-lasting and more cohesive group marriages are, in fact, those in which, as Dr. Downing reports, the initial sexual spree "generally gives way to the quiet, semipermanent, monogamous relationship characteristic of many in our general society."

Not surprisingly, therefore, Dr. Ellis finds that most group marriages are unstable and last only several months to a few years; and sociologist Lewis Yablonsky of California State College at Hayward, who has visited and lived in a number of communes, says that they are often idealistic but rarely successful or enduring. Over and above their specific difficulties, they are utopian—they seek to construct a new society from whole cloth. But all utopias thus far have failed; human behavior is so incredibly complex that every totally new order, no matter how well planned, generates innumerable unforeseen problems. It really is a pity: group living and group marriage look wonderful on paper.

. . .

All in all, then, the evidence is overwhelming that old-fashioned marriage is not dying and that nearly all of what passes for rebellion against it is a series of patchwork modifications enabling marriage to serve the needs of modern man without being unduly costly or painful.

While this is the present situation, can we extrapolate it into the future? Will marriage continue to exist in some form we can recognize?

It is clear that, in the future, we are going to have an even greater need than we now do for love relationships that offer intimacy, warmth, companionship and a reasonable degree of reliability. Such relationships need not, of course, be heterosexual. With our increasing tolerance of sexual diversity, it seems likely that many homosexual men and women will find it publicly acceptable to live together in quasi-marital alliances.

The great majority of men and women, however, will continue to find heterosexual love the preferred form, for biological and psychological reasons that hardly have to be spelled out here. But need heterosexual love be embodied within marriage? If the world is already badly overpopulated and daily getting worse, why add to its burden—and if one does not intend to have children, why seek to enclose love within a legal cage? Formal promises to love are promises no one can keep, for love is not an act of will; and legal bonds have no power to keep love alive when it is dying.

Such reasoning—more cogent today than ever, due to the climate of sexual permissiveness and to the twin technical advances of the pill and the loop—lies behind the growth of unwed unions. From all indications, however, such unions will not replace marriage as an institution but only precede it in the life of the individual.

It seems probable that more and more young people will live together unwed for a time and then marry each other or break up and make another similar alliance, and another, until one of them turns into a formal, legal marriage. In 50 years, perhaps less, we may come close to the Scandinavian pattern, in which a great many couples live together prior to marriage. It may be, moreover, that the spread of this practice will decrease the divorce rate among the young, for many of the mistakes that are recognized too late and are undone in divorce court will be recognized and undone outside the legal system, with less social and emotional damage than divorce involves.

If, therefore, marriage continues to be important, what form will it take? The one truly revolutionary innovation is group marriage—and, as we have seen, it poses innumerable and possibly insuperable practical and emotional difficulties. A marriage of one man and one woman involves only one interrelationship, yet we all know how difficult it is to find that one right fit and to keep it in working order. But add one more person, making the smallest possible group marriage, and you have three relationships (A-B, B-C and A-C); add a fourth to make two couples and you have six relationships; add enough to make a typical group marriage of 15 persons and you have 105 relationships.

This is an abstract way of saying that human beings are all very different and that finding a satisfying and workable love relationship is not easy, even for a twosome, and is impossibly difficult for aggregations of a dozen or so. It might prove less difficult, a generation hence, for children brought up in group-marriage communes. Such children would not have known the close, intense, parent-child relationships of monogamous marriage and could more easily spread their affections thinly and undemandingly among many. But this is mere conjecture, for no communal-marriage experiment in America has lasted long enough for us to see the results, except the famous Oneida Community in Upstate New York; it endured from 1848 to 1879, and then its offspring vanished back into the surrounding ocean of monogamy.

Those group marriages that do endure in the future will probably be dedicated to a rural and semiprimitive agrarian life style. Urban communes may last for some years but with an ever-changing membership and a lack of inner familial identity; in the city, one's work life lies outside the group, and with only emotional ties to hold the group together, any dissension or conflict will result in a turnover of membership. But while agrarian communes may have a sounder foundation, they can never become a mass movement; there is simply no way for the land to support well over 200,000,000 people with the low-efficiency productive methods of a century or two ago.

Agrarian communes not only cannot become a mass movement in the future but they will not even have much chance of surviving as islands in a sea of modern industrialism. For semiprimitive agrarianism is so marginal, so back-breaking and so tedious a way of life that it is unlikely to hold most of its converts against the competing attractions of conventional civilization. Even Dr. Downing, for all his enthusiasm about the "Society of Awakening," as he calls tribal family living, predicts that for the foreseeable future, only a small minority will be attracted to it and that most of these will return to more normal surroundings and relationships after a matter of weeks or months.

Thus, monogamy will prevail; on this, nearly all experts agree. But it will almost certainly continue to change in the same general direction in which it has been changing for the past few generations; namely, toward a redefinition of the special roles played by husband and wife, so as to achieve a more equal distribution of the rights, privileges and life expectations of man and woman.

This, however, will represent no sharp break with contemporary marriage, for the marriage of 1971 has come a long way from patriarchy toward the goal of equality. Our prevalent marital style has been termed companionship marriage by a generation of sociologists; in contrast to 19th Century marriage, it is relatively egalitarian and intimate, husband and wife being intellectually and emotionally close, sexually compatible and nearly equal in personal power and in the quantity and quality of labor each contributes to the marriage.

From an absolute point of view, however, it still is contaminated by patriarchalism. Although each partner votes, most husbands (and wives) still think that men understand politics better; although each may have had similar schooling and believes both sexes to be intellectually equal, most husbands and wives still act as if men were innately better equipped to handle money, drive the car, fill out tax returns and replace fuses. There may be something close to equality in their homemaking, but nearly always it is his career that counts, not hers. If his company wants to move him to another city, she quits her job and looks for another in their new location; and when they want to have children, it is seldom questioned that he will continue to work while she will stay home.

With this, there is a considerable shift back toward traditional role assignments: He stops waxing the floors and washing dishes, begins to speak with greater authority about how their money is to be spent, tells her (rather than consults her) when he would like to work late or take a business trip, gives (or withholds) his approval of her suggestions for parties, vacations and child discipline. The more he takes on the airs of his father, the more she learns to connive and manipulate like her mother. Feeling trapped and discriminated against, resenting the men of the world, she thinks she makes an exception of her husband, but in the hidden recesses of her mind he is one with the others. Bearing the burden of being a man in the world, and resenting the easy life of women, he thinks he makes an exception of his wife but deep-down classifies her with the rest.

This is why a great many women yearn for change and what the majority of women's liberation members are actively hammering away at. A handful of radicals in the movement think that the answer is the total elimination of marriage, that real freedom for women will come about only through the abolition of legal bonds to men and the establishment of governmentally operated nurseries to rid women once and for all of domestic entrapment. But most women in the movement, and nearly all those outside it, have no sympathy with the anti-marriage extremists; they very much want to keep marriage alive but aim to push toward completion the evolutionary trends that have been under way so long.

Concretely, women want their husbands to treat them as equals; they want help and participation in domestic duties; they want help with child rearing; they want day-care centers and other agencies to free them to work at least part time, while their children are small, so that they won't have to give up their careers and slide into the imprisonment of domesticity. They want an equal voice in all the decisions made in the home—including job decisions that affect married life; they want their husbands to respect them, not indulge them; they want, in short, to be treated as if they were their husbands' best friends —which, in fact, they are, or should be.

All this is only a continuation of the developments in marriage over the past century and a quarter. They key question is: How far can marriage evolve in this direction without making excessive demands upon both partners? Can most husbands and wives have full-time uninterrupted careers, share all the chores and obligations of homemaking and parenthood and still find time for the essential business of love and companionship?

From the time of the early suffragettes, there have been women with the drive and talent to be full-time doctors, lawyers, retailers and the like, and at the same time to run a home and raise children with the help of housekeepers, nannies and selfless husbands. From these examples, we can judge how likely this is to become the dominant pattern of the future. Simply put, it isn't, for it would take more energy, money and good luck than the great majority of women possess and more skilled helpers than the country could possibly provide. But what if child care were more efficiently handled in state-run centers, which would make the totally egalitarian marriage much more feasible? The question then becomes: How many middle-class American women would really prefer full-time work to something less demanding that would give them more time with their children? The truth is that most of the world's work is dull and wearisome rather than exhilarating and inspiring. Women's lib leaders are largely middle-to-upper-echelon professionals, and no wonder they think every wife would be better off working full time—but we have yet to hear the same thing from saleswomen, secretaries and bookkeepers.

Married women *are* working more all the time—in 1970, over half of all mothers whose children were in school held jobs—but the middle-class women among them pick and choose things they like to do rather than *have* to do for a living; moreover, many work part time until their children have grown old enough to make mothering a minor assignment. Accordingly, they make much less money than their husbands, rarely ever rise to any high positions in their fields and, to some extent, play certain traditionally female roles within marriage. It is a compromise and, like all compromises, it delights no one—but serves nearly everyone better than more clear-cut and idealistic solutions.

Though the growth of egalitarianism will not solve all the problems of marriage, it may help solve the problems of a *bad* marriage. With their increasing independence, fewer and fewer wives will feel compelled to remain confined within unhappy or unrewarding marriages. Divorce, therefore, can be expected to continue to increase, despite the offsetting effect of extramarital liaisons. Extrapolating the rising divorce rate, we can conservatively expect that within another generation, half or more of all persons who marry will be divorced at least once. But even if divorce were to become an almost universal experience, it would not be the *antithesis* of marriage but only a part of the marital experience; most people will, as always, spend their adult lives married —not continuously, in a single marriage, but segmentally, in two or more marriages. For all the dislocations and pain these divorces cause, the sum total of emotional satisfaction in the lives of the divorced and remarried may well be greater than their great-grandparents were able to achieve.

Marital infidelity, since it also relieves some of the pressures and discontents of unsuccessful or boring marriages—and does so in most cases without breaking up the existing home—will remain an alternative to divorce and will probably continue to increase, all the more so as women come to share more fully the traditional male privileges. Within another generation, based on present trends, four of five husbands and two of three wives whose marriages last more than several years will have at least a few extramarital involvements.

Overt permissiveness, particularly in the form of marital swinging, may be tried more often than it now is, but most of those who test it out will do so only briefly rather than adopt it as a way of life. Swinging has a number of built-in difficulties, the first and most important of which is that the avoidance of all emotional involvement—the very keystone of swinging—is exceedingly hard to achieve. Nearly all professional observers report that jealousy is a frequent and severely disruptive problem. And not only jealousy but sexual competitiveness: Men often have potency problems while being watched by other men or after seeing other men outperform them. Even a regular stud, moreover, may feel threatened when he observes his wife being more active at a swinging party than he himself could possibly be. Finally, the whole thing is truly workable only for the young and the attractive.

Hunt's prediction about the future increase in swinging seems, at this time, to be erroneous. Current study of the swinging scene seems to indicate a substantial decline in interest. Sociologists estimated that there were about a million and a half people experimenting with group sex in 1972. At the end of 1974 they estimated that this number had fallen to about a half million. In 1972 there were about twenty swinging clubs in Southern California, but by 1975 that had fallen to eight. "All those swing clubs are failing and falling apart," says Dr. Gilbert Bartell, author of *Group Sex*. "These are depressed and unsettled times. There is a more somber feeling among people, a retreat away from sexual frivolity."[2,3]

There will be wider and freer variations in marital styles—we are a pluralistic nation, growing more tolerant of diversity all the time—but throughout all the styles of marriage in the future will run a predominant motif that has been implicit in the evolution of marriage for a century and a quarter and that will finally come to full flowering in a generation or so. In short, the marriage of the future will be a heterosexual friendship, a free and unconstrained union of a man and a woman who are companions, partners, comrades and sexual lovers. There will still be a certain degree of specialization within marriage, but by and large, the daily business of living together—the talk, the meals, the going out to work and coming home again, the spending of money, the lovemaking, the caring for the children, even the indulgence or nonindulgence in outside affairs—will be governed by this fundamental relationship rather than by the lord-and-servant relationship of patriarchal marriage. Like all friendships, it will exist only as long as it is valid; it will rarely last a lifetime, yet each marriage, while it does last, will meet the needs of the men and women of the future as no earlier form of marriage could have. Yet we who know the marriage of today will find it relatively familiar, comprehensible—and very much alive.

Conclusion

In the preceding readings we have tried to give a broad description of the many pressures now influencing the American family. In addition, we have tried to place the resultant family stresses into a meaningful time and cultural perspective. The continuing argument as to whether or not the family will survive the pressures placed upon it by modern technology seems inappropriate. The family has survived for thousands of years because it is a flexible institution rather than a rigid one. It will continue to survive although in some modified form for the same reason.

The family represents man's interests in human interaction and reproduction. Such interests have been and will always be a significant part of man's life. Just how he fulfills these interests depends on his society and values at a given time in history. Hence family structure is always of many forms if one views man across societies and across time. The truly unique quality of man is the fact that he is born fairly free of instinctual biological behavioral determinents; thus his family structure is not dictated by his biology, rather it is largely determined by his culture. He is equally at home in an Eskimo igloo, a Navajo hogan, and a middle-class suburban home. To conclude that the family system is disappearing, because some one form of it is changing, fails to grasp the essential flexibility of man and hence his family institution. The question is not whether the family will disappear as an institution, rather the important questions revolve around trends in family structure and functions: what forces are behind these changes, and what effect will change within the family and changes in the larger society have upon one another?

References

Introduction

1. "Who Gets Married Today and Why," *Redbook,* February 1974.
2. David R. Mace, "Marriage Enrichment: Wave of the Future?" *The Family Coordinator* 24 (April 1975): 133.

Section 1   Tomorrow's Morality

Reading 1   Science, Sex, and Tomorrow's Morality

1. J. B. Gurdon, "Adult Frogs Derived from the Nuclei of Single Somatic Cells," *Developmental Biology* 4 (1962): 256–73.
2. *Time.* 9 April 1971, p. 38.

Reading 2   Does the Family Have a Future?

1. "The Third World: Seeds of a Revolution," *Time,* 13 July 1970.
2. "The World Food Crisis," *Time,* 11 November 1974.
3. George B. Leonard, "The Man And Woman Thing," *Look,* 25 December 1968.

Reading 4   Are Marriage and the Family About to Disappear?

1. Pitirim Sorokin, *The Crisis of Our Age* (New York: Dutton, 1941), pp. 130–40.
2. Pitirim Sorokin, *Social and Cultural Dynamics,* vol. 4 (New York: Harper & Row, 1937), p. 776.
3. Carle Zimmerman, *Family and Civilization* (New York: Harper & Row, 1947).
4. See Una Sait, *New Horizons for the Family* (New York: Macmillan, 1938), chap. 20, for a thorough discussion of the radical marriage theories of the twenties.
5. Bertrand Russell, *Marriage and Morals* (New York: Liveright, 1929).
6. *Ibid.,* p. 315.
7. Benjamin Lindsey and Wainwright Evans, *The Companionate Marriage* (New York: Liveright, 1927).
8. Barrington Moore, *Political Power and Social Theory* (Cambridge: Harvard, 1958), chap. 5.
9. Bertrand Russell, *Marriage and Morals* (New York: Liveright, 1929), p. 133.
10. See Rollo May, *Love and Will* (New York: W. W. Norton & Co., 1970), for a thorough discussion of these aspects of love in American society.
11. Ira Reiss, "How and Why America's Sex Standards are Changing." *Trans-Action,* March 1968, p. 26.

Reading 5   Marriage Has Improved

1. "Married Couples Living to Advanced Ages," *Statistical Bulletin,* 49:9–11, June, 1968. See also "Survival and the Life Cycle," *Statistical Bulletin,* 47:5–7, September 1966.

2. There may well be a temporary flurry of divorces when the Viet Nam war ends. The return of men long absent from wives and families brings this aftermath. The refined divorce rate (rate based only on women of marriageable age) is already showing an increase. See *Monthly Vital Statistics: Divorce Statistics, 1966*, vol. 17, no. 10 Supplement, January 6, 1969.

3. Robert E. Parke, Jr., and Paul C. Glick, "Prospective Changes in Marriage and the Family," *Jr. of Marriage and The Family*, 29:249–56, May 1967.

4. Rustum Roy and Della Roy, *Honest Sex* (New York: New Library, 1968).

5. "Survival and the Life Cycle," *Statistical Bulletin*, 47:5–7, Metropolitan Life Insurance Co., September 1966.

6. William J. Goode, *World Revolution and Family Patterns* (New York: Free Press of Glencoe, 1963).

7. Parke and Glick, *op. cit.*

8. U.S. Department of Commerce, Bureau of the Census. "Population Characteristics," series P–20, no. 122, March 22, 1963. Table 1, p. 9.

9. Jack Anderson, "Taking Stock of Our Country," *Santa Barbara News-Press*, C–8, 2 January 1975.

10. Don Kendall, Associated Press, "Food Stamps Used by 13.5 Million," *Santa Barbara News-Press*, A–12, 3 November 1974.

11. John C. Belcher, "The One-Person Household: A Consequence of the Isolated Nuclear Family," *Journal of Marriage and Family Living* 29:534–40.

12. In January 1969, *Reader's Digest* reported the remarkable progress in Soviet housing, but also stressed the poor quality of the housing, and the great current shortage. Even with this progress, 40 percent of Moscow citizens still live in "communal flats" where they share kitchen and toilet facilities. Three or more family members live in two small rooms. Divorced persons may still have to live together with a blanket hung between beds. These are standards which would be judged far down in the poverty level in the United States. Although Soviet housing shortage represents the extreme, apartments are in chronic short supply in many European countries, making it difficult for the young to marry and live separate from relatives.

13. Marital Status and Family Status, March 1967, "Population Characteristics," series P–20, no. 170, February 23, 1968, United States Census, p. 1.

Section 2   The Romantic Ideal: Love and Marriage in America

1. M. Rowland and L. Young, "Survey of Sexual Behavior at Stanford," unpublished manuscript, Stanford University, November 1968.

2. Lawrence Casier, "This Thing Called Love," *Psychology Today*, December 1969.

3. Ibid.

4. Ibid.

5. Erich Fromm, *The Art of Loving* (New York: Harper, 1956), p. 59.

Reading 8   The True Love of John and Mary

1. Robert O. Blood, Jr., *Marriage*, 2nd ed. (New York: The Free Press, 1969), pp. 17–18.

2. Carlfred Broderick, "Going Steady: The Beginning of the End," *Teen-Age Marriage and Divorce*, Farber and Wilson, eds. Reprinted by permission of the author and Diablo Press, 1967.

3. Ibid.

4. John R. Clarke, *The Importance of Being Imperfect* (New York; David McKay Co., 1961).

Reading 9   Love and Marriage in Modern America: A Functional Analysis

1. Morton M. Hunt, *The Natural History of Love* (New York: Alfred A. Knopf, 1959), p. 3.

2. Theodor Reik, *A Psychologist Looks at Love* (New York: Holt, Rinehart, and Winston, 1944), p. 3.

3. Ibid., p. 4.

4. Sigmund Freud, *Group Psychology and the Analysis of the Ego* (London: Hogarth, 1922), p. 72.

5. William J. Goode, "The Theoretical Importance of Love," *American Sociological Review* 24(1959):38.

6. This is to differentiate from other behavioral complexes to which the same word is applied: love of art, money, God, and so forth.

7. Willard Waller and Reuben Hill, *The Family* (New York: The Dryden Press, 1951), p. 101.

8. Hunt, *op. cit.,* 363.

9. For an opposing position, see Goode, *op. cit.*

10. Ralph Linton, *The Study of Man* (New York: Appleton-Century, 1936), p. 175.

11. Andrew Truxal and Francis Merrill, *The Family in American Culture* (New York: Prentice-Hall, Inc., 1974), p. 139.

12. Hunt, *op. cit.,* 341.

13. Raoul De Sales, "Love in America," *The Atlantic Monthly* 161 (1938): 645–51.

Reading 10   "What Is This Thing Called Love?"

1. D. Byrne, O. London, and K. Reeves, "The Effect of Physical Attractiveness, Sex, and Attitude Similarity on Interpersonal Attraction," *Journal of Personality* 36 (1968): 269–71.

2. Sigmund Freud, "The Most Prevalent Form of Degradation in Erotic Life," *Collected Papers* 4, ed. E. Jones (London: Hogarth Press, 1925), pp. 203–16.

3. S. Schachter, "The Interaction of Cognitive and Physiological Determinants of Emotional State," *Advances in Experimental Social Psychology* I, ed. Berkowitz (New York: Academic Press, 1964), pp. 49–80.

4. G. Maranon, "Contribution a l'etude de l'action emotive de l'andrenaline," *Revue Francaise Endocrinalogia* 2 (1924): 301–25.

5. S. Schachter and J. Singer, "Cognitive, Social and Physiological Determinants of Emotional State," *Psychological Review* 69 (1962): 379–99.

6. H. T. Finck, *Romantic Love and Personal Beauty: Their Development, Causal Relations, Historic and National Peculiarities* (London: Macmillan, 1891).

7. J. W. Brehm, M. Gatz, G. Geothals, J. McCrimmon, and L. Ward. "Psychological Arousal and Interpersonal Attraction," mimeographed, available from authors, 1970.

8. E. Walster, "The Effect of Self-Esteem on Romantic Liking," *Journal of Experimental Social Psychology* 1 (1965): 184–97.

9. L. Jacobs, E. Walster, and E. Berscheid, "Self-esteem and Attraction," *Journal of Personality and Social Psychology* 17 (1971): 84–91.

10. V. Vassilikos, *The Plant; the Well; the Angel; A Trilogy,* translated from Greek by Edmund and Mary Keeley, 1st American ed. (New York: Knopf, 1964).

11. E. Aronson and D. Linder, "Gain and Loss of Esteem as Determinants of Interpersonal Attractiveness," *Journal of Experimental Social Psychology* 1 (1965): 156–71.

12. I. Duncan, *Isadora* (New York: Award Books, 1968).

13. W. H. Masters and V. E. Johnson, *Human Sexual Response,* (Boston: Little, Brown 1966).

14. S. Valins, "Cognitive Effects of False Heart-rate Feedback," *Journal of Personality and Social Psychology* 4 (1966): 400–8.

15. Margaret Mead, in *The Anatomy of Love* by A. M. Krich (New York: Dell, 1960).

Reading 11   A Marriage Wake: Myths That Die Hard

1. Aron Krich, "Marriage and the Mystique of Romance," *Redbook,* November 1970.

Section 3.   The Romantic Ideal: Ethnic, Cultural, and Class Differences

1. Stuart Queen and Robert Habenstein, *The Family in Various Cultures,* 4th ed. (New York: J. B. Lippincott, 1974), p. 5.

2. Morton M. Hunt, *The Natural History of Love* (New York: Alfred A. Knopf, 1959).

3. Etsu Sugimato, *A Daughter of the Samurai* (Garden City, New York: Doubleday, 1935), pp. 115–16.

4. Thomas Price, "African Marriage," I.M.C. Research Pamphlet no. 1 (London: SMC Press Ltd. 1954), p. 15.

Reading 12   The Modern Chinese Communist Family

1. Victor H. Li, "Law and Penology: Systems of Reform and Correction," ed. Michel Oksenberg, *China's Developmental Experience,* New York, Columbia University, *Proceedings of the Academy of Political Science,* vol. XXXI, no. 1 (March 1973), pp. 152–53.

2. My appreciation to Dr. Wu Chen-i, professor of psychiatry, Peking Medical College, and Dr. Shen Yu-chun, director of the Department of Psychiatry, Peking Medical College, for elucidating the concept of "revolutionary optimism."

3. Michel Oksenberg, *China: The Convulsive Society,* Headline Series, The Foreign Policy Association, no. 203 (December 1970), p. 8.

4. Slater, p. 5.

5. Ralph Keyes, *We, the Lonely People: Searching For Community* (New York: Harper and Row, 1973), p. 33.

6. Slater, p. 7.

Reading 13   The Matrilineal Hopi Indian Family

1. Mischa Titiev, *Old Oraibi* (1944), pp. 45–46. by permission of Harvard University Press.

2. The term "clan" is used by many writers to describe this unit. Since there are no clear-cut residential groups organized by blood lines and integrated into operating political and social units among the Hopi, the use of "sib" seems more appropriate.

3. Titiev, *op. cit.,* p. 13.

4. Titiev, *op. cit.,* p. 137.

5. Titiev, *op. cit.,* p. 41.

6. Laura Thompson, *Culture in Crisis: A Study of the Hopi Indians* (1950), p. 135.

7. Thompson and Joseph, *op. cit.,* pp. 40 ff.

8. Ibid, p. 41.

1. Brigitte Linner, *Sex and Society in Sweden* (New York: Random House, 1967).

2. J. Robert Moskin, "The New Contraceptive Society," *Look Magazine,* 5 February 1969.

Reading 14   Marital Sexuality in Four Cultures of Poverty

1. Oscar Lewis, *Life in a Mexican Village: Tepoztlan Restudied* (Urbana: U. of Illinois Press, 1951). p. 326

2. Lewis, *op. cit.,* p. 326.

3. Geoffrey Gorer, *Exploring English Character* (New York: Criterion Books, 1955), pp. 115–16.

4. Lewis, *op. cit.,* p. 326; Slater and Woodside, *op. cit.,* p. 172.

5. J. Mayone Stycos, *Family and Fertility in Puerto Rico: A Study of the Lower Income Group* (New York: Columbia U. Press, 1955), p. 143.

6. Ibid., pp. 42–43; Landy, *op. cit.,* p. 108 and pp. 159–60.

7. B. M. Spinley, *The Deprived and the Privileged: Personality Development in English Society* (London: Routledge and Kegan Paul, 1953), p. 87.

8. Cf., Oscar Lewis, *Five Families: Mexican Case Studies in the Culture of Poverty* (New York: Basic Books, 1959); and *The Children of Sanchez: Autobiography of a Mexican Family* (New York: Random House, 1961).

9. Spinley, *op. cit.,* pp. 62–63.

10. Stycos, *op. cit.,* p. 142.

11. Ibid., p. 99.

12. Spinley, *op. cit.,* p. 87.

13. Arnold W. Green, "The 'Cult of Personality' and Sexual Relations," *Psychiatry* IV (1941), pp. 343–44.

14. Lewis, *Life in a Mexican Village, op. cit.,* pp. 399–405.

15. Ibid., p. 407.

16. Stycos, *op. cit.,* pp. 91–97.

17. Ibid., pp. 134–35.

18. Lewis, *Life in a Mexican Village, op. cit.,* pp. 326–27.

19. Eliot Slater and Moya Woodside, *Patterns of Marriage: A Study of Marriage Relationships in the Urban Working Classes* (London: Cassell and Co., 1951).

20. Lee Rainwater, *And The Poor Get Children: Sex, Contraception and Family Planning in the Working Class* (Chicago: Quadrangle Books, 1960).

21. Lewis, *Life in a Mexican Village, op. cit.,* p. 326.

22. Lewis's studies of urban Mexican couples suggest that a more complex sexual relationship is common. (*Five Families, op. cit.; The Children of Sanchez, op. cit.*).

23. Stycos, *op. cit.,* pp. 134–42.

24. Lee Rainwater, *Family Design: Marital Sexuality, Family Size and Contraception* (Chicago: Aldine Publishing Co., 1964).

25. Spinley, *op. cit.,* p. 61.

26. Slater and Woodside, *Patterns of Marriage,* pp. 168–69.

27. Slater and Woodside (Ibid.) note that women frequently shift from "he" to "they" when discussing sexual relationships with the husband, a usage apparent also in the American interviews. Apparently, a good many women find it difficult in connection with sex to think of the husband as other than a representative of demanding men as a type.

28. The Kinsey data *(op. cit.)* suggest that late in marriage (36–40 age period) at the lowest educational level, men have extramarital relations four times as often as women; at the intermediate level slightly more than twice as often; and at the highest educational level, only 50 per cent more often.

29. Margaret Mead, *Male and Female* (New York: William Morrow, 1949), pp. 201–22.

30. Stycos, *op. cit.,* p. 149.

31. Lewis, *Life in a Mexican Village,* pp. 319–25.

32. Reuben Hill, J. M. Stycos, and Kurt W. Back, *The Family and Population Control* (Chapel Hill: U. of North Carolina Press, 1959).

33. Elizabeth Bott, *Family and Social Network* (London: Tavistock Publications, 1957).

34. Madeline Kerr, *The People of Shipstreet.* (London: Routledge & Kegan Paul, 1958).

35. Davis and Gardner, *op. cit.;* Rainwater, Handel, and Coleman, *op. cit.*

36. Various Puerto Rican sources such as Stycos, *op. cit.; The People of Puerto Rico,* ed. by Julian Steward. (Urbana; U. of Illinois Press, 1956); Landy, *op. cit.,* suggest that there is

some tendency for the wife to retain a tie with a maternal figure after marriage, but not in the same organized way that is traditional in Tepoztlan or common with the "Mum" system in England.

37. Erik Erikson, *Childhood and Society* (New York: W. W. Norton, 1950).

38. See the closely related discussion by William J. Goode, "The Theoretical Importance of Love," *American Sociological Review* 24 (1959), pp. 38–47, and by Max Gluckman, *Custom and Conflict in Africa* (Oxford: Basil Blackwell, 1955) in which these authors argue that romantic love between a couple tends to interfere with other important solidarities in a society and that therefore societies tend to operate in ways that keep love from disrupting existing social arrangements. While the efforts of society to control love are clearest in connection with mate selection, these efforts continue after marriage also and have some bearing on the kind of sexual relationship that commonly exists among couples in a society.

39. Bott, *op. cit.*

40. Rainwater et al., *op. cit.*

41. In a study of Detroit wives' feelings about their marriages, Robert O. Blood and Donald M. Wolfe, *Husbands and Wives: The Dynamics of Married Living* (Chicago: Free Press, 1960), pp. 221–35), it was found that the wife's satisfaction with the "love and affection" she receives from her husband increases steadily with social status. This seems related to the fact that there is a greater degree of sharing, communication, and joint participation in social relations at the higher than on the lower-status levels.

42. Melford Spiro, "Social Systems, Personality and Functional Analysis," *Studying Personality Cross-Culturally,* ed. Bert Kaplan (Evanston: Row and Peterson, 1961).

43. Spinley, *op. cit.,* p. 87.

44. Green, *op. cit.,* pp. 343–44.

45. Spinley, *op. cit.,* pp. 81–82.

46. Kerr, *op. cit.,* p. 88.

47. Nathan Murillo, "The Mexican American Family," *Chicanos: Social and Psychological Perspectives,* N.N. Wagner and Marsha Haug, eds. (St. Louis: C. V. Mosby Co., 1971), pp. 99–102.

Reading 15   Mexican Family Roles

1. José Gómez Robleda, *Psicologia del mexicano,* (México, D. F.: Instituto de Investigaciones Sociales, Universidad Nacional, 1962), pp. 57–58.

2. Francisco González Pineda, *El mexicano; psicologia de su destructividad,* (México: Editorial Pax-México, S.A., Segunda Edición, 1963), p. 158.

3. Cf. Martha Wolfenstein and Nathan Leites, *Movies; A Psychological Study* (Glencoe, Illinois: Free Press, 1950).

4. Bermúdez, *op. cit.,* p. 58; and José Gómez Robleda, *Psicologia del mexicano,* p. 97.

5. Bermúdez, *op. cit.,* pp. 93–94.

6. Whetten has expressed an opposite opinion: "Little information is available concerning the roles played by Mexican family members. Few objective studies have been made. There appears to be wide variation in customs among social classes and among different regions of the country. One hesitates to generalize on the basis of meager information." Nathan Whetten, *Rural Mexico* (Chicago: University of Chicago Press, 1948), p. 393.

7. Bermúdez, *op. cit.,* p. 101.

8. Ibid., p. 48.

9. González Pineda, *op. cit.,* pp. 53–54.

10. An excellent description of the male peer group—both youth and adult—among Mexican-Americans has been given in the chapter on the *palomilla* in Arthur Rubel, *Across the*

Tracks; Mexican-Americans in a Texas City (Austin: University of Texas Press, 1966), pp. 101–18.

11. González Pineda, *op. cit.,* p. 252.

12. Ibid., pp. 51–52; and Ma. Luisa Rodríguez Sala de Gomezgil, *El estereotipo del mexicano; estudio psicosocial,* México: Instituto de Investigaciones Sociales (Universidad Nacional, 1965), p. 182.

13. Ramírez, *op. cit.,* pp. 85–86; John H. Bushnell, "La Virgen de Guadalupe as Surrogate Mother," *American Anthropologist* 60 (April 1958), pp. 261–65; also William Madsen, *The Virgin's Children* (Austin: University of Texas Press, 1960).

Reading 16 The Contemporary Black American Family

1. Robert Staples, "Towards a Sociology of the Black Family: A Theoretical and Methodological Assessment," *Journal of Marriage and Family* (February 1971), pp. 119–135.

2. The point of view that the African cultural heritage was not destroyed by slavery is presented in Melville Herskovits' *The Myth of the Negro Past* (1941).

3. Stanley M. Elkins, *Slavery* (1959). A review of historical projections and modern research findings and formulations on the American Negro personality is found in Thomas F. Pettigrew's useful *A Profile of the Negro American* (1964).

4. Pettigrew, *op. cit.,* pp. 3–55.

5. Frazier, *op. cit.,* p. 89 ff.

6. For a detailing of these problems see Nathan Glazer and Daniel P. Moynihan, *Beyond the Melting Pot* (1963), pp. 24–85.

7. The latter two types are closely related to the "externally adapted" and the "acculturated" family types developed by Jessie Bernard. They derive from current black life-styles that are somewhat reflective of, but also cut across, economic classes. See Jessie Bernard, *Marriage and Family Among Negroes* (1966), chapter 2, pp. 27–66.

8. Andrew Billingsley and Amy Tate Billingsley, "Illegitimacy and Patterns of Negro Family Life," *The Unwed Mother* ed. Robert W. Roberts (1966), pp. 131–57.

9. Ernest W. Burgess, Harvey J. Locke, and Mary Margaret Thomes, *The Family: From Institution to Companionship* (1963), p. 89.

10. E. Franklin Frazier, *op. cit.* See particularly chapters IX and X, pp. 163–214.

11. Jessie Bernard, *op. cit.,* p. 9. ff.

12. Ibid., p. 12. Reprinted by permission of the publishers, Prentice-Hall, Inc., Englewood Cliffs, N.J.

13. Ibid., p. 27 ff.

14. Ibid., pp. 79–85.

15. David M. Heer, "The Prevalence of Black-White Marriages in the United States, 1960 and 1970," *Journal of Marriage and Family* (May 1974), pp. 246–58.

16. Joseph H. Douglass, "The Urban Negro Family" in *The American Negro Reference Book, op. cit.,* p. 341.

17. Bernard, *op. cit.,* p. 118.

18. For a harsh, possibly overdrawn, indictment of middle-class Negro life, including indulgence of children, see E. Franklin Frazier, *Black Bourgeoisie,* (1957 1962). For a more recent, balanced but not uncritical depiction, see St. Clair Drake, "The Social and Economic Status of the Negro in the United States" (1967).

19. Ernest W. Burgess et al., *op. cit.,* p. 91. See also Andrew and Amy Tate Billingsley, op. cit., pp. 152–55.

20. Charles Silberman, *Crisis in Black and White* (1964), p. 30. See also Chapter II, pp. 17–35.

21. Karl E. Taeuber and Alma F. Taeuber, *Negroes in Cities* (1965), pp. 37–48; also "The Negro Population in the United States," in *The American Negro Reference Book, op. cit.,* pp. 96–160.

22. G. Franklin Edwards, "Communities and Class Realities," in *The American Negro,* volume 2; *Daedalus* (Winter 1966), p. 4.

23. Ibid.

24. Two central references which have been drawn upon here are Daniel P. Moynihan's *The Negro Family: The Case for National Action* (1965); and Lee Rainwater's "Crucible of Identity," in *The American Negro,* Volume 2; *Daedalus* (Winter 1966), pp. 172–216.

25. Daniel P. Moynihan, op. cit.

26. Note that it is not held that *all* slum dwelling or central city blacks of lower socio-economic classes elect the matricentric family pattern; nor do all middle- and upper-class blacks find themselves in the acculturated type. These quite different family types represent modal tendencies, one more grounded in normative elements than the other. Middle-class mothers may still cling to the matriarchal role. On the other hand, some unemployed or casually employed fathers become adjusted to their economic contingencies and play dominant, often authoritarian, paternal roles. See for example, "The Culture of Unemployment: Some Notes on Negro Children," by Michael Schwartz and George Henderson in *Blue Collar World,* Arthur B. Shostak and William Gomberg, eds. (1964), pp. 459–68.

27. See Eugene Litwark's "The Use of Extended Family Groups in the Achievement of Social Goals: Some Policy Implications," in *Social Problems* 7 (Winter 1959–60), pp. 177–86.

28. Lee Rainwater, *op. cit.,* p. 183. The remainder of this section follows closely this excellent research report. See also the related research of Rainwater's colleague David A. Schulz, reported in *Coming Up Black: Patterns of Ghetto Socialization* (1969).

29. Ibid., pp. 183–84.

30. Ibid., pp. 185–87.

31. Ibid., p. 186.

Section IV   The Family and its Alternatives

1. Alvin Toffler, *Future Shock* (New York: Random House, 1970).

2. Brock Chisholm, "For Every Child's Health," *Children and Today's World,* Assoc. for Childhood Education International, Washington D.C., 1967, 22–29.

Reading 17   Family Patterns and Human Rights

1. William J. Goode, *World Revolution and Family Patterns* (New York: The Free Press, 1964).

2. The best-known study in English is T. W. Adorno, E. Frenkel-Brunswik, D. J. Levinson and R. N. Sanford, *The Authoritarian Personality* (New York: Harper & Row, Publishers, 1950). See the critiques in Richard Christie and Marie Jahoda, eds., *Studies in the Scope and Method of the Authoritarian Personality* (New York: The Free Press, 1953).

3. R. Nichols, "A Factor Analysis of Parental Attitudes of Fathers," *Child Development,* 1962, 33, 797–8.

4. W. Hartup, "Some Correlates of Parental Imitation in Young Children," *Child Development,* 1962, 33, 94.

5. Needless to say, Allport himself objects to the pale qualities of the term "tolerant," but no good English word exists which conveys the meaning of "supporting human rights."

Perhaps there is no such word in other Western languages, either. See Gordon W. Allport, *The Nature of Prejudice* (New York: Doubleday & Co., Inc., 1958), especially chapter 27. See also chapters 10 and 25.

6. Gabriel A. Almond and Sidney Verba, *The Civic Culture* (Boston: Little, Brown and Co., 1965), 274–76, 284, 286–87.

7. Allport, *op. cit.,* 399–400.

8. On the class differences in the support of civil liberties, see Samuel A. Stouffer, *Communism, Conformity and Civil Liberties* (Gloucester, Mass.: Peter Smith, 1963), especially chapter 2 and appendix E.

9. Almond and Verba, *op. cit.,* 284.

10. Almond and Verba, *op. cit.,* 212–14.

11. J. Cooper and J. Lewis, "Parent Evaluation as Related in Social Ideology and Academic Achievement," *Journal of Genetic Psychology* (1962): 101, 135.

12. J. Howard Kauffman, "Interpersonal Relations in the Traditional and Emergent Families Among Midwest Mennonites," *Marriage and Family Living* (August 1961), 23, 251.

13. In this connection, see the complexities suggested by comparisons among British, German, and American child-rearing patterns, in Lipset, *op. cit.,* 277–81, especially his suggestion that perhaps a different type of personality is needed for stable democracy in different kinds of societies.

Reading 18   The Self-Actualizing Person in the Fully-Functioning Family: A Humanistic Viewpoint

1. This refers not merely to the Hippie groups but what may prove to be more significant to experiments in intense group experiences and new social arrangements for the family.

2. A. Maslow, "Deficiency Motivation and Growth Motivation," in M. R. Jones (Ed.), *Nebraska Symposium on Motivation,* 1955.

3. C. R. Rogers, "A Theory of Therapy, Personality, and Interpersonal Relationships, as Developed in the Client-Centered Framework," in S. Koch (Ed.), *Psychology: A Study of a Science,* vol. 3 (New York: McGraw-Hill, 1959).

4. *Ibid.,* p. 98.

5. H. S. Sullivan, *Conceptions of Modern Psychiatry* (New York: W. W. Norton & Company, Inc., 1940).

6. K. Horney, *Self Analysis* (New York: W. W. Norton & Company, Inc., 1942).

7. T. Parsons and R. F. Bales, *Family, Socialization and Interaction Process* (Glencoe: The Free Press, 1955).

8. E. Fromm, *Man for Himself* (New York: Holt, Rinehart & Winston, Inc., 1947).

9. R. Flacks, "Student Activists: Result, Not Revolt," *Psychology Today* 1 (1967):18–23, 61.

10. *Ibid.*

11. *Ibid.,* p. 20.

12. E. S. Haldane and G. R. T. Ross, trans., *The Philosophical Works of Descartes,* vol. 1 (New York: Dover Publication, Inc., 1911).

Reading 19   The Sex Role Revolution: Reexamination of Femininity and Masculinity

1. Janet Saltzman Chafetz, *Masculine/Feminine or Human?* (Itasca, Ill.: F. E. Peacock Publishers, Inc., 1974), p. 201.

2. Robin Lakoff, "Language and Woman's Place," *Language in Society,* II, 1 (April 1973): 45–80.

3. "On the Beat," *Santa Barbara News-Press,* 18 August 1974, C-1.

4. For brief surveys of the literature, see Lenore J. Weitzman, "Sex-Role Socialization," in Jo Freeman, ed., *Women: A Feminist Perspective,* (Palo Alto, CA.: Mayfield Publishing Co., 1975), p. 108; and Chafetz, *op. cit.,* p. 72.

5. Inge K. Broverman et al., "Sex-Role Stereotypes: A Current Appraisal," *Journal of Social Issues* 28, 2 (1972), as reprinted by Warner Modular Publications 600 (1973): 61, 63, 64.

6. Chafetz, *op. cit.,* p. 35. Dr. Sandra Bem of Stanford University is currently engaged in this kind of research.

7. See the excellent summary essay by Naomi Weisstein, "Psychology Constructs the Female," in Vivian Gornick and Barbara K. Moran, eds., *Woman in Sexist Society* (New York: New American Library, 1971), pp. 207–24.

8. Broverman et al., *op. cit.,* p. 65.

9. *Ibid.,* p. 70.

10. Kirsten Amundsen, *The Silenced Majority* (Englewood Cliffs, N.J.: Prentice-Hall, 1971), p. 33; Chafetz, *op. cit.,* p. 124.

11. See the significant studies among college women by Matina Horner, "Toward an Understanding of Achievement-Related Conflicts in Women," *Journal of Social Issues* 28, 2(1972), as reprinted by Warner Modular Publications 608 (1973).

12. For a fuller treatment, see Chafetz, *op. cit.,* p. 166ff.

13. *Ibid.,* p. 166.

14. *Ibid.*

15. An exception is Ashley Montagu, *The Natural Superiority of Women* (New York: Macmillan Co., 1968). For a discussion of research bias, Jessie Bernard, "Sex Differences: An Overview," *Warner Modular Publication* 26 (1973): 1–18.

16. John Money and Anke Ehrhardt, *Man and Woman, Boy and Girl* (Baltimore: Johns Hopkins University Press, 1972) as reported in J. Richard Udry, *The Social Context of Marriage* (Philadelphia: J. B. Lippincott Co., 1974), p. 45ff.

17. Weitzman, *op. cit.,* p. 107.

18. Nancy Chodorow, "Being and Doing: A Cross-Cultural Examination of the Socialization of Males and Females," in Gornick and Moran, eds., *op. cit.,* 264ff.

19. *Ibid.,* p. 261f.

20. Nancy Chodorow's article, from which the material in this section is drawn, attempts to correlate all these variables.

21. Esther M. Lloyd-Jones, "The Self-Actualized Woman," in Mary Louise McBee and Kathryn Blake, *The American Woman: Who Will She Be?* (Beverly Hills, Calif.: Glencoe Press, 1974), p. 41.

22. *Ibid.,* p. 41f.

23. *Ibid.,* p. 40.

24. Harvey Cox, *The Secular City* (New York: Macmillan Co.), 1965.

Reading 20   The Alternatives: Changing Sexual and Family Mores

1. Bertrand Russell, "Our Sexual Ethics," first published in 1936. Quotes taken from *Why I am Not a Christian* (New York: Simon & Schuster, 1957), pp. 171–72.

2. Edward Pahlman, "Childlessness, Intentional and Unintentional: Psychological and Social Aspects," *Journal of Nervous and Mental Disease* 151 (1970): 2–11.

3. J. E. Veevers, "Voluntary Childlessness: A Neglected Area of Family Study," *Family Coordinator* 22 (April 1973): 199–206.

4. Anna Silverman and Arnold Silverman, *The Case Against Having Children* (New York: David McKay, 1971).

5. Ellen Peck, *The Baby Trap.* (New York: Bernard Geis Assn., 1971).

6. *Time,* 16 September 1974, pp. 54–63.

7. Caroline Bird, an essay in *Marriage: For and Against* (New York: Hart Publishing, 1973), p. 169.

8. U.S. Bureau of Census. Current Population Reports, Series P-23, no. 42, *The Social and Economic Status of the Black Population of the United States.* Washington D.C.: U.S. Government Printing Office, 1972.

9. Duane Denfield, "Dropouts from Swinging," *Family Coordinator* 23 (January 1974): 45–49.

10. Robert R. Bell, book review of the above book appearing in the *Journal of Marriage and the Family* 34 (Feb. 1972): 193–94.

11. Gilbert D. Bartell, *Group Sex* (New York: Peter Wyden, 1971).

12. Judith L. Lyness et al., "Living Together: An Alternative to Marriage," *Journal of Marriage and the Family* 34 (May 1972): 305–11.

13. Dan J. Peterman et al., "A Comparison of Cohabiting and Noncohabiting Students," *Journal of Marriage and the Family* 36 (May 1974): 344–55.

14. Carl Danziger and Mathew Greenwald, *Alternatives: A Look at Unmarried Couples and Communes,* Institute of Life Insurance, Research Services, 277 Park Avenue, New York, New York 10017, 1973.

15. G. Kapecky, "Unmarried . . . But Living Together," *The Ladies Home Journal* (July 1972) p. 66.

16. Margaret Mead, "Personal Communication," a monthly column in *Redbook,* 25 November 1966.

17. Ira L. Reiss, essay in *Marriage: For and Against* (New York: Hart, 1972), p. 246.

1. *Time,* 1972.

2. U.S. Bureau of Census, Current Population Reports, series P-20, no. 168, 22 December 1967. Data refers to March, 1966.

Reading 23   Parents Without Partners

1. See Anne W. Simon, *Stepchild in the Family* (New York: Odyssey Press, 1964), p. 69.

2. Alvin Schorr has an analysis of this data in *Poor Kids* (New York: Basic Books, 1966), esp. pp. 16–22. One estimate concludes that over 6 million children in the United States are growing up in fatherless homes. See Elizabeth Herzog and Cecilia Sudia, "Fatherless Homes," *Children* 15 (1968): 177–82.

3. For an excellent discussion of the changing attitudes toward divorced persons, see William L. O'Neill, *Divorce in the Progressive Era* (New Haven, Conn.: Yale University Press, 1967).

4. Schorr, "And Children of the Nation Come First," *Poor Kids,* chap. 2.

5. On the financial problems of divorced women, see William J. Goode, "Postdivorce Economic Activities," *After Divorce* (New York: Free Press, 1956), chap. 16.

6. Ibid.; see chap. 16 for a discussion of the problem of support payments after divorce.

7. The financial problems of the divorced man were analyzed in a 1968 study (unpublished) conducted by the writer and several graduate students from the School of Social Work, University of Wisconsin. Eighty divorced men were interviewed at length. Financial problems were one of the constant complaints of these men.

8. On the employment of wives at the point of divorce, see Goode, *After Divorce,* pp. 71–74.

9. A discussion of the financial crises of AFDC mothers may be found in Sydney E. Bernard, *Fatherless Families: Their Economic and Social Adjustment* (Waltham, Mass.: Brandeis University, 1964); see also Louis Kriesberg, *Mothers in Poverty* (Chicago: Aldine Publishing Co., 1970).

10. For an analysis of the employment of mothers with minor children, see F. Ivan Nye and Lois Wladis Hoffman, *The Employed Mother in America* (Chicago: Rand McNally & Co., 1963), pp. 7–15.

11. See Reuben Hill, *Families Under Stress* (New York: Harper & Bros., 1949).

12. Goode (*After Divorce,* chap. 21) discusses some of the postdivorce problems of the father and his children.

13. In the 1968 unpublished study of 80 divorced men cited earlier (see no. 7 above), the lack of contact with their children was one of the problems most often referred to by these fathers.

14. This woman was a professional social worker—hence, some of her language is a bit technical.

15. For a discussion of the concept of "social deviation," see Marshall B. Clinard, *Sociology of Deviant Behavior* (New York: Rinehart & Co., 1968), pp. 3–27.

16. On the attitudes of people toward the divorced person in our society, see Morton M. Hunt, *The World of the Formerly Married* (New York: McGraw-Hill Book Co., 1966), passim; see also Goode, "Social Adjustment," *After Divorce,* chap. 17.

17. It is possible, of course, for a woman who was once married to become an unmarried mother at a later date—as a widow or as a divorced woman.

18. Alvin Schorr explores the inadequacy of the AFDC welfare program in his study, *Explorations in Social Policy* (New York: Basic Books, 1968).

19. In the 1968 study of divorced men, conducted at the University of Wisconsin, there was frequent concern expressed by the men about the welfare of their children after the divorce (see no. 7 above).

20. The 80 detailed interviews from this study are not yet fully analyzed.

21. See Goode, *After Divorce,* chap. 21, for a discussion of how the divorced women in his sample felt about rearing children after the marriage had been terminated.

22. One of the better discussions of desertion is the paper by William M. Kephart, "Occupational Level and Marital Disruption," *American Sociological Review* (August 1955). Among other things, Kephart believes desertion to be more common than is generally thought. He also found that desertion was by no means limited to the lower socioeconomic levels.

23. The writer has been unable to find any empirical research that compares the psychological trauma of divorce with that of desertion.

24. On the courtship and remarriage problems of divorced and separated women, see Jessie Bernard, *Remarriage* (New York: Dryden Press, 1956); also Goode, "Steady Dating, Imminent Marriage, and Remarriage," *After Divorce,* chap. 19. Hunt, *World of the Formerly Married,* also analyzes these problems at length.

25. On the unmarried mother, see the following: Clark Vincent, *Unmarried Mothers* (New York: Free Press, 1961); Robert W. Roberts, ed., *The Unwed Mother* (New York: Harper & Row, 1966).

26. Bernard, (*Fatherless Families*) states that women under 35 with no husbands in the household are responsible for more children than are the households headed by men under 35. See also Schorr, *Poor Kids,* p. 21. In chap. 7, "Fatherless Child Insurance," Schorr has an excellent analysis of the economic problems faced by unmarried mothers in our society.

27. See Rose Bernstein, "Are We Still Stereotyping the Unmarried Mother?" *Social Work* 5 (January 1960): 22–38.

28. U.S. Bureau of the Census, *Characteristics of Families,* Series P-20, no. 242 (Washington, D.C., 1972), p. 25, table 5.

29. Robert B. Bell, *Marriage and Family Interaction,* 3d ed. (Homewood, Ill.; Dorsey Press, 1971), pp. 419-20.

30. Bernard Farber, *Family Organization and Interaction* (San Francisco: Chandler Publishing Co., 1964), p. 457.

31. Ibid.

32. Alfred Kadushin, "Single Parent Adoptions: An Overview and Some Relevant Research" (New York: Child Welfare League of America, 1968); see also Benjamin Schlesinger, ed., *The One-Parent Family* (Toronto: University of Toronto Press, 1970).

33. Kadushin, "Single Parent Adoptions," p. 40.

34. On the "double bind" and its potential impact on children, see Virginia Satir, *Conjoint Family Therapy* (Palo Alto, Calif.: Science & Behavior Books, 1964); also Jay Haley, *Strategies of Psychotherapy* (New York: Grune & Stratton, 1963).

35. Alfred Kadushin, *Child Welfare Services* (New York: Macmillan Co., 1967), p. 363.

36. Ibid.

37. See ibid., chapter 9, for an analysis of foster-parent programs; see also David Fanshel, *Foster Parenthood: A Role Analysis* (Minneapolis: University of Minnesota Press, 1966).

38. Kadushin, *Child Welfare Services.*

39. Ibid., p. 425.

40. Ibid., p. 396.

41. Both Fanshel and Kadushin agree on the difficulty of the foster-parent role.

42. Kadushin, *Child Welfare Services,* p. 437.

43. Ibid., chap. 10, "Adoption," presents a thorough review of the literature on adoption.

44. See H. David Kirk, *Shared Fate* (New York: Free Press, 1964). While this book is useful, we feel that Kirk would have gained a better perspective on parental problems if he had compared a group of natural parents with a group of adoptive parents.

45. See E. E. LeMasters, "Parenthood as Crisis," *Marriage and Family Living* 19 (1957): 352–55. In this study of natural parents having their first child, we found about the same apprehension that Kirk found in his adoptive parents. This paper received the Ernest Burgess Award from the National Council on Family Relations.

46. Kadushin, *Child Welfare Services,* pp. 482–83. Kadushin also found that older "problem" children could be adopted successfully; see his *Adopting Older Children* (New York: Columbia University Press, 1970).

Reading 24   Communes and Cluster Families as Viable Alternatives to the Nuclear Family

1. James W. Ramey, "Emerging Patterns of Innovative Behavior in Marriage," *The Family Coordinator* 21 (October 1972): 449.

2. Carl Rogers, *Becoming Partners: Marriage and Its Alternatives* (New York: Delacorte Press, 1972).

3. Robert N. Whitehurst, "Some Comparisons of Conventional and Counterculture Families," *The Family Coordinator* 21 (October 1972): 400.

4. "The American Family: Future Uncertain," *Time,* 28 December 1970.

5. Ira L. Reiss, Essay in *Marriage: For and Against* (New York: Hart, 1972) p. 246.

6. L. Rabkin and K. Rabkin, "Kibbutz Children," *Psychology Today* (September 1969).

7. *Time,* 1 February 1971.

8. "Developing an Extended Family," Unitarian Church, Santa Barbara, California, 1974.

Reading 25   The Future of Marriage

1. Arlie R. Hochschild, *The Unexpected Community* (Englewood Cliffs, New Jersey: Prentice-Hall, 1973).

2. Associated Press. "Swinging Scene's Advocates Decline in State, Nation." *Santa Barbara News Press,* 3 November 1974.

3. "The Sexes," *Time,* 25 November 1974.

Index